An Update on Business Laws for Commerce and Management

AN UPDATE ON BUSINESS LAWS FOR COMMERCE AND MANAGEMENT

A Textbook for Diploma in Commercial Practice, B.Com, BBM, MBA, MSW, CA-CPT, CS foundation and other Management and Professional Courses

By

VASANTHI REENA WILLIAMS
Ph.D, MBA, M.COM, LLB, PGDMM, DCP, MNIPM, MIMA, MQCFI
Teresian College, Post Graduate Centre, Mysore, Karnataka

UNIVERSITY SCIENCE PRESS
(An Imprint of Laxmi Publications Pvt. Ltd.)
An ISO 9001:2008 Company
BENGALURU • CHENNAI • COCHIN • GUWAHATI • HYDERABAD
JALANDHAR • KOLKATA • LUCKNOW • MUMBAI • RANCHI • NEW DELHI
BOSTON (USA) • NAIROBI (KENYA)

AN UPDATE ON BUSINESS LAWS FOR COMMERCE AND MANAGEMENT

Printed and bound in India
Typeset at Shubham Composer, Delhi
First Edition : 2014
ISBN 978-93-80856-02-5

Branches

✆	Bengaluru	080-26 75 69 30	
✆	Chennai	044-24 34 47 26,	24 35 95 07
✆	Cochin	0484-237 70 04,	405 13 03
✆	Guwahati	0361-254 36 69,	251 38 81
✆	Hyderabad	040-27 55 53 83,	27 55 53 93
✆	Jalandhar	0181-222 12 72	
✆	Kolkata	033-22 27 43 84	
✆	Lucknow	0522-220 99 16	
✆	Mumbai	022-24 93 12 61	
✆	Ranchi	0651-220 44 64	

PUBLISHED IN INDIA BY

UNIVERSITY SCIENCE PRESS
(An Imprint of Laxmi Publications Pvt.Ltd.)
An ISO 9001:2008 Company
113, GOLDEN HOUSE, DARYAGANJ,
NEW DELHI - 110002, INDIA
Telephone : 91-11-4353 2500, 4353 2501
Fax : 91-11-2325 2572, 4353 2528
www.laxmipublications.com info@laxmipublications.com

C—
Printed at: Repro Knowledgecast Limited, Thane

This Book Is Dedicated To
My Family

PREFACE

The study of Business Management is incomplete without the study of Business Laws. Law is an instrument of social control. The study of Business Laws helps in understanding the legal aspects and rules governing business transactions. Business Law is a branch of Civil Law. It governs and addresses the legal theoretical framework consisting of Rules and Regulations affecting business or Commercial transactions and economic activities. The subject is therefore very important for students studying Commerce/Business subjects. This book is also useful to others who wish to understand the concept of Business Laws for their individual information.

This textbook is designed to provide the readers a basic understanding of Laws relating to business focusing on the students studying Mercantile Law at the Diploma Level, Graduation Level (B.Com, BBM and BBA) at the Post Graduation Level and also for those taking up professional courses like CA-CPT and CS-foundation. The book also includes ample illustrations and decided legal cases for the reader to understand related topics. This book would be useful for every person as it is necessary to have some knowledge of law for his everyday transactions. The knowledge of Mercantile Law or Business Laws would make a person appreciate the legal entanglements pertaining to their transactions, avoid legal litigations, and obtain timely expert advice.

With the intention of making the subject of Law interesting and help students having Business Law as a subject either at the Under Graduation level or Post Graduation level, the text is divided into 4 chapters for easy segregation, topicwise. The reader is encouraged to analyze and evaluate legal provisions and to adopt a practical approach to seeking solutions. Suggestions for the improvement of the book will be gratefully acknowledged.

—Author

ACKNOWLEDGEMENT

For every endeavor , there is always an inspiration & motivation. My main motivator is my Sister Ms. Teresa ,who has been a pillar of strength and encouragement.

My sincere thanks to Mr. V.R. Raghunathan, Advocate, Mysore (Retd.) Senior Manager (HR), M/s BEML Ltd., Mysore and Hon. Secretary of National Institute of Personnel Management (NIPM), Mysore for his constant motivation, valuable suggestions in my academic pursuits and also for the reflections on making this book more useful to the readers.

My thanks are also due to my students, friends and their families for the encouragement, timely feedback and support, directly and indirectly assisting in the completion of this book on time.

Last, but not the least, I thank the publisher for publishing this book and ensuring it reaches those who need it the most.

—Author

CONTENTS

1

MERCANTILE LAW

1.1 INTRODUCTION TO LAW

The term 'law' is used in many senses. Depending upon the context in which the term is used, we speak of the laws of science, ethics, games and sport, etc. In the context of physical and natural sciences the term law means uniformity in nature and in other branches of knowledge, the term refers to rule of external human action. Therefore, whether it is scientific law, social law or moral law, the term 'law' in its widest sense means a rule of action.

Law, in simple terms mean 'rules'. Rules include a set code of conduct to regulate external human actions and conduct in their dealing with each other and with the government. Man is a social being and comes into contact with people in different capacities. In all his associations, he is expected to observe a code of conduct. The basic objective of law is to make human associations possible and conducive to the welfare of the society. For example, with a vehicle mechanic for repair of the vehicle, with a tailor to get a dress stitched, with the government as a taxpayer or with the seller of goods, as a buyer. In all these associations, he is expected to observe code of conduct – these are called rules. The objective of these rules is to make human association conducive for the welfare of the State and its people.

Since law is a rule of conduct for the regulation of civil society, it is considered in its strictest sense, as a body of principles that govern human conduct and the observance of which can be enforced in Courts. The force used is known as 'sanction'. It is this sanction which the State administers to secure obedience to its laws. The main object of law being, creation and protection of legal rights.

The purpose of law is to maintain order and secure justice within a given society, maintain status quo in society, ensuring stability and security of social order, enable individuals, maximum of freedom to assert themselves and determine the sphere within which the existence and activity of each individual will be secure and free. The main goal of law is justice. Law is an effective instrument for securing justice because it has the sanction of the State power behind it. The different branches of law are (*i*) Constitutional Law (*ii*) Administrative Law (*iii*) Civil Law and (*iv*) Criminal Law.

(A) Definition of Law

Salmon defines Law as "*A body of principles recognized and applied by the State in the administration of justice*".

Holland defines Law as "*A rule of external human action enforced by the Sovereign Political Authority*".

According to Austin, "*A Law is a rule of conduct imposed and enforced by the Sovereign*". Thereby law is the general body of rules commanding general obedience, enforced by a sovereign political authority. Being a command, law must be obeyed regardless of the fact whether it is in conformity with morality or not and however ethically bad it might be.

The dictionary describes law as "*A rule or body of rules of conduct inherent in human nature and essential to or binding upon human society*". It can also be said that, Law is a rule of conduct or procedure established by custom, agreement, or authority. It is a set of rules or principles dealing with a specific area of a legal system *e.g.*, Business Law, Tax Law, Labour Law etc. It is a piece of enacted legislation which creates a condition of social order and justice which enforces a system of judicial administration giving effect to the laws of a community. A set of rules that is enforceable by the Courts, regulating the government of a State, the relationship between the organs of government and the subjects of the State, and the relationship or conduct of subjects towards each other.

From these definitions certain features of law can be easily outlined as (*i*) a body of rules (*ii*) external acts of human beings governed by rules. (*iii*) a sovereign political authority enforcing rules (law presupposes existence of a State). (*iv*) law is generally imposed by some authority (*v*) law can be enforced in a court of law. Legally, a set of rules alone is not sufficient unless;

1. It is enforced by the State.
2. The State to enforce such law is a Sovereign State;
3. It receives due recognition.
4. It attempts to achieve some sort of security and uniformity in its application.

Rules which have the above mentioned characteristics are called 'law'. Law includes all the rules and principles which regulate our relations with other individuals and with the State. In developing the science of law, the Roman Jurists evolved three fundamental and closely related concepts, namely:

(*i*) Natural Law - *jus naturale.*

(*ii*) Law common to nations – *jus gentium.*

(*iii*) Civil Law – *jus civile.*

Civil law, which was to be in conformity with natural law, was interpreted to mean customary law of a particular State. Although the Law of Nations was considered to be distinct from Natural Law, they were merged together by the Dutch Jurist Hugo Grotius, who is regarded as the Father of International Law. Therefore we may conclude that, Law is a body of rules that controls the external acts of human beings or of society. The body that controls and imposes such acts is the sovereign political authority. Lastly, law can be enforced in a court of law.

(B) Definition of Business Law

Business Law is a body of legal rules which relate to the conduct of business. It is also known as Mercantile Law or Commercial law. The term 'Business', 'Commercial' and 'Mercantile' are synonymous. According to Slater, *"The phrase Mercantile Law or Commercial Law is generally used to denote those portions of the law which deal with the rights and obligations arising out of transactions between mercantile persons"*. It comprises a vast number of laws pertaining to business transactions, and these laws govern the relation of businessmen to society. Mercantile Law, also called Business Law or Commercial Law is an important branch of Civil Law. It consists of legal rules which govern and regulate business, trade and commerce. These rules bring about definiteness in the commercial transactions.

Business Law or Mercantile Law cannot be regarded as a separate branch of law. It is a branch of general law and relates to industry, trade and commerce. It includes law relating to, the Law of Contracts, Law relating to Sale of Goods, Partnership, Company, Negotiable Instruments, Bill of Lading and Charter Party, Insurance, Common Carriers, Arbitration and Insolvency. Exceptionally, however, the laws relating to tortuous liability and certain aspects of criminal law often become relevant in business transactions. It determines the validity of contracts and prescribes the mode and manner of their performance. An individual, a partnership or a company carrying on business is a mercantile person. Mercantile transactions relate mostly to movable property.

(C) Scope of Business Law

Mercantile transactions relate to goods or movable property having a corpus or a body in material form like a common commodity of commerce, and non-corporeal movable like negotiable instruments, insurance policies, trademarks, copy rights, shares etc. Therefore, the phrase 'Business Laws' or 'Mercantile Law' is obviously a reference to transactions of trade and commerce. Business Laws concerns the study of rights and obligations arising out of mercantile transactions between mercantile persons. They may be sole-traders, common man, partnership concerns or a Joint Stock Company. Although Mercantile Law or Business Law is mainly concerned with mercantile transactions between mercantile persons, in a few cases, however, some enactments grouped as Mercantile Law, are made applicable to non-mercantile transactions between non-mercantile persons also.

Although the scope of Mercantile Law is very vast, the Indian Contract Act is the most important part of Mercantile Law. It provides a basis for the other branches of Mercantile Law. The Sale of Goods Act, Partnership Act, Company Law, etc. are all founded on the general principles of Contract Act. Therefore, the study of Contract Act is very important for understanding Mercantile Law. It deals with general principles, essential elements of a valid contract, performance of contracts and breach of contract. Certain other aspects of Mercantile Law are Sale of Goods Act, Partnership Act, Companies Act, Negotiable Instruments Act, Insolvency Law, Law of Arbitration and so on.

For the proper working of society, there must exist a code of conduct. In ancient times society was not organized. The rights of the individuals were not recognized. Gradually, society evolved and the State came into being. To regulate the State, there should be a specific code of conduct, to be followed by everyone. Thereby law evolved as a system of rights and obligations including rules and principles, which regulate our relations with other persons and with the State.

These rules and regulations took the form of statutes. To enforce the law and to resolve the conflicts arising there from, courts of law were setup by the State. Laws were made to govern almost every walk of life. Criminal laws were made to control criminal activities in the society like Indian Penal Code which enumerates which activities are considered criminal and what will be the punishment for committing a crime. Likewise, Mercantile Law was evolved to govern and regulate trade and commerce. Hence, the term Mercantile Law can be defined as that branch of law, which comprises laws concerning trade, industry and commerce. It is an ever growing branch of law, which adapts itself with the changing circumstances of trade and commerce. In a world dominated by commerce and trade, lawmakers are constantly endeavoring to find ways and means of making trade transactions and agreements follow certain codes and fair practices. All managers are bound to know their rights and obligations when entering into any agreement or contract.

(D) Sources of Business Law

The following diagram describes the sources of Law:

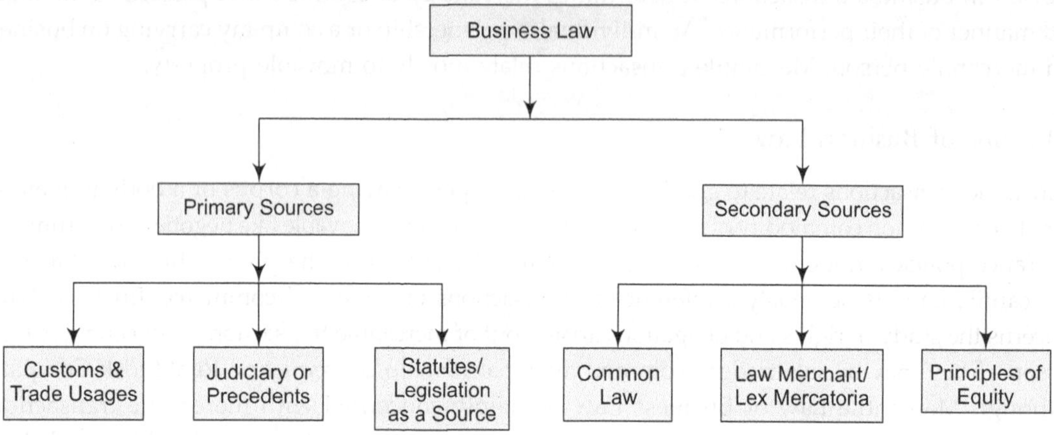

Primary Sources

Customs and Trade Usages: Customs are long established practice and considered as an unwritten law. Any conduct, act or usage that is practiced by a group of people for a long period of time becomes a custom. Therefore, customs are also considered as one of the sources of law. However, in order to be binding, a custom need to have the following requisites; the custom must have existed and practiced for a long time. The requirement of long usage is essential since it is from this that a custom derives its force as governing the rights of the parties in place of the general law.

(*a*) The custom has to be reasonable and practiced continuously from time immemorial.

(*b*) The custom must not be opposed to public policy and morality.

(*c*) The custom needs to be certain, definite and consistent.

(*d*) The custom must have an obligatory force and supported by general public opinion.

(*e*) The custom should be enjoyed peaceably without any dispute in a Court of Law.

Custom law is the name given to the customary law *i.e.*, customs and usages recognized and enforced by the common law courts. Customs and usages which were evolved, recognized and adopted as rules of conduct by the community, acquired the name 'common law', when they became common over a wide area and, when found expression in the judicial pronouncements, they became legal principles of law. 'Custom', in simple words, means a usage or practice common to many or to a particular place. It is a long established practice considered as unwritten law. A particular act, usage or conduct practiced by a group of people for a long period becomes a custom. In order to be valid and have a binding force, a custom must have the following requisites, namely; Firstly, immemorial antiquity; the custom must have existed for so long that it goes beyond the memory of man. The requirement of long usage is essential since it is from this that a custom derives its force as governing the parties' rights in place of the general law. Secondly, a custom must be reasonable *i.e.*, it must not be contrary to reason, it must be practiced continuously from time immemorial, must not be opposed to public policy and morality. A custom must be certain and definite, it should be consistent. It must have an obligatory force and supported by the general public opinion. And lastly enjoyed peaceably without any dispute in a Law Court or otherwise.

Judiciary or Precedents: A substantial portion of common law is the product of decided cases accumulated in volumes of law reports. A judicial precedent may, according to Salmond, be either authoritative or persuasive. The decisions of the Supreme Court of India, for instance, are authoritative for all courts in India, while a decision of the High Court, although authoritative to its subordinate courts, are only persuasive to the other High Courts and subordinate courts. The doctrine of *stare decisis* (to stand by past decisions) is the name given to the rule that subordinate courts must follow the precedents declared by superior courts. Judges of the superior courts incorporate in their judgment *ratio decidendi* (principle or reason for the decision), and the judgement is binding on the subordinate courts in similar cases. While *ratio decidendi* is a vital part of the judgment, *obiter dicta* (things said by the way) are not essential to the decision. A substantial portion of the English Common Law is the product of decided cases accumulated in volumes of law reports.

According to Salmond, a judicial precedent may be either authoritative or persuasive. While *ratio decidendi* is authoritative to all the subordinate courts, *obiter dicta* may be persuasive. The decisions of the Supreme Court of India, are authoritative for all courts in India, while a decision of High Court, although authoritative to its subordinate courts, are only persuasive to the other High Courts and subordinate courts. The Indian Mercantile Law more often than not is codified by parliamentary enactments. English judicial decisions apply only in the event where Indian law is silent on a particular point and the customs and usages prevailing in India permit such application. Otherwise, such decisions are merely persuasive and of guidance only.

Judicial precedents are an important source of law based on the principle that what has been decided in an earlier case is binding in a similar future case, unless there is a change in the circumstances. It is also called as Doctrine of Precedents or Doctrine of *Stare-Decisis,* which means adherence to the earlier decision and not unsettling things, which are already established. *'Obiter dictum'* means an incidental and collateral opinion, which is uttered by a judge while delivering a judgment. It is a mere saying by the way, a chance remark, which is not binding upon future Courts. The judicial precedents are an important source of law. Sometimes, there is no provision which can answer a particular question of law. In such cases the court will look into the previous decisions on similar matters to find the relevant law.

Statutes or Legislation as a source: Statute law takes precedence over common law and equity. It consists of law laid down by Acts of Parliament. Statute law takes precedence over common law and equity. This is because the supremacy of the parliament empowers it to make any law within the constitutional framework. It also has the power to nullify the decisions of the courts of law. Statute law is given effect to by courts of law, which interpret and explain the law. In the course of interpretation, a rule of law may be enunciated, and if done so, it becomes a precedent for the subordinate courts. The doctrine of *stare decisis,* meaning, to stand by past decisions, is the name given to the rule that subordinate courts must follow the precedents declared by superior courts. Judges of the superior courts incorporate in their judgment, *ratio decidendi,* which means principle or reason for the decision, and the judgment is binding on the subordinate courts in similar cases. While *ratio decidendi* is a vital part of the judgment, *obiter dicta* meaning, things said by the way, are not essential to the decision. Statute law is given effect to by courts of law, which interpret and explain the law.

The term legislation is used in different senses. In a wide sense, it includes all methods of law making and, therefore, would include laws made by judges also. In the strict sense, it may be defined as the promulgation of legal rules by an authority (Parliament or a State Legislature) that has the power to do so. In modern times, legislation is the most important source of law in all countries.

English Mercantile Law: This is the most important source of the Indian Mercantile Law. The principal source of the English Mercantile Law is the Common Law of England as modified and supplemented by Equity and Statute Law. The bulk of the Indian Mercantile Law is based on and follows, the English Mercantile Law. In the absence of any specific law, usage or custom on a particular point arising before a Court, rules of the English law *i.e.,* of justice, equity and good conscience are applied. The Courts in India are, however, selective in the application of the English Law. It is interesting to know that in England there is no English Contract Act in the form of a statute. It has been derived from common law, the usage of merchants and traders in different spheres of trade, substantiated or ratified by decisions in the Court of Law.

Secondary Sources

Common Law: In other words, it is the customs, traditions and usages which were recognized and adopted as rules of conduct, evolved as 'common law'. The common laws are the usages recognized and enforced by common law courts. Such customs became common over a period of time and found expression in the judicial pronouncements; they became legal principles of law. The Court of Exchequer, the Court of Common Pleas and the Court of King's Bench were the common law courts which grew out of the King's Council known as the ***Curia Regis*** over a period of time after the Norman Conquest way back in the year 1066. When the Courts of England were being centralized, the common laws were acknowledged and established as law by the end of the reign of Henry III. The English common law is unwritten and not codified by the Parliament. It is gathered only from law reports.

Law Merchant /Lex Mercatoria: One of the most important sources of English Mercantile Law is the Law Merchant or *'Lex Mercatoria'*, a name given to the legal principles based on customs and usages that developed first as a separate system of law and subsequently became part of the common law. The fixed and stereotyped English common law could not provide justice for disputes amongst merchants. The reason for the dissatisfaction was the different domicile of the merchants who came to trade. As such they were not acquainted with the common law and it was difficult for them to refer their disputes to the Courts of Common Pleas at the Westminster Hall in London. Hence, there grew among the western European merchants, during the 14th and 15th centuries, a large number of customs and usages, supplemented by borrowing from Roman law. Since, the law merchant received in its growth contributions from every country of Western Europe; it was regarded as a special type of *jus gentium*.

Principles of Equity: According to Salmond, equity may mean morality, honesty, fairness or principles of natural justice. Equity is a system of law parallel to the rules of common law and statute law. According to the principles of Equity, relief is granted under the principles based on morality, honesty, fairness or principles of natural justice. Slater calls it supplemental law since it modifies common law in some respects and supplements it in others so as to make the English legal system more complete. There were valid reasons for suitors to be dissatisfied due to the following reasons, namely:

(*a*) The common law remedy with regard to money compensation in the form of damages was not a satisfactory relief.

(*b*) The common law was inadequate to serve the growing needs of suitors and the law of contracts was undeveloped.

(*c*) The defendant was too powerful, especially if he were a man of wealth and power.

(*d*) Where foreign merchants were suitors, the court lacked jurisdiction to try the case.

Therefore, such dissatisfied suitors began to present petitions to the King, who in turn passed them on to be heard by the Chancellor, who was regarded as the 'Keeper of the King's Conscience'. The Chancellor began to sit as a separate court known as the Court of Chancery and granted relief based on notions of justice, equity and good conscience. The reliefs granted by the Court of Chancery came to be known as equitable remedies as contrasted with the common law remedy. However, where common law and equity conflicted, it was propounded that equity should prevail.

Custom and usage of a trade play an important role in business dealings of that trade. To have a binding force, the custom or usage must be certain, reasonable and well known. Now it is more than a century that the Mercantile Laws are governing trade and commerce. The law of contract is the foundation upon which the superstructure of modern business is built. It is common knowledge that in business transactions quite often promises are made at one time and the performance follows later. In such a situation if either of the parties were free to go back on its promise without incurring any liability, there would be endless complications and it would be impossible to carry on trade and commerce. Hence the law of contract was enacted which lays down the legal rules relating to promises, their formation, their performance, and their enforceability. Explaining the object of the law of contract Sir William Anson observes, "*The law of contract is intended to ensure that what a man has been led to expect shall come to pass, that what has been promised to him shall be performed*".

The law of contract is applicable not only to the business community but also to others. Everyone of us enters into a number of contracts almost every day, and most of the time we do so without even realizing what we are doing from the point of law. A person seldom realizes that when he entrusts his scooter to the mechanic for repairs, he is entering into a contract of bailment; or when he buys a packet of biscuits, he is making a contract of the sale of goods; or again when he goes to the cinema to see a movie, he is making yet another contract; and so on. Besides, the law of contract furnishes the basis for the other branches of Mercantile Law. The enactments relating to sale of goods, negotiable instruments, insurance, partnership and insolvency are all founded upon the general principles of Contract Law. That is why the study of the law of contract precedes the study of all other subdivision of Mercantile Law.

The Contract Act has remained unchanged during the last many years. But it is equally usual with this subject that its body of case law is constantly swelling. A number of decisions have brought about changes in the approach to problems which were all along considered as more or less settled affairs. For example, contracting through tenders was considered to be a secret process of finding the minimum quotation. But now it has been held that all the tenders can be invited to the negotiation table and given an opportunity to revise their figures openly. The courts have also laid down as to how the bounties hidden in a Government contract should be distributed. Negligent professional advisers have been held liable for the miseries, which they bring about under the weight of their wrong advice. Setoff is an equitable right and its exclusion has been held to be unreasonable. The Doctrine of Promissory Estoppels has become an independent working principle with this restriction that no estoppels can be claimed in reference to things which contain legal violations. A balance sheet would import estoppels and constitute a promise to pay a time barred debt. The Doctrine of Undue Influence has been applied to cases involving economic duress by threatening breach of contract and compelling the party to come for renegotiations. The Supreme Court relieved an illiterate person from the consequences of his signature (A signature obtained by misreading of the document to him). Price escalation clauses have to be used with restraint and reason. Termination of Government agencies and trade in securities held by Government institutions must be done with a sense of responsibility so as not to cause any damage to public distributions and markets.

Terms of contract which may shock the conscience of the court are likely to fall foul of Sec. 23 and may, therefore, be regarded as unlawful. Similarly, contracts against public welfare would be regarded as unlawful within the meaning of Sec. 23. Terms excluding jurisdiction of courts are to be strictly construed and not left to inferences and accordingly an action may be allowed in a jurisdiction where a carrier has his subordinate office. A Supreme Court decision discovers and establishes principles as to jurisdiction in the context of international arbitration agreements. Compensation can be awarded in a suit filed for specific enforcement where the contract has become incapable of being specifically enforced. Writ jurisdiction has not been permitted to be used as a method of enforcing contracts.

The Indian Contract Act was enacted from the 1st day of September, 1872. It is applicable to the whole of India except the State of Jammu and Kashmir. The Indian Mercantile Law being mostly codified by parliamentary enactments, English judicial decisions apply if the Indian Law is silent on a point and the customs and usages prevailing in India permit such application. Otherwise, such decisions are merely persuasive and of guidance only.

The Indian judiciary owes its origin to the English judicial system that existed before independence. The Constitution of India provides the three-tier judiciary, which is independent of the executive and the legislature. The Indian Constitution provides a unified court system. Its objective is to render justice to those who seek legal remedy. The unique feature of the Indian Constitution is that it distributes powers between the Center and the States.

QUESTIONS

1. How would you define the term 'Law'?
2. Define Business or Mercantile Law.
3. Explain the scope of Business Law.
4. What are the sources of Business/Mercantile/Commercial law?

2

THE INDIAN CONTRACT ACT, 1872

2.1 INTRODUCTION TO THE INDIAN CONTRACT ACT 1872

The term CONTRACT is derived from the Latin term *'contracum'*, which means to *'draw together'*. Section 2(h) of the Indian Contract Act defines a contract as *"an agreement enforceable by law"*. Salmond defines a contract as *"an agreement creating and defining obligations between the parties"*. The definitions therefore imply that there should be an agreement between two parties which can be enforced in a court of law.

What is an agreement? An agreement can be described as a promise or a set of promises. Section 2(e) of the Act defines an agreement as *"every promise and every set of promises, forming consideration for each other, is an agreement."* Accordingly, a contract is an agreement and an agreement is a set of promise between two parties. A contract therefore requires two parties, one making an offer called the *promisor* or *offerer*, to another person called the *promisee* or *offeree*. The law of contracts is primarily concerned with self-imposed obligations. Therefore, the parties to a contract do enjoy freedom of contract and the rights and duties created by them can be enforced even though the terms of the contract are harsh or unfair to one party.

Illustration: *A offers to sell his bicycle to B for ₹ 500. Here, A is making a proposal or offer to B. A is the offerer and B is the offeree. If B accepts the offer made by A, a contract comes into existence. Both A and B shall abide by their respective promises as this agreement between the two is enforceable in a court of law.*

It is through the device of contracts that credit required in modern business is created and put to use. Therefore, a study of Mercantile Law necessarily starts with a study of the rules of law governing contracts. The law of contracts is the basis for other enactments covered by the term 'Mercantile Law'. As a common man, we enter into a number of contracts in our day to day activities and as such, it is necessary for us to familiarize ourselves with the law relating to contracts. The word 'Contract' is the customary and standard method of defining the rights and duties between the persons who give and taken or the buyer and seller, in a transaction. The law of contract is applicable not only to the business community, but also to others. The law of contract furnishes the basis for the other branches of Mercantile Law. The enactments relating to sale of goods, negotiable instruments, insurance, partnership and insolvency are all founded upon the general principles of contract law.

In its singular sense, the phrase 'Law of Contract' refers to a body of rules applicable to all contracts regardless of their content or form. As per the Indian Contract Act, the plural term is more relevant since the Act contains not only the general principles of contract but also the rules of law governing special contracts. The Indian Contract Act contains a number of limiting principles subject to which the parties may create rights and duties for themselves. In fact the parties to the contract are the makers of law for themselves. The law takes cognizance of their promise to each other (so far as it is not against the law or public policy) and enforces the promise made against the party who has defaulted in his performance. Therefore, the law of contract is primarily concerned with self imposed obligations.

Entering into a contract was in accordance with the philosophy of laissez-faire, in the 18th and 19th centuries. Accordingly, it was propounded that men had an absolute and immutable right to make their own contracts for themselves and the law was not expected to interfere with such a right by limiting the power of contracting. The judge was called upon to interfere only to assist the aggrieved party when the other party did not perform his part of the promise or contractual obligation. The parties to a contract enjoy freedom of contract as the rights and duties are created by them. They can frame any rules they desire. In fact the parties to the contract create the rights and duties for themselves. Once such an agreement is entered into between the parties, it can be enforced even though the terms of the contract are harsh or unfair to one party. According to Sir William Anson, *"The law of contract is intended to ensure that what a man has been led to expect shall come to pass; that what has been promised to him shall be performed"*.

The Indian Contract Act, came into force on the first day of September 1872. This Act is mainly based on English Common Law. The Act extends to the whole of India except the State of Jammu and Kashmir. The law is not exhaustive. It deals with the general principles of law of contracts and contains special contracts only but does not deal with all branches of the law of contract. There are separate Acts which deal with contracts relating to Negotiable Instruments, Sale of Goods, Partnership, Transfer of Property, Insurance, etc.

(A) Scheme of the Act

The Act is divided into:

1. General Principles of Law of Contract (Section 1 to 75).
2. Special Contract
   (*a*) Contract of Indemnity and Guarantee (Section 124 to 147).
   (*b*) Contract of Bailment and Pledge (Section 148 to 181).
   (*c*) Contract of Agency (Section 182 to 238).

The Indian Contract Act 1872

General Principles of law of contract
(Section 1 to 75).

Specific kinds of contract
(a) Contract of Indemnity and Guarantee (Section 124 to 147).
(b) Contract of Bailment and Pledge (Section 148 to 181).
(c) Contract of Agency (Section 182 to 238).

Section 1 to 75 of the Act deals with the different stages in the formation of a contract, its essential features, its performance or breach and the remedies for breach of contract. **Sections 76 to 123 were repealed from the Indian Contract Act and separate Acts called the Sale of Goods Act and Partnership Act were enacted in the year 1930 and 1932 respectively**. Special contracts, namely, indemnity and guarantee, bailment and pledge and Agency are covered under Sections 124 to 238. It is interesting to note that The Sale of Goods Act, The Indian Partnership Act, The Negotiable Instruments Act, Insurance Act, The Companies Act, etc., are not covered under the Contract Act, though they are also formed by contracts and fall within the purview of the term.

Where the Contract Act is silent on any matter, the Hindu or Mohammedan Law relating to contracts shall apply accordingly. The case in point is, the Hindu Law of Contracts known as *damdupat,* according to which, a Hindu creditor cannot recover from a Hindu debtor, interest in excess of the principal amount, is still in force in Maharashtra and Calcutta. Therefore, although the Indian Contract Act, by its very title, appears to cover the whole law of contracts, it does not itself profess to be a complete code and comprehensive. The Act therefore is not a complete code and is not exhaustive.

The extent of application of the common law to contracts in India has been examined by the Indian Law Courts in the course of a number of legal decisions. English cases are helpful only in enlightening how the English Courts have decided cases under similar circumstances. As such those cases have only a persuasive value. If the language of an Indian statute is such that it is obscure, and it cannot be understood without the help of English Law, or a particular matter cannot be brought within the provisions of the Act, it may be permissible to seek assistance from English decisions, but not when the words or the language is clear and unambiguous.

(B) Definition

Sir William Anson defines a contract as "*A legally binding agreement made between two or more persons, by which rights are acquired by one or more to acts or forbearances on the part of the other or others.*"

Section 2(h) of the Indian Contract Act, defines a contract as an agreement enforceable by law. Pollock defines a contract as "*Every agreement and promise enforceable at law is a contract*". According to Salmond, a contract is "*An agreement creating and defining obligations between the parties.*"

All the definitions imply that a contract is a legally enforceable agreement. The law however does not enforce every promise. Since enforceability apparently depends upon the existence of an agreement, it becomes necessary to know what an agreement is and what type of an agreement is enforceable by a court of law.

2.2 AGREEMENT AND ITS REQUIREMENTS

Making an offer or a proposal is the starting point in the process of concluding an agreement between two parties. Section 2(a) of the Act defines a proposal as "*When one person signifies to another his willingness to do or to abstain from doing anything with a view to obtaining the assent of that other to such act or abstinence, he is said to make a proposal.*"

According to Section 2 (c) 'the person making the proposal is called the '*promisor*' and the person accepting the proposal is called the '*promisee*'. Clause (e) of Section 2(h) of the Indian Contract Act, defines an agreement as, "*Every promise and every set of promises, forming consideration for each other, is an agreement*". Therefore, it can be stated that a 'promise' is an agreement. Section 2(b) defines a promise as, "*When the person to whom the proposal is made signifies his assent thereto, the proposal is said to be accepted. A proposal, when accepted, becomes a promise.*".

An agreement is the result of offer and acceptance. An agreement thereby needs two elements namely, proposal or offer and acceptance of the proposal or offer. Therefore, an agreement means offer by one party and the acceptance of the offer by the other to whom the offer has been made.

Requirement:

1. Two Parties , One party making an Offer and the other party accepting the offer

Offer + Acceptance = Agreement → Contract

2. Agreement should be enforceable by law. (Creation of obligation).
3. *Consensus ad idem.*
4. Promise to do or not to do something. (Act or abstinence).

Illustrations: *(1) Mr. Ram agrees to sell his house at Delhi to Mr. Shyam for ₹50,00,000. This gives rise to a legal obligation on the part of Mr. Ram to transfer ownership of the property at Delhi to Mr. Shyam and correspondingly a legal obligation on the part of Mr. Shyam to pay the stated amount to Mr. Ram. The failure on the part of either party to fulfill their part of the promise entitles the aggrieved part to file a suit against the offender and make it enforceable through a court of law. This is an example of a legally enforceable agreement.*

(2) Mr. A, husband of Mrs. Z, promises to present her a diamond necklace. If Mr. A fails to fulfill his promise, Mrs. Z, wife of Mr. A cannot sue her husband as it is a social obligation and hence cannot be enforced in a court of law.

For the formation of a contract, there must be an agreement. The agreement should be enforceable by Law. This being so, an agreement requires two parties, one to make a proposal, and the other to accept the proposal. The person making the proposal is called the '*promisor*' and the person accepting the proposal is called the '*promisee*'.

Illustration: *A tells B, 'I am willing to sell my Scooter to you for ₹30, 000' or 'will you buy my scooter for ₹30,000'. Here A is said to be making an offer or proposal to B.*

Since a proposal is only a signification or intimation by one person to another, of his willingness to do or not to do a specific act, the proposal may either be in the form of a statement or a question. Further, the proposal need not necessarily be for doing an act. It may be for not doing or abstaining from doing an act. Thus, an agreement is a two-sided bargain, to do or not to do something on one side in return for something being promised or done or not done on the other side. Technically the terms; act (to do something); abstinence or forbearance (not to do something) can be used to describe a proposal.

Secondly, the next important aspect to be noted in connection with agreement is the meeting of minds of the two parties which forms a common intention. The legal term denoted for meeting of minds is called '*consensus ad idem*'. It signifies that the parties agree about the same thing in the same sense. An accepted proposal becomes a promise.

Illustration: *A owns 2 scooters , one Kinetic Honda and another Activa. A tells B, 'I am willing to sell my Scooter to you for ₹ 30,000'. A wants to sell his Kinetic Honda Scooter to B. B however thinks he is purchasing the Activa Scooter. Here there is no consensus ad idem and consequently no contract.*

Therefore, when we analyse the definitions of contract, we find that a contract essentially consists of two elements. They are- (*i*) an agreement and (*ii*) its enforceability by law. An agreement is an accepted proposal. Consequently, to form an agreement, there must be a proposal or offer by one party and acceptance of the proposal or offer by another.

Thus Agreement = Offer + Acceptance and an Agreement enforceable by law is a contract. But an agreement becomes enforceable only when it gives rise to an obligation between both the parties to the contract. For the formation of a contract, the process of proposal or offer by one party and the acceptance thereof by the other is necessary. Accordingly, when we use the term contract, we should be careful to pick out only such of those agreements as create legal obligations.

Illustrations: *(1) Thus when Sunitha offers to take Anitha for a movie and Anitha accepts the offer, a contract is created but without any legal implications. Hence, it is social offer and if Sunitha does not keep up her promise, Anitha cannot sue her for performance.*

(2) A goes to a shopping mall, buys a gift for her friend using her credit card. She then proceeds to a courier service provider and sends the gift to her friend paying cash. Later she bought a sari for herself by issuing a personal cheque in exchange.

Here these contracts at the shopping mall, courier service provider and the sari shop come under transactions having economic consequences. Though there were no spoken words or promises to do anything, yet the act of providing the debit card or the issue of cheque or the payment by cash, all amounts to individual contracts, creating obligation on the part of the buyer and seller.

When one person signifies to another his willingness to do or abstain from doing anything with a view to obtaining the assent of the other to such act or abstinence, he is said to make a proposal. Thereby, when the person to whom the proposal is made signifies his assent thereto, the proposal is said to be accepted. In order to convert a proposal into a promise, the acceptance must be absolute and unqualified. This means, that an acceptance with a variation is not acceptance, it is simply a counter proposal. When the proposer prescribes any particular manner of acceptance, then the person to whom the offer is made, should accept the offer only in the mode prescribed and where no manner is prescribed, it should be in a usual and reasonable manner.

(A) *'Consensus Ad Idem'* In an Agreement

The essence of an agreement is the meeting of the minds of the parties in full and final agreement. An agreement requires mutual understanding between the parties. Mutual understanding means drawing the minds of the parties to form a common intention. Thus, *Consensus ad idem* or identity of minds signifies that the parties are agreeable about the same thing in the same sense. Accordingly, an agreement is said to be formed between two parties only when their minds coincide or when there are *ad idem* or when they agree upon the same thing in the same sense. Unless there is *Consensus ad idem*, there can be no contract.

Illustration: *Raj who owns two cars one blue and the other white, is selling his blue car to Mahesh. Mahesh thinks he is purchasing the white car. There is no Consensus ad idem and consequently no contract.*

2.3 OBLIGATION

Obligation which is also known as the '*vinculum juris*', is the legal tie bond which binds the parties to a contract and imposes the necessity of doing or abstain from doing a definite act or acts. Since obligation is the legal tie binding two or more determinate individuals, it requires two parties. Obligation should not be uncertain or indefinite. The obligation should relate to legal matters and not to social affairs. Therefore an agreement becomes enforceable only when it gives rise to an obligation. This means that a contract should consist of two constituent elements, namely, agreement and obligation. A party to a contract cannot claim any benefit of the obligation unless the same is arising from a contract. An agreement, to become a contract, must give rise to a legal obligation or duty. The term obligation is defined as a legal tie which imposes upon a definite person or persons the obligation of doing or refraining from doing a definite act or acts. An agreement which gives rise to a social obligation is not a contract.

Illustration: *Ravi agrees to sell his car to Babu for ₹1,50,000. The agreement gives rise to an obligation on the part of Ravi to deliver the car and Babu to pay the price of the car to Ravi. This agreement gives rise to legal obligation and hence this is a contract.*

An agreement may be a social agreement or a legal agreement. If Ram invites Shyam to dinner and Shyam accepts the invitation, it is a social agreement and does not give rise to contractual obligation and cannot be enforced in a court of law. It is only those agreements which are enforceable in a court of law which are contracts.

Illustrations: *(1) Geeta's father promises to pay her ₹1000 every month as pocket allowance. Later he refuses to pay. Geeta cannot recover the amount as it is a domestic agreement and there is no intention on the part of the parties to create a legal relation.*

(2) Harish invites all his friends home for his birthday party. When his friends arrive at his house they find it locked and Harish nowhere present. They cannot file a suit against Harish as it is a social agreement and there is no intention on the part of the parties to create a legal relation.

(A) Distinguishing between a Social Obligation and a Legal Obligation

The validity of an enforceable agreement or obligation depends upon whether the agreement satisfies all the essential requisites laid down in the Act. Merely because there is an agreement giving rise to a legal obligation, does not necessary follow that the agreement becomes enforceable by law and hence, could be called a *valid contract*. Section 10 of the Act lays down the essential elements required in an agreement to make it enforceable in a court of law. According to the Section "all agreement are contracts if they are made by the free consent of the parties competent to contract, for a lawful consideration and with a lawful object, and are not hereby expressly declared to be void".

(B) Who can Enter into a Contract?

- Any person who is of sound mind- *i.e.*, if at the time of making the contract, he is capable of understanding and forming a rational judgement as to its effect upon his interest.
- Any person who has attained the age of majority according to the law to which he is subject.
- Any person who is not disqualified from contracting by any law to which he is subject.
- Any person who is competent to enter into a contract.

The following persons are therefore incompetent to enter into a contract:

- Minor.
- Person of unsound mind.
- Person who has been disqualified by law to which he is subject.

2.4 CLASSIFICATION OF CONTRACTS

Section 2 of the Act, which is called the 'interpretation clause', under clause (h) defines a contract and also provides the basis for the classification of contracts. The following diagram depicts the classification of contacts on the basis of enforceability, validity and performance.

Classification of Contracts

Enforceability (Validity)	Mode of creation (Formation)	Extent of Execution (Performance)
- Valid	- Express	- Executed
- Voidable	- Implied	- Executory
- Void contracts	- Constructive/Quasi contracts	- Unilateral.
- Illegal /Unenforceable		- Bilateral

(A) Classification According to Validity

From the point of view of the **validity** or **enforceability** of a contract, it may be valid, voidable, void, unenforceable or illegal. A contract is based on an agreement and an agreement becomes a contract when all the essential elements are present. Such an agreement becomes a valid contract, enforceable in a court of law. In such a case, the contract is a perfectly valid contract and further, such a contract creates a right in *personam,* which can be enforced against the party on whom a legal obligation to do or not to do a definite act is imposed.

However, when one or more of the essential elements of a contract is or are missing, the contract becomes either **voidable, void, illegal or unenforceable**.

According to Sec 2(i) of the Act, *"All agreements, which are enforceable at the option of any one of the parties, and the other party has no such option, such contracts are known as voidable contracts"*. A **voidable contract** is an agreement that is binding and enforceable, but because of the lack of one or more of the essentials of a valid contract, it may be repudiated. Thus, a voidable contract is one which is enforceable at the option of one of the parties to it, but not the other. The party entitled either to affirm it or reject it, is naturally the aggrieved party. As such, it is he at whose option the contract becomes enforceable. Usually a contract becomes voidable when the consent of one of the parties to the contract is obtained by coercion, undue influence, misrepresentation or fraud. Such a contract is voidable at the option of the aggrieved party, that is, the party whose consent was so obtained. But the aggrieved party must exercise his option of rejecting the contract.

(*i*) Within a reasonable time and

(*ii*) Before the rights of third parties intervene, otherwise the contract cannot be repudiated.

Illustration: *Anil is induced to sell his scooter through undue influence at a very low price. Here, Anil's consent has been obtained by use of force. The contract is voidable at his option. Anil may avoid the contract or elect to be bound by it.*

A contract becomes voidable in other cases also. If a contract contains reciprocal promises and one of the parties to it prevents the other from performing his promise, the party so prevented, can set aside the contact.

Illustrations: *(1) A building contractor enters into a contract with a land owner for constructing a compound wall. However when the building contract comes to the site for executing his work, the land owner does not permit him or prevents the contractor form performing his promise. In such a situation, the building contractor can set aside the contract.*

(2) Similarly, if a party promises to do a certain thing within a specified time, but fails to do it, the other party may avoid the contract, if time were the essence of the contract.

Clause (g) of Section 2 lays down that an agreement not enforceable by law is said to be void. A **void agreement** does not create any legal rights or obligations. According to this definition, there can only be a void agreement but not a void contract, since the term contract suggests or proposes the idea of enforceability. A void agreement is a nullity in the eyes of law, and thereby does not create any legal rights or obligations on the parties.

Illustration: *An agreement with a minor or an agreement without consideration.*

However, in certain cases an agreement which is otherwise valid, becomes void subsequently owing to certain reasons such as impossibility of performance or illegality. Thus, it is in the context of distinguishing between a void agreement and a void contract that the term has been found to be convenient for usage. If an agreement is void from the time it is entered into, the agreement is said to be void *'ab initio'* or *'prima facie'*. In case of such agreements, it is inappropriate to use the term 'contract'. An agreement with a minor, is *void-ab-initio* or from the beginning, so also agreements in restraint of trade, in restraint of marriage, wagering agreements etc.

A contract which was valid when it was first entered into but subsequently becomes unenforceable due to impossibility of performance, change of law or other reasons is called a **void contract**. If the performance of a contract becomes impossible owing to the operation of law, the contract becomes a **void contract**. A contract which is enforceable by law may sometimes cease to be enforceable subsequently, for such reasons as impossibility or illegality. Such contracts become void only when they cease to be enforceable. Till such time, they are perfectly valid. Such contracts are known as *'ex post facto'*. Section 2 (j) of the Act lays down that, *"A contract, which ceases to be enforceable by law becomes void when it ceases to be enforceable."* This clause is with reference to a void contract.

Illustration: *Raj contracts to import goods from a foreign country, which is perfectly valid. However, if war breaks out between the countries, it becomes impossible owing to the operation of law, to import goods. The contract therefore cannot be enforced and becomes a void contract.*

Supervening impossibility (also called as 'act of god', where the performance of a contract becomes impossible due to natural calamities like flood, earthquake, destruction of the subject matter due to lightening etc.) as contemplated in Section 56 of the Act, and impossibility of performance on which a contingent contract depends, according to Section 32 of the Act, render the contract void subsequently. Correspondingly, if the performance of the contract becomes impossible owing to the operation of law, the contract becomes void. A contract becomes void even when the party entitled to set aside the contract chooses to do so.

	Void Agreement		Voidable Agreements
1.	A void agreement is nullity in the eyes of law. It is void *ab initio.*	1.	A voidable agreement is enforceable at the desire of the affected party.
2.	The aggrieved party in a void agreement cannot enforce it in a court of law.	2.	A voidable agreement is valid in the beginning but declared void by the party having the option to make it void.
3.	An agreement is void only when it is made with a person who is not competent to enter into a contract, an agreement without consideration or based on mistake or against public policy or immoral.	3.	When the consent of a part is obtained through coercion, undue influence, fraud or misrepresentation, it becomes a voidable agreement.
4.	Goods or property cannot be transferred to a third party.	4.	Goods or property can be transferred if the affected party has not made the voidable contract void by exercising his option.

(B) Illegal Contracts or Unenforceable Contracts

Illegal Contracts or Unenforceable Contracts are contracts which the law forbids to be made. It cannot be enforced in a court of law because of some technical defect such as the absence of the contract in writing or where the remedy has been barred by lapse of time or insufficiency of stamp etc. All illegal agreements are void but all void agreements or contracts are not necessarily illegal. An agreement is said to be illegal and void if its object or consideration is fraudulent, injures another person, is forbidden by law or the courts regard it as immoral and opposed to public policy. A contract becomes unenforceable for want of attestation, registration, absence of legal formalities (in writing), insufficient stamp, want of proof, or because of the period of limitation.

Illustrations: *(1) An agreement to destroy evidence or commit a robbery.*

(2)X hires K to injure A and pays him ₹ 10,000.

(C) Classification According to Formation of Contracts

Express contract: When a contract is made by words spoken or written, the contract is said to be express. In an express contract, the terms are made clear either in writing or orally or both at the time of entering into an agreement. An express contract is one that is explicitly set forth in words, either spoken or written. It does not arise from action or implications between the parties to the contract.

Illustration: *A tells B through an SMS that he offers his Vespa Scooter for ₹40,000 and B informs A on telephone that he accepts the offer. This is an express contract.*

Implied Contract: When an offer or acceptance is made otherwise than in words, such a contract is said to be implied. An implied contract is one which is inferred from the acts or conduct of the parties or course of dealings between them. It is not the result of any express promise or promises between the parties but of their particular acts.

Illustrations: *(1) A who was instructed to deliver a basket of oranges to B, delivers the basket of oranges to X by mistake. In this case, B is obligated to return the basket of oranges to A. But, if B does not return the basket of* *oranges to A, and instead keeps it for himself, then an implied contract comes into existence. That is, by B's acceptance of the basket of oranges, he is bound to pay A the cost of the basket of oranges.*

(2) There is an implied contract when A (i) gets into a public bus, or (ii) orders for a meal in a restaurant etc.

(3) In Upton Rural District Council Vs. Powell- a fire broke out in Powell's farm and he called upon the Upton District fire brigade to put out the fire which the latter did. Powell's farm however did not come under the jurisdiction of the fire service zone, although Powell believed it to be so. Held, he was liable to pay for the service that was rendered by the fire brigade as there was an implied promise to pay.

Quasi contract: These contracts are also referred to as constructive contracts. Such contracts do not come into existence by virtue of an agreement express or implied between the parties but the law infers or recognizes a contract due to the actions between the parties, under special circumstances. Strictly speaking, a quasi-contract is not a contract at all. A quasi contract is based upon the equitable principle that a person shall not be allowed to retain unjust benefit at the expense of another. These contracts contain certain relations resembling those created by a contract. (**Note:** Quasi Contracts have been dealt with in detail at the end of this chapter)

Illustration: *Sheela visits her classmate's house to show her new dress, but forgets to take it back. Her classmate wears the dress as her own. Here, the moment Sheela's classmate wears Sheela's dress; she is obliged to pay Sheela, the cost of the dress. Though there is no agreement between the parties, but due to actions between the parties, the law recognizes it as a contract.*

(D) Classification According to Performance

Executed Contract: 'Executed' means that which is done. An executed contract is one in which both the parties have performed their respective obligations. When a promisor and promisee perform their part of the promise or, if the consideration for the promise in a contract is accomplished, such a contract is said to be executed. A contract is said to be executed when the parties to the contract perform their respective part of the promise.

Illustration: *A agrees to stitch a shirt for B for ₹150. When A finishes stitching the shirt and B pays the price to A, i.e, when both the parties perform the obligation, the contract is said to be executed.*

Executory Contract: When the obligation or promise made by one or either parties to the contract is yet to be performed, such a contract is called an *Executory contract*. 'Executory' means that which remains to be carried into effect. An executory contract is one in which both the parties have yet to perform their obligations. (a contract may sometimes be partly executed and partly executory)

Illustration: *Where C a contractor, agrees to build A's house from the 15th of next month and A in consideration promises to pay ₹10,00,000 for the cost of construction , the contract is Executory because it is yet to be carried out. This is because there is an act which still remains to be done by both parties.*

Unilateral contract is a contract in which only one party has to perform his part of the promise. A unilateral or one-sided contract in one in which only one party has to fulfill his obligation at the time of the formation of the contract, the other party having fulfilled his obligation at the time of the contract or before the contract comes into existence. Such contacts are also known as contracts with 'executed consideration'.

Illustration: *Sharath advertises a reward of ₹1500 to anyone who finds his lost purse. Girish, knowing about the offer finds the purse and gives it to Sharath. As soon as Girish finds the purse, he has performed his part of the obligation and it remains for Sharath to pay the reward to Girish.*

Bilateral contract is a contract in which the promise of both the parties to the contract is outstanding. When the obligation on the part of both the parties is yet to be performed, these contracts are known as contracts with executory consideration.

Illustration: *Ram agrees to build a house for Shyam after Shyam deposits a sum of ₹30,00,000 in his bank account.*

2.5 ESSENTIAL ELEMENTS OF A VALID CONTRACT

The validity of an enforceable agreement depends upon whether the agreement satisfies all the essential requirements laid down in the Act. Section 10 of the Act lays down the essentials of a valid contract. According to this Section, "*All agreements are contracts if they are made by the free consent of the parties competent to contract, for a lawful consideration and with a lawful object and are not hereby expressly declared to be void.*" The definition states that contracts are agreements, but all agreements need not be contracts. It is only those agreements that satisfy or fulfill the essential elements laid down by the Act that can be called a contract enforceable in a court of law.

According to the Act, the essential elements required to make an agreement, a valid contract are as follows: (*i*) Proposal or (Offer) and Acceptance of the offer made, with an intention to create a legal relationship. (*ii*) Lawful consideration (*iii*) Competent to contract or contractual capacity. (*iv*) Free Consent (*v*) Lawful object (*vi*) Agreement must not have been expressly declared to be void. (*vii*) Possibility of performance. (*viii*) Terms of the agreement must be certain (*ix*) Legal formalities. It is only when all the elements are present in the agreement made, that the contract becomes a valid contract, enforceable in a court of law.

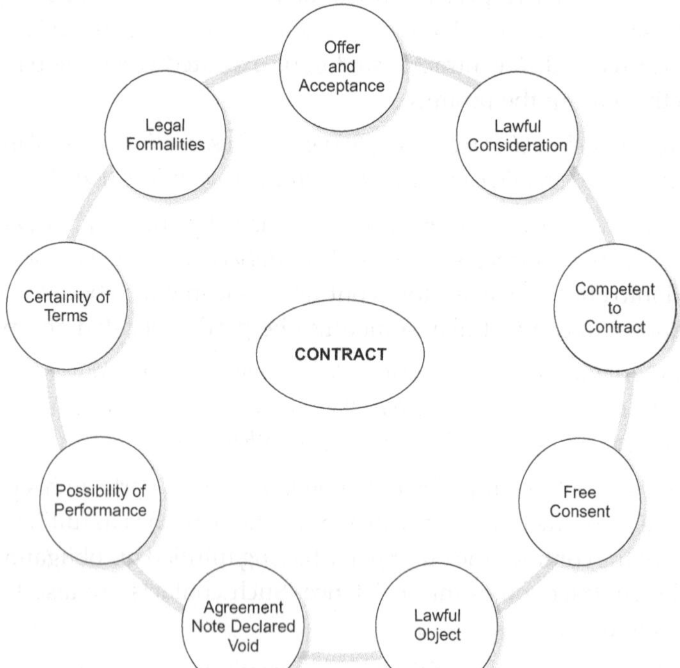

(A) Offer and Acceptance

The first essential element of a valid contract is the presence of an agreement between the parties. Sec 2(a) of the Act defines a proposal as, *"When one person signifies to another his willingness to do or to abstain from doing anything, with a view to obtaining the assent of that other to such act or abstinence, he is said to make a proposal."*

The person making the offer is called the *offerer* and the person to whom such an offer is made is called *offeree.* The offer made may not be only to obtain the assent to do a particular act but also an assent to abstain from doing a particular act which will also constitute a valid proposal.

Illustrations: *(1) A says to B, will you purchase my car for ₹ 95,00,000. A, in this case, is making an offer to B as he signifies to B his willingness to sell his car to B for ₹ 95,00,000 with a view to obtaining B's assent to purchase the car.*

(2) A promises to pay B ₹ 500 provided B does not complain to his parents about A's absence from college. A's proposal or offer to pay ₹ 500 is done with a view to obtaining the assent of B, not to do something.

There must be two parties to an agreement *i.e.,* one party making the offer and the other party accepting it. The terms of the offer must be definite and the acceptance of the offer must be absolute and unconditional. The acceptance must also be according to the mode prescribed and must be communicated to the offerer. In order to judge whether there is an agreement between two parties, it is necessary to find out whether there is *'consensus ad idem'* or identity of mind between the parties.

Illustration: *Mr. A has two Tata Nano cars , one Yellow and the other White. He offers to sell his Yellow car to Mr. Z for 90,000 . Mr. Z accept the offer thinking it to be in respect of the White Tata Nano car. Here, the agreement between Mr. A and Mr. Z, is not enforceable, owing to the absence of consensus ad idem or identity of minds and hence void.*

Although the intention to create a legal relationship is not mentioned in Section 10 of the Act, it is an important ingredient according to the English law. Since the same is recognized by courts in India, it is necessary that the agreement sought to be enforced should contemplate legal relation between the parties to the contract. In the absence of such an intention, the agreement cannot be enforced. When two parties enter into an agreement, their intention must be to create legal relationship between them. If there is no such intention on the part of the parties, there is no contract between them. Agreement of a social or domestic nature are not contracts and cannot be enforced in a court of law.

Illustrations: *(1) An agreement to attend a social or religious function, to dine at a friend's house, to watch a movie with a friend, etc., does not confer any right of action since it does not create any legal obligation.*

(2) Balfour Vs. Balfour – A husband promised to pay his wife a household allowance of £30 every month. Later the parties separated and the husband failed to pay the amount to his wife. The wife sued for the allowance. Held, agreements such as these were outside the realm of contract altogether.

Offer

An offer may be express (written or by words spoken) or implied *i.e.,* understood by the conduct of the parties, or the circumstances of the case. When the offer is implied, it is called an implied offer.

Illustration: *A transport company runs a bus on a particular route. There is an implied offer by the transport company to carry passengers for a certain fare. The acceptance of the offer is complete as soon as a passenger boards the bus.*

When an offer is made to a definite person, it is called a *specific offer*. It can be accepted only by the person to whom it is made. When an offer is made to the world at large, it is called a general offer.

Illustration: *In the famous case Carlill Vs. Carbolic Smoke Ball Co., A company advertised a reward of £100 to any person who contracted influenza after using the smoke balls manufactured by the company, in accordance to its printed directions. One Mrs Carlill used the smoke balls according to the directions of the company but contracted influenza. The company however refused to pay the reward promised stating that she should have given prior intimation before accepting the offer. The court held that she could recover the amount as it was a general offer, not to any specific person but to the whole world and by buying the smoke balls, she had accepted the offer.*

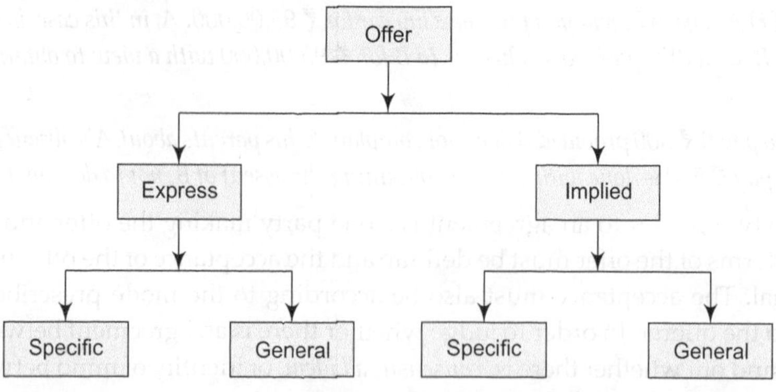

An offer may be classified according to the mode it is put forward. Accordingly, an offer may be either an express offer or an implied offer. An offer which is expressed by words written or spoken is called an '*express offer*', whereas when an offer is deciphered or interpreted by the conduct of the parties, is called '*implied offer*'.

An offer can be further classified according to the type of proposal, which could be either 'Specific' or 'General'. An offer is said to be specific when addressed to a specific individual or a group of individuals. And when an offer is addressed to an unascertain body of individuals, or to the public at large, it is said to be general offer. According to Salmond, a specific offer is called 'offer to individuals' and a general offer is called '*offer at large*'.

Illustrations: *(1) Geeta, advertises in the newspaper offering a reward of ₹1000 to anyone who brings back her lost dog. The offer can be accepted by anyone, and is a general offer.*

(2) In Carlill Vs. Carbolic Smoke Ball Co. (1893), a leading case on general offer, the defendants who were the proprietors and vendors of a medical preparation advertised in several newspapers, offering a reward of £100 to anyone who contracted influenza after using their smoke ball, three times daily for two weeks, as per the instructions printed on the cover. Ms.Carlill, the plaintiff, bought one of the balls on the faith of the advertisement and used it as per the directions mentioned but still got affected with influenza. The company initially refused to pay the amount as there was no communication of the acceptance of the offer by the lady. However, the court ruled that the company was liable to pay the amount declared.

(3) G makes an offer to P for the sale of his car for ₹200,000. This is a specific offer.

(i) Legal Rules as to Offer

(*a*) Offer must be such as is capable of being accepted and giving rise to legal relationship. A social invitation, even if it is accepted, does not create legal relationship because it is not so intended. In making an offer, whether the offerer intended to enter into a binding contract or not, can be known from the nature of the agreement and the surrounding circumstances.

Illustration: *In Balfour Vs.Balfour (1919), Mr. Balfour, who was serving the Government of Ceylon, went to England with his wife on leave. After the expiry of the period of leave, Mr. Balfour had to go back to Ceylon, but his wife could not accompany him for medical reasons. Consequently, he promised orally to pay an allowance of £30 a month for her maintenance until she rejoined him. On his failure to make the payment, the wife sued him for the recovery of the promised amount. Her suit was dismissed by the Court of Appeal on the ground that the agreement was only an arrangement between husband and wife, and the parties never intended to make a bargain.*

(*b*) Terms of offer must be definite, unambiguous and certain but not loose and vague. If the terms of an offer are vague or indefinite, its acceptance cannot create any contractual relationship.

Illustrations: *(1) In Taylor Vs. Partington (1855), an agreement to take a lease of a house for three years at £85 per annum, if the house was 'put into thorough repair, and the drawing rooms handsomely decorated, according to the present style', could not be enforced as the terms were vague and uncertain.*

(2) A agrees to sell to B 100 litres of oil; there is nothing whatever to show what kind of oil was intended. Hence, the agreement is void for uncertainty. However, if A deals only with coconut oil, and agrees to sell to B 100 litres of oil, there is an enforceable contract because A deals with only one kind of oil.

The terms of the contract may, therefore be ascertained from the custom of trade or from previous transactions between the same parties.

(*c*) An offer may be distinguished from the following:

(*i*) A declaration of intention and an announcement. A declaration by a person that he intends to do something gives no right of action to another.

Illustration: *A father wrote to his would-be son-in-law that his daughter would have a share of what he left. Held it was merely a statement of intention.*

(*ii*) An invitation to make an offer or do business. Just as a statement of intention, the process of agreement is usually preceded by a stage of negotiations. In the course of negotiations or preliminary discussion, if one party declares his intention of doing something, his declaration does not, by itself become an offer. Display of goods by a shop keeper in his window, with prices marked on the goods is not an offer but merely an invitation to the public to make an offer to buy the goods at the marked price.

Illustration: *If Raj asks Preetham, 'do you want to buy my car?' or ' I am willing to sell my car', he is not making an offer by only declaring his intention to sell his car.*

(*iii*) Tenders and quotations. An advertisement inviting tenders and quotations of the lowest prices is also an invitation to offer but not an offer capable of acceptance. A tender may be either (a) definite offer to specify goods or services or (b) a standing offer.

When tenders are invited for the supply of specified goods or services, it is tender as a definite offer. Each tender submitted is an offer. The party inviting tenders may accept any tender he chooses and thus bring about a binding contract.

Illustration: *A invites tenders for the supply of 100,000 bricks. X, Y and Z submit the tenders. A accepts X's tender. There is a binding contract between A and X.*

Where goods or services are required over a certain period (continuous period), a trader may invite tenders on a standing offer which is a continuing offer. The acceptance of a standing offer has the effect that, as and when the goods or services are required, an order is placed with the person who submitted the tender and each time a distinct contract is made.

Illustration: *A, a hotel manager invites tender for the supply of groceries, vegetables and milk for his hotel, for a period of one year. This is a continuous offer and the person with whom the contract is entered will have to supply the goods as per the requirement of the hotel, for a period of one year.*

(*d*) Offer must be communicated. An offer, to be complete, must be communicated to the person to whom it is made. Unless an offer is communicated to the offeree by the offerer or by his duly authorized agent, there can be no acceptance of it.

An acceptance of an offer, in ignorance of the offer is no acceptance and does not confer any right on the acceptor.

Illustration: *In Fitcher Vs Snedakar, S offered a reward to anyone who returned his lost dog. F brought the dog to S without having heard of the offer. Held, F was not entitled to the reward.*

(*e*) Offer must be made with a view to obtaining the assent. The offer to do or not to do something must be made with a view to obtaining the assent of the other party addressed and not merely with a view to declaring the intention of making an offer.

(*f*) Offer should not contain a term the non-compliance of which may be assumed to amount to acceptance. The person making the offer cannot conclude that if the acceptance is not communicated by a certain time, the offer would be considered as accepted. An offer may contain any term or condition, however onerous or difficult the same might be, and it is for the acceptor to accept all the conditions or reject them in toto. The offerer may prescribe any mode of acceptance, but he cannot prescribe the form or time of refusal so as to fix a contract on the acceptor.

Illustration: *A sends an email to B, offering to sell his laptop for ₹12,000 and further states that if B does not reply to the email, A shall consider that B has accepted the offer. Acceptance should be communicated, mere silence does not amount to acceptance.*

(*g*) *Cross Offer:* When an offer made by one person in ignorance of a similar offer made to each other are known as *cross offers*. Two identical offers do not make a contract. In such a case, although the offer made by the second person is on similar terms as that of the first person, and as such, there appears to be identity of minds between the two, such instances amounts to cross offer and do not bring a concluded contract between the two.

Illustration: *In Tinn Vs. Hoffman & Co. (1873), the defendants wrote to the plaintiff on 28th November 1871, offering to sell 800 tons of iron at 69 sh. Per ton. On the same day, the plaintiff wrote to the defendants offering to buy 800 tons at 69 shillings. The two letters crossed in post and neither of them knew anything about the offer of the other, since there was no communication of each others offer. The plaintiff contended that there was a good contract for 800 tons at 69 shillings. It was held that the defendant would not be bound as a result of the simultaneous offers, each being made in ignorance of the other.*

(*h*) *Counter offer:* When the initial offer made by one party is accepted with some conditions to the original offer, such an acceptance becomes a counter offer and cannot be considered as acceptance. The person making the offer has the right to decide on the terms and conditions of the offer. The person accepting the offer should accept it without any conditions. However, if the acceptance is made against the offer, it is termed as a counter offer. Such an offer cannot be considered an offer; nevertheless, if the person making the original offer accepts the terms of the counter offer, a contract may come into existence. At such point in time, the person making the counter offer becomes the offerer and the person who had made the original offer becomes the acceptor or offeree.

(ii) Termination of an Offer

1. By lapse of stipulated time or reasonable time. An offer lapses either because of efflux of time or of the death or insanity of the proposer. If the offerer has fixed a period of time within which alone the acceptance is to be effected, and the acceptance is not made within that time, the offer automatically lapses after the expiry of that period.

   However, if the offer does not stipulate any period of time for acceptance, the offer may be accepted within a reasonable time. What is reasonable time will depend upon the circumstances of each case and it is for the court to determine reasonable time.

2. An offer also lapses on the death or insanity of the proposer. Under the Indian law, an acceptance in ignorance of the death or insanity of the offerer gives rise to a contract. Secondly, if the offer has been accepted, death may not cause the cancellation of the contract, unless the offerer's personal skill is a vial element in the contract.

   Illustration: *A an artist contracts with B, to paint his portrait for ₹20,000. B accepts the offer but after a few days, A is struck with paralysis and cannot paint. Here the personal skill of the offerer is required and hence leading to termination of the offer.*

3. Failure to fulfill conditions of the offer. If the acceptance is not made in the mode prescribed. According to Sub-section 3 of Section 6 of the Act, an offer is terminated *"by the failure of the acceptor to fulfill a condition precedent to acceptance."*

   Illustration: *In Pipraich Sugar Mills Ltd. Vs. Pipraich Sugar Mills Mazdoor Union (1956), the management offered to pay a certain sum to the employees on condition that they withdraw the strike notice . It was held that a conditional offer to pay a certain sum by the employer to the employees lapses when the condition is not accepted.*

4. By rejection of the offer. An offer stands automatically terminated if the offeree refuses to accept it. Rejection may be express or implied. Sometimes instead of rejecting the offer made, the offeree may make a counter-offer, which has the same effect as the rejection of the original offer.

5. By revocation. An offer is terminated by the offerer withdrawing his offer. Such a withdrawal is known as revocation. So long as the offer remains unaccepted, the offerer is free to revoke his offer at any time. This is true even though the offerer knows that the offeree is planning to accept the offer. Section 5 of the Act states that *"a proposal may be revoked at any time before the communication of acceptance is complete as against the proposer but not afterwards."* An offer can be revoked even though the offerer has promised to hold it open for a certain period. Similarly, even if the offer stipulates that it will not be withdrawn without the consent of the other party, it can be revoked at any time before it is accepted. Again, notice of revocation of an offer might be from a third party, and as such, offeree cannot accept the offer after receiving such notice.

   Illustration: *If A proposes by letter to sell his house to B, and B accepts the proposal by a letter, A may revoke his proposal at any time before or at the moment when B posts his letter of acceptance, but not afterwards.*

6. By subsequent illegality or destruction of the subject matter. If the thing offered is destroyed or substantially impaired before acceptance, or as a result of a change in the law, the thing offered cannot be bought and sold and results in revocation of the offer.

   Illustration: *A agrees to supply B with 100 bags of coffee seeds. Before B can accept the offer, the Government rule states that coffee seeds cannot be sold in the open market. The offer made by A stands cancelled.*

(iii) Acceptance

Sec 2(b) defines acceptance as *"when the person to whom a proposal is made signifies his assent thereto, the proposal is said to be accepted. A proposal when accepted becomes a promise."* Acceptance may be either express or implied. It is express when it is communicated by words spoken or written or by doing some required act. It is implied when it is gathered from the circumstances or conduct of the party making the acceptance.

Illustration: *A offers to sell his book to B for ₹ 50. B accepts the offer to purchase the book for ₹50. This amounts to acceptance by B.*

(iv) Legal Rules as to Acceptance

The acceptance of an offer is the very essence of a contract. To be legally effective, it must satisfy the following conditions:

1. **It must be absolute and unqualified**: Acceptance of a proposal with conditions, variations and reservations, will not constitute an acceptance of the offer. Acceptance with variations in a 'counter proposal' or 'counter offer' becomes a contract if the counter offer is accepted by the original proposer or offeror.

   Illustration: *In Hyde Vs. Wrench (1840), the defendant offered to sell his farm to the plaintiff for £1,000. The plaintiff replied 'I will give you £950'. This was refused by the defendant. Subsequently, the plaintiff replied, 'very well, I will give you the £1,000 you ask'. When the defendant declined to stick to his original offer, the plaintiff sued him for specific performance of the contract. The court held that the offer to buy for £950 in response to the offer to sell for £1,000 was only a counter-offer which amounted to rejection of the original offer and it was not possible to revive the original offer. Hence there was no contract between the parties.*

2. **It must be communicated to the offeror**: Acceptance and intimation of acceptance of offer is mandatory for a concluded contract. Mental assent is no acceptance at all. It may also be implied from the conduct of the acceptor. If there is no communication of acceptance, no contract is created. It cannot be implied from silence.

   Illustration: *A tells B that he intends to sell his house to C but tells C nothing of his intention. There is no contract, even if C is willing to buy A's property.*

3. **It must be according to the mode prescribed or in the usual or reasonable mode:** If the acceptance is not according to the mode prescribed, nor in some usual and reasonable mode (where no mode of acceptance is prescribed), the offeror may intimate to the offeree within a reasonable time that the acceptance is not according to the mode prescribed and may insist that the offer must be accepted in the prescribed mode only. If he does not inform the offeree, he is deemed to have accepted the acceptance. [Sec 7(2)].

4. **It must be given within a reasonable time**: If any time limit is specified, then the acceptance must be given within that specified time. However, if time is not specified, then the acceptance must be given within a reasonable time. Acceptance must be given before the offer lapses or before the offer is withdrawn.

   Illustration: *In Ramsgate Victoria Hotel Co. Ltd. Vs. Montefiore (1866), the defendant applied for shares in the plaintiff's company on 8th June. The company did not write to him allotting the shares until 23rd November, when he was informed that shares were allotted to him. His refusal to accept the shares led to the dispute. It was held that he was not bound to accept the shares as his offer lapsed owing to the delay by the company in notifying its acceptance.*

5. Acceptance cannot precede an offer: If the acceptance precedes an offer, it is not a valid acceptance and does not result in a contract.
6. The Acceptance must show intention on the part of the acceptor to fulfill terms of the promise. If no such intention is present, the acceptance is not valid.

   Illustration: *In Gostho Behari Sirkar Vs. Surs Estates Ltd (1960), the appellant concluded an agreement in Calcutta according to which he agreed to buy property belonging to the defendant for ₹1,30,000, and the defendants also agreed to sell the property 'free from encumbrances and the title thereof being found good and marketable'. The correspondence between the solicitors of the two parties also made a reference to the drawing up of a draft agreement for sale and the same to be sent by the plaintiff's solicitor to the defendant's solicitor, subject to the plaintiff being satisfied with the area of the land, the total rent realised from the premises. On the defendants revocation of the agreement, and the sale of property to another person, the plaintiff sued for specific performance. The trial judge dismissed the suit on the ground that there was a concluded contract between the two parties.*
7. Acceptance must be made /given by the offeree : an offer can be accepted only by the person to whom it is made. However, if somebody else is invested with the authority to accept the offer on behalf of the person to whom it is made, it is a valid acceptance.

(v) Communication

An offer or proposal to be complete must be communicated. Through communication the promisor signifies his willingness and the promise signifies his consent. Only when the offer is communicated, it can be accepted. Lack of knowledge of an offer does not constitute acceptance of an offer. There could be no consent or assent of which the party has never heard. Therefore, it is essential that in order to establish an undisputed proposal and acceptance, the same must be communicated to the other party, the offeree or to whom the offer is being made.

(vi) Outcome of Communication

(i) **By any act:** An act includes an action by conduct, by words spoken or written. Communication can, therefore be in the form of a letter, telegram, telex, email, telephone, etc. Any act by a person by which he intends to communicate or which has the effect of communication, will constitute communication.

Illustration: *When A enters into a public transport bus, it is a communication of acceptance by action, that A is willing to pay the travel fare and the stationing of the bus at the bus stop communicates by action that the bus company intends to take A to the destination mentioned on the board of the bus.*

(ii) **By omission:** An omission includes conduct or forbearance (not doing an act). An abstinence or forbearance on the part of one person which has the effect of communicating will constitute communication. A mere mental act or a thought does not constitute communication.

Illustration: *Ganesh decides to sell his house to Mahesh and to none other. However, this intention of Ganesh is not communicated to Mahesh. There is no communication and hence cannot constitute an offer or acceptance.*

Conditions if any should be communicated so as to give reasonable notice thereof to the person dealing with the contract. A condition printed behind the receipt for goods received, or conditions printed on the reverse of an airline ticket , railway or bus ticket, conspicuously on the face or back of it with sufficient notice thereof, would constitute a valid communication. A condition should be communicated prior to the date of the contract.

Communication of Proposal: The communication of a proposal is complete when it comes to the knowledge of the person to whom it is made [Sec 4]. There can be acceptance only when there is knowledge of the offer. Offer should be brought to the knowledge of the person to whom it is made.

Illustration: *A proposes, by letter, to sell his house to B at a certain price. The communication of the proposal is complete only when B receives the letter.*

(vii) Communication of Acceptance

Communication of acceptance is complete:

(*a*) As against the proposer: when it is put in the course of transmission to him, so as to be out of the power of the proposer. In the case of acceptance through post or by email, the contract is complete on the date when the letter of acceptance is posted, whether or not the letter is received by the offeror is absolutely immaterial. The offeror, however, becomes bound only when a properly addressed and adequately stamped letter of acceptance is posted. The contract is complete when acceptance of offer is put in the course of transmission to the offeror.

(*b*) As against the acceptor: when it comes to the knowledge of the proposer [Sec 4].

Illustration: *B accepts A's proposal by a letter sent by post. The communication of the acceptance is complete as against A, when the letter is posted, and completed against B, when the letter is received by A.*

Communication should be duly posted to the correct address. In case of delay due to negligence of the postal authorities, the parties are not bound. As a general rule, the contract would be complete as soon as acceptance is posted. The time and place of making the contract is determined by the time, when and where the letter of acceptance is posted.

(viii) Revocation of Proposal and Acceptance

Revocation means to withdraw or to take back. Revocation may be of a proposal or an acceptance. After a transaction has ripened into a contract, it requires the consent of both the parties to either revoke it or modify it. Revocation or modification of the contract by one party without the consent of the other party nullifies the contract. Mutual consent is necessary.

Illustration: *A enters into a contract with B for the purchase of 60 meters of red coloured cotton material on a certain date. B does not have the required material and sends only 40 meters of red coloured cotton material and 20 meters of yellow coloured cotton material. If A has not been intimated or notified about the modification, he need not accept the consignment and the contract stands revoked. However, if B has intimated to A prior to sending the consignment that there is shortage of the red coloured cotton material and A agrees to accepting 20 meters of yellow coloured cotton material, only then contract comes into existence.*

Revocation of proposal: A proposal may be revoked at any time before the communication of its acceptance is complete as against the proposer, but not afterwards [Sec 5]. Therefore, in case of posting of a letter of acceptance, the same can be revoked by an email reaching earlier than the letter. In case both the letter of acceptance and revocation by email arrive simultaneously, both cancel each other and as such there would be no binding contract. Revocation is effective only when it comes to the knowledge of the person to whom the offer is made.

When a proposal is revoked, the offer comes to an end. A proposal can be revoked in any of the following ways mentioned under Sec 6 of the Act.

(*a*) By communication of notice of revocation by the proposer to the other party.

(*b*) By lapse of time prescribed in such proposal for its acceptance. If no time is prescribed, then the offer shall lapse within a reasonable time, without communication of the acceptance.

(*c*) By failure of the acceptor to fulfill a condition precedent to acceptance. or,

(*d*) By death or insanity of the proposer, if the fact of his death or insanity comes to the knowledge of the acceptor before acceptance.

Revocation of Acceptance: An acceptance may be revoked at any time before the communication of the acceptance is complete as against the acceptor, but not afterwards [Sec 5].

Illustration: *A offers to sell his car to B for a certain sum of money. B accepts the offer and sends his acceptance by post. However he is informed by his friend Z that the value of the car in the market is much less than the amount quoted by A. Now, B wants to revoke his acceptance to A. B can do so by either making a telephone call or by sending a telegram or an SMS to A, before his initial acceptance which has been sent by post reaches A. This revocation is effectual only when it is made before the original acceptance can reach the offeror but not afterwards.*

(ix) Communication of Revocation

Communication of revocation is complete:

(*a*) As against the person who makes it, when it is put into a course of transmission to the person to whom it is made so as to be out of the power of the person who makes it;

(*b*) As against the person to whom it is made, when it comes to his knowledge.

Illustrations: *(1) A revokes his proposal by telegram. The revocation is complete as against A when the telegram is dispatched. It is complete as against B when B receives it.*

(2) B revokes his acceptance by telegram. B's revocation is complete, as against B when the telegram is dispatched and as against A when it reaches him.

From a quotation in Anson's Law of Contracts, "*Acceptance is to an offer, what a lighted match is to a train of gun-powder. It produces something which cannot be recalled or undone*". This statement states that when an offer is accepted by the person to whom it is made, it becomes a contract and it cannot be revoked. But an offer may be cancelled by the offerer before it is accepted by the offeree. The statement suggests the following facts.

- An offer will be effective until it is withdrawn. The offeree must know the withdrawal of the offer before he accepts the offer.
- If the letter of acceptance is not properly addressed, stamped and posted, it cannot be considered as acceptance. Hence, the offer can be revoked.
- Sometimes the letter of acceptance may be written but not posted. Before the letter of acceptance is posted, a letter revoking the offer may reach the offeree. This is also when an offer is revoked as there has been no acceptance communicated to the offeror.
- Mental acceptance or an acceptance made in the mind of the offeree but not communicated does not amount to acceptance.

(B) Lawful Consideration

Consideration is '*something in return for something*'. Consideration is one of the essential elements to support a contract. Subject to certain exceptions, an agreement made without consideration is '*Nudum Pactum*', which means, a nude contract and hence void. A promise to do something or to give something without anything in return would not be enforceable at law and considered *nudum pactum i.e.*, a bare or naked agreement not enforceable by law, subject to certain exceptions specified in the Act. Hence it is important that an agreement must be supported by consideration.

Consideration is a technical term used in the sense of *'quid pro quo'*, *i.e.*, something in return. When a party to an agreement promises to do something, he must also get something in return. This 'something' is called consideration in a contract. The reason for the insistence upon consideration by the law is to discourage promises made without realizing the consequences. Courts of law do not enforce gratuitous promises. Consideration that is unlawful also is considered void and hence unenforceable. An agreement to be enforceable by law must be supported by consideration.

Consideration means an advantage or benefit moving from one party to the other. It means 'something in return'. It may be an act or abstinence (agreeing not to do something) or promise to do or not to do something. It may be past, present or future. But it must be real and lawful.

Illustration: *M promises to pay ₹5000 to D if he forges his father's signature. Here the consideration for M is the forged signature by D which is unlawful against the consideration of ₹5000 to D for his act. Hence this agreement is void with respect to the unlawful consideration.*

Definition: Sec 2(d) of the Indian Contract Act defines Consideration as "*when, at the desire of the promisor, the promisee or any other person (a) has done or abstained from doing or (b) does or abstains from doing or (c) promises to do or abstain from doing something, such act or abstinence or promise is called consideration for the promise.*"

The definition can be analysed as follows:

(*a*) Consideration is an act (of doing something). It states that consideration is affirmative.

Illustration: *A promises B to guarantee payment of price of the goods which B sells on credit to X. Here selling of goods by B to X is consideration for A's promise.*

(*b*) An abstinence or forbearance or refraining from doing something.

Illustration: *A promises B not to file a suit against him if he pays him ₹10,000. The abstinence of A is the consideration for B's payment.*

(*c*) A return promise.

Illustration: *A agrees to sell his motorbike to B for ₹ 35,000. Here B's promise to pay the sum of ₹ 35,000 is the consideration for A's promise to sell the motorbike, and A's promise to sell his motorbike is the consideration for B's promise to pay the sum of ₹35,000.*

Therefore, one of the essential conditions for the enforceability of a contract is consideration. The rule is expressed by the Latin maxim *'ex nudo pacto non oritur actio'*, which means "out of a bare promise, no cause of action can arise". Therefore, a gratuitous promise, such as a promise to make a gift or charity which is not supported by consideration cannot be enforceable by the promisee. A consideration may be some benefit to one party or some detriment to the other. It may be therefore summed up as 'No consideration, no contract'.

(i) Legal Rules Regarding Consideration

(*a*) *It must move at the desire of the promisor*: An act constituting consideration must have been done at the desire or request of the promisor. If it is done at the instance of a third party or without the desire/will of the promisor, it will not be a good consideration.

Illustrations: *(1)A saves B's goods from fire without being asked to do so. A cannot demand payment for his services.*

(2) In Durgaprasad Vs. Baldeo,(1880), the plaintiff constructed a market at the request of the District Collector. The defendants who occupied the shops, promised to pay to the plaintiff a commission on articles sold through their agency, in consideration of the plaintiff having spent money on the construction of the market. In a suit by the plaintiff for the recovery of commission, it was held that promise was not supported by consideration, since the market was constructed not at the request of the shop keepers but at the instance of the District Collector.

(b) Consideration may move from the promisee or any other person—stranger to a contract: A consideration may move from the promisee or any other person. Consideration from a third party is a valid consideration under English law, however, consideration must move from the promisor only. It follows that a person who receives benefit under a contract may not, unless he has supplied consideration, enforce his rights under the contract, Accordingly, no stranger to the consideration may sue on a contract.

Illustration: *In Chinnayya Vs. Ramayya (1881). In this case on the 9th of April 1877 Raja Surraneni Lakshmi Vankana Rao made over her share in the Zamindari of Milavaram to the defendant her daughter, by a registered deed of gift with a stipulation that her daughter should pay annually ₹653 to her uncles as the mother was paying formerly and the amount should be paid until the daughter gave them a village which yielded the same amount. On the same date, the defendant executed an agreement in favour of the plaintiff, the brothers of the donor, promising to carry out the terms of the deed of gift. Since the defendant declined to fulfill her promise, this suit was brought to recover the amount due with interest. The defendant pleaded that there was no consideration for that agreement and hence, it was not binding on her. It was held that consideration had already moved from her mother and hence the defendant was liable to pay the dues.*

(c) It may be an act, abstinence or forbearance or a return promise: Forbearance to sue. If a person who could sue another for the enforcement of a right agrees not to pursue his claim, this constitutes a good consideration for a promise by the other person. This results in a benefit to the person not sued and a detriment to the person who could sue.

A reasonable and bonafide compromise of a disputed claim is a kind of forbearance. Request of a debtor to his creditors to accept a lesser amount in satisfaction of their debt is a consideration.

Illustration: *A borrows from B ₹100 at 20% p.a and fails to pay the amount. When B is about to file a suit, A agrees to pay a higher rate of interest. B as a result does not file the suit. This forbearance on the part of B not to file a suit is sufficient consideration and B can enforce the promise made by A, i.e., to pay a higher rate of interest.*

(d) It may be past, present or future

(*i*) Past consideration: when consideration by a party for a present promise was given in the past *i.e.,* before the date of promise, it is said to be past consideration. In English law, past consideration is not consideration.

Illustration: *A renders some service to B's family on B's request. After a month, B promises to compensate A for the service rendered to him. It is past consideration and A can recover the promised amount.*

(*ii*) Present or executed consideration: when consideration is given simultaneously with promise *i.e.,* at the time of promise, it is said to be present consideration.

Illustration: *Shopkeeper and customer-cash sales. When the customer pays the price of the goods and the shopkeeper delivers the goods to the customer, it is present and executed consideration.*

(*iii*) Future or executory consideration: when consideration from one party to the other is to pass subsequently to the making of the contract, it is future or executory consideration.

Illustration: *D promises to deliver certain goods to P after a week; P promises to pay the price after a fortnight. The promise of D is supported by the promise of P. Consideration in this case is future.*

(e) *It need not be adequate*: The Contract Act states that a contract should be supported by consideration. So long as consideration exists, the courts are not concerned as to its adequacy. It further states that adequacy or otherwise of consideration is only the look-out of the promisor and not the duty of either the law or the courts to determine the consideration and its adequacy.

Illustration: *A sold his radio to B for ₹5. This is a perfectly valid contract as long as B has not threatened or forced A to sell his radio of just ₹5 to him.*

(f) *It must be real and not illusory*: Although consideration need not be adequate, it must be real, competent and of some value in the eyes of law. There is no real consideration in the following cases, namely;

(i) Physical impossibility (*A tells B that if he can carry two cooking cylinder and run 100 meters , he will reward him ₹20,000)*

(ii) Legal impossibility (*A promises to get his son married to B's daughter , a minor , who is 14 years of age)*

(iii) Uncertain consideration (*X tells his friend that he will pay him ₹10,000 if he finds water while digging in the farm)*

(iv) Illusory consideration. (*S promises to pay V five gold coins if he finds gold in his field)*

(g) *It must be something which the promisor is not already bound to do*: A promise to do what one is already bound to do , either by general law or under an existing contract, is not a good consideration for a new promise, since it adds nothing to do the pre-existing legal or contractual obligation. Likewise, a promise to perform a public duty by a public servant is not a consideration.

Illustration: *In Ramachanddra Chintamani Vs Kalu Raju, there was a promise to pay to the vakil an additional sum if the suit was successful. Held, the promise was void for want of consideration. The vakil was under a pre-existing contractual obligation to render the best of his services under the original contract and therefore the promise to pay an additional sum was not called for.*

(h) *It must not be illegal, immoral or opposed to public policy*: The consideration given for an agreement must not be unlawful. Where it is unlawful, the courts do not allow an action on the agreement.

Illustration: *A rents out his house to B for the purpose of gambling.*

(ii) Stranger to a Contract

It is a general rule of law that only parties to a contract may sue and be sued on that contract. This rule is known as the doctrine of privity of contract. Privity of contract means relationship subsisting between the parties who have entered into contractual obligation. It implies a mutuality of will and creates a legal bond or tie between the parties to a contract. If consideration is furnished not by the promise but by a third person, the promisee becomes a stranger to the consideration, and as such, he cannot enforce the promise. Similarly, a person who is not a party to a contract cannot claim any right under the contract even though the contract may be for his benefit. Such a person is known as a stranger to contract. Under Indian Law, a stranger to contract cannot sue.

Illustration: *In a leading case on this point, Dunlop Pneumatic Tyre Co. Ltd Vs Selfridge & Co. Ltd (1915), the plaintiffs sold a number of their tyres to Dew & Co, on the terms that Dew & Co would not resell them below the listed prices and that, in the event of a sale to trade customers, they would obtain a similar undertaking from them.*

Dew & Co. sold the tyres to Selfridge & Co, who undertook to observe the restrictions and to pay to Messrs Dunlop & Co £5 for each tyre sold in breach of the agreement. Selfridge & Co. supplied tyres to two of their own customers below the listed price. Consequently, Dunlop & Co. sued Selfridge & Co to recover two sums of £5 each as liquidated damages and asked for an injunction to restrain further breaches of agreement. It was held that Dunlop Co could not maintain the suit as it was a stranger to the contract.

A person who is not a party to a contract cannot sue upon it even though the contract is for his benefit and he provided consideration. Secondly, a contract cannot confer rights or impose obligations arising under it on any person other than the parties to it. Thus, if there is a contract between A and B, X cannot enforce it.

Exceptions: The following are the exceptions to the rule that a stranger to a contract cannot sue:

(*a*) **A Trust or Charge:** A person called the beneficiary, in whose favour a trust or other interest in some specific immovable property has been created can enforce it even though he is not a party to the contract. Where a trust is created by a contract, the beneficiary can enforce his rights which the trust has conferred on him even though he is not a party to the contract creating the trust.

Where a charge is created on specific immovable property in favour of a person; although the third party and a stranger to the document creating a charge on specific immovable property, he can enforce the charge since he is beneficially entitled to it.

Illustrations: *(1) A husband who was separated from his wife executed a separation deed by which he promised to pay to the trustees all expenses for the maintenance of his wife. It was held, that the agreement created a trust in favour of the wife and could be enforced.*

(2) In Nawab Khwaja Muhammad Khan vs. Nawab Husaini Begum (1909), the plaintiff, a Mohamedan lady sued her father-in-law to recover arrears of an allowance called karch-i-pandan, which the father-in-law had promised to pay her in perpetuity by virtue of an agreement entered into by him with the father of the lady, prior to her marriage with the son of the defendant, and in consideration of the same. A specific property had also been charged for this purpose. The plaintiff and her husband lived together for some years, and owing to differences between the two, she left her husband's home and later filed a suit for the recovery of the promised amount.

Although the defendant admitted that he had promised to pay ₹500 a month in perpetuity to the plaintiff for her 'betel-leaf' expenses from the date of the marriage, he disclaimed the liability on the ground that the plaintiff was not a party to the agreement and that she had forfeited her right to the allowance by her misconduct and refusal to live with her husband. The subordinate judge dismissed the suit on the ground that the plaintiff had refused to live with her husband. On appeal, the High Court held that the lady had a clear right to sue under the agreement and accordingly it reversed the order of the trial court and the court ordered that she was entitled to the allowance as it was because of the agreement to pay the allowance that the marriage took place in the first place.

(*b*) **Marriage settlement, partition or other family arrangement:** When an arrangement is made in connection with marriage, partition and other family arrangements and a provision is made for the benefit of a person, he may sue although he is not a party to the agreement. When a provision is made for the maintenance of female member of a Hindu family on a partition of the joint family property, or for settlement of claims between members of a family, or for the marriage expenses of a female member, such members, though not parties to the agreement, can sue on the footing of the agreement.

Illustration: *(1) In Shuppu Ammal vs. Subramanian (1909), two Hindu brothers, upon the partition of the family property agreed, at the time of partition that they should contribute ₹300 in equal shares, invest the amount on the security of immovable property and pay the interest towards the maintenance of the mother. In a suit by the mother, it was held by the Madras High Court that 'a person who was not a party to a document but in whose favour a charge was created by such document was entitled to maintain a suit to enforce its terms, either as the actual beneficiary or as the charge-holder.'*

(2) In Daropti Vs Jagpat Rai, Jagpat's wife deserted him because of his ill-treatment. Jagpat then entered into an agreement with his father-in-law to treat his wife property or to pay her monthly maintenance. Subsequently, she was again ill-treated and driven out. Held, she was entitled to enforce the promise made by Jagpat to her father.

(*c*) **Acknowledgement or estoppels:** where the promisor by his conduct, acknowledges or otherwise constitutes himself as an agent of a third party, a biding obligation is thereby incurred by him towards the third party. When , in a contract between two parties, the promisor is required to make a payment to a third party, and such promisor acknowledges the payment by conduct or otherwise to that third party, the latter can sue the promisor, although there is no privity of contract between the promisor and himself.

Illustrations: *(1) In Debanrayan Dutt Vs. Chunilal Ghose (1914), the plaintiff advanced ₹300 to a person on the security of a pattah relating to immovable property. The person who borrowed money, then transferred by a registered instrument all his property, movable and immovable , to the defendant for ₹2,000. There was a provision and declaration in the instrument that out of this consideration money of ₹2,000, ₹300 due to the plaintiff should be paid by the defendant. On the day on which the instrument was executed, the defendant acknowledged the obligation to pay ₹300 to the plaintiff, and the acknowledgement was communicated to and accepted by the plaintiff. The court held the view that, 'where the transferee of a debtor's liability has acknowledged his obligation to the creditor for the debt to be paid by him under the provisions of the registered instrument conveying to him all the movable and immovable properties of the original debtor, and the acknowledgement was communicated to the creditor and accepted by him, the arrangement between the creditor and the transferee did not amount to a novation (new contract) within the meaning and the creditor is entitled to sue the transferee on the registered instrument.'*

(2) A who is the friend of B, accompanies him to a party. B within hearing range of A states that A is his partner in business and A does not say anything. Later B defaults his creditors and the creditors claim their dues form A. A is stopped from denying that he is not a partner and is bound towards B's creditors.

(*d*) **Assignment of a contract:** The assignee of rights and benefits under a contract not involving personal skill can enforce the contract subject to the equities between the original parties. Thus the holder in due course of a Negotiable Instrument can sue for the amount on it even though there is no contract between him and the person liable to pay. When rights under a contract are assigned, the assignee can sue upon the contract for the enforcement of his rights.

(*e*) **Contracts entered into through an agent:** The principal can enforce the contract entered into by his agent provided the agent acts within the scope of his authority and in the name of the principal. A contract entered into by an agent, acting within the scope of his authority, can be enforced by the principal.

(*f*) **Covenants running with the land:** In cases of transfer of immovable property, the purchaser of land, with notice that the owner of the land is bound by certain conditions or covenants created by an agreement affecting the land, shall be bound by them although he was not a party to the original agreement which contained the conditions or covenants. This is also called as the '*easement right*'.

(iii) Exceptions to the Rule, 'A Contract Without Consideration is Void'

The general rule is stated in the maxim *'ex nudo pacto non oritur actio' i.e.*, an agreement made without consideration is void. However, Section 25 and Section 185 deals with the exceptions to this rule. In such cases, agreements are enforceable even though they are made without consideration. The exceptional cases are:

1. **An act of natural love and affection [Sec 25(1)]:** A written and registered agreement based on natural love and affection between near relatives is enforceable even if it is without consideration.

   Illustration: *In Rajlukhy Vs. Bhoothnath, A Hindu husband, after referring to quarrels and disagreement between him and his wife , executed a registered document in favour of his wife, agreeing to pay her maintenance (however, no consideration moved from his wife). It was held that the agreement was void as the relationship between the husband and wife had soured.*

   A written agreement between a daughter who lives abroad and her mother to send her a fixed sum of money every month for her mother's expenses is valid and can be enforced in a court of law.
2. **Compensation for voluntary services [Sec 25(2)]:** A promise to compensate, wholly or in part, a person who has already voluntarily done something for the promisor, is enforceable, even though without consideration.

   Illustration: *A finds B's purse and gives it to him. B promises to give a reward of ₹ 1,000 to B. This is an enforceable contract.*
3. **A Promise to pay a time-barred debt [Sec 25(3)]:** a promise by a debtor to pay a time-barred debt is enforceable provided it is made in writing and is signed by the debtor or by his agent generally or specially authorized on that behalf. A debt is barred by limitation if it remains unpaid or unclaimed for a period of three years. Such a debt becomes legally irrevocable.

   Illustration: *A owes B ₹ 10,000, but the debt is barred by the Limitation Act. A signs a written promise, to pay B ₹ 6,000 on account of the debt. This is a valid contract which can be enforced.*
4. **A completed gift:** The rule 'no consideration, no contract' does not apply to completed gifts.
5. **Agency [Sec 185]:** Consideration is not necessary to create an agency.
6. A promise though gratuitous would be enforceable if , on the faith of the promise, the promisee suffers loss.

(C) Competent to Contract

Persons entering into a contract should be legally competent to do so. A person is said to be legally competent if he has attained the age of majority, is of sound mind and not disqualified from contracting by any law to which he is subject. The law declares that certain classes of persons do not have the capacity to enter into legally binding agreements, further the law seeks to protect their interests from being exploited by deceitful and corrupt persons. The parties to the agreement must be capable of entering into a valid contract.

Contractual competence is defined under Section 11 of the Act which states the *"every person is competent to contract who is of the age of majority according to the law to which he is subject, and who is of sound mind, and is not disqualified from contracting by any law to which he is subject"*. Every person is competent to contract if he is

- Of the age of majority (not a minor) according to the law to which he is subject.
- Of sound mind (not a lunatic, idiocy, etc.)
- Not disqualified from contracting by any law to which he is subject (a convict, alien enemy, etc.)

In other words, the Act disqualifies three classes of persons from entering into a valid contract. They include minors, persons of unsound mind and those who are specially disqualified by the law to which they are subject. One of the essential elements of a valid contract is that the parties to the contract must be competent to contract. Flaw in capacity to contract may arise from minority, lunacy, idiocy, drunkenness etc. and status *i.e.*, foreign sovereigns, Ambassadors, alien enemies, convicts, professional persons, insolvents etc. If a party suffers from any flaw in capacity, the agreement is not enforceable, except in some special cases. An agreement becomes a contract when is it is entered into between the parties who are competent to contract [Sec 10].

Illustration: *A minor borrows ₹500 on a fraudulent representation that he is a major. If he fails to repay the amount, the creditor cannot recover the amount. This is because, the minor can plead minority and he cannot be prevented from setting up such a plea. The same holds good for persons of unsound mind, namely lunatics, idiots', persons under intoxication etc.*

(i) Contract with a Minor

According to Sec 3 of the Indian Majority Act, 1875, a minor is a person who has not completed eighteen years of age. In the following two cases, he attains majority after attaining twenty one years of age;

1. Where a guardian of a minor's person or property has been appointed under the Guardians and Wards Act, 1890. or
2. Where the superintendence of the minor's property is assumed by a Court of Wards.

The rules governing minors' agreements are based on two fundamental rules;

(*a*) **First Rule:** the law protects minors against their own inexperience and against the possible improper designs of those more experienced. The law protects their rights, property and acquits them in their dealings. The Judges are their counselors, the jury their servants and the law their guardian.

(*b*) **Second Rule:** in pursuing the above object, the law should not cause unnecessary hardship to persons who deal with minors.

1. Minor Agreement

1. An agreement with a minor or an agreement by a minor is void and inoperative *ab-initio*.

   Illustration: *In Mohiri Bibi Vs Dharmadas Ghose (1903), a minor mortgaged his house with a money lender to secure a loan of ₹20,000, out of which the mortgagee (money lender) paid the minor a sum of ₹8,000. Subsequently, the minor sued for setting aside the mortgage, stating that he was underage when he executed the mortgage. Held, the mortgage was void and therefore, it was cancelled. Further, the money lenders request for the repayment of the amount advanced to the minor as part of the consideration for the mortgage was also not accepted.*

2. A minor can be an agent or a beneficiary. Incapacity of a minor to enter into a contract means incapacity to bind him by a contract. There is nothing which debars him from becoming a beneficiary.

   Illustration: *Mahesh a minor, aged 17 agreed to purchase a second-hand scooter for ₹5000 from Suresh. He paid ₹1,000 as advance and agreed to pay the balance the next day and collect the scooter. When he came* *with the money the next day, Suresh told him that he had changed his mind and offered to return the advance amount. Suresh cannot avoid the contract, though Mahesh, the minor, may , if he wants to.*

3. **Ratification:** A minor's agreement cannot be ratified by him on attaining the age of majority. Since a minor's agreement is a nullity in the eyes of law, the question of its ratification by the minor after attaining the age of majority does not arise. Ratification relates back to the date of making the agreement. Thus, consideration given during minority is no consideration.

   Illustration: *In Indran Ramaswamy Vs. Anthiyappa Chettyar, M a minor, borrows ₹ 5000 from L and executes a promissory note in favour of L. After attaining majority, he executes another promissory note in settlement of the first note. The second promissory note is void for want of consideration.*

4. **Restitution:** If a minor has received any benefit under a void agreement, he cannot be asked to compensate or pay for it. This means that an agreement with a minor is absolutely void and therefore a minor need not pay back any money he has received, even though he fraudulently misrepresents that he is of full age.

   Illustration: *M a minor, obtains a loan by mortgaging his property. He is not liable to refund the loan amount and further, even the mortgaged property cannot be made liable for repayment of the debt.*

5. **A minor can always plead minority:** Even if the minor has, by misrepresenting his age, induced the other party to enter into a contract with him, the minor cannot be sued either for the performance of the contract or in tort (civil wrong) for fraud because if the injured party were allowed to sue for fraud, it would be giving the other party an indirect means of enforcing the void agreement.

6. **Specific Performance:** There can be no specific performance of the agreements entered into by him as they are void-ab-initio. A minor's agreement being void from the inception, there cannot be any contract to be specifically enforced. Therefore none of the parties can ask for specific performance. A contract entered into on behalf of a minor by his parent or guardian or the manager of his estate can be specifically enforced by or against the minor provided the contract is;

   (*a*) Within the scope of the authority of the parent, guardian or manager and

   (*b*) For the benefit of the minor.

7. **Minor as a partner:** A minor cannot enter into a contract of partnership. A minor cannot be a partner in a firm since partnership arises on the basis of a contract. However the Act states that a minor may be admitted to the benefits of an already existing partnership, with the consent of the other partners. He can neither take part in the management of the affairs of the partnership firm.

8. **A minor cannot be adjudged insolvent:** This is because he is incapable of contracting debts.

9. **Beneficial contracts:** Agreements entered into by a minor for his benefit are valid and enforceable. Such agreements may be enforced even against a minor, but only to make his property liable and not his person. A minor is liable for necessaries supplied to him. It includes necessary services (like medical services, education, services of a lawyer, etc) rendered to him or anyone whom he is legally bound to support, which includes his siblings, widowed mother who is incapable of taking care of herself and the family or the father who is incapacitated due to lunacy, etc.

   Illustration: *In Roberts Vs.Gray (1913), the defendant, an infant entered into a contract with the plaintiff, a famous billiards player, to go on a world tour with him. The plaintiff incurred expenses necessary for making preparations for the tour. The defendant repudiated the contract before the tour began. The court upheld an award of ₹1,500 damages for the breach made by the minor.*

10. **Minor as an agent:** A minor can be an agent but he cannot employ an agent. An agent is merely a connecting link between his principal and the third party. As soon as the principal and the third party are brought together, the agent drops out. A minor binds the principal by his acts without incurring any personal liabilities. As an agent, he can represent the principal and bind him for his act done in the course of the contract of agency. However, the minor is not personally liable for any wrongful act, although the principal is responsible to third parties for the acts of the minor-agent.
11. **Tortious liability:** A minor is liable in tort (civil wrong). Minors are liable for negligently causing injury or damage or for converting property that does not belong to them. When a tort arises out of a contract , a minor is not liable in tort as it is an indirect way of enforcing an invalid contract.

    Illustration: *(1) In Burnard Vs. Haggis (1863), an infant hired a horse for riding and was expressly forbidden from jumping it. The defendant allowed his companion to use the horse for jumping. Consequently, the horse was injured and died. It was held that 'using the horse in this manner positively forbidden by the contract, was a mere trespass, for which the defendant (minor) was liable.'*

    (2) In another decided case Ballet Vs. Mingay (1943), in which , a minor hired a microphone and amplifier and lent the same without authority to a friend, was held liable on the ground that the wrongful act was independent of any bailment.
12. A minor's parents or guardian are not liable for the contract entered into by the minor, even though the contract is for the supply of necessaries to the minor. But if the minor is acting as an agent for the parents or guardian, then the parents/guardian shall be liable under the contract.

2. Minors' Liability for Necessaries

A minor is liable to pay out of his property for necessaries supplied to him or to any one to whom he is legally bound to support [Sec 68]. The claim arises not out of contract but out of what are called quasi-contractual obligations. A contract to supply goods is not enforceable against the minor since the contract is void. Moreover, in an action against the minor for necessaries, the plaintiff must prove that at the time of sale and delivery, the minor did not already possess an adequate supply of goods of the class in question. Again, it is only the property of the minor which is liable for meeting the liability arising out of such contracts. He is not personally liable.

The law has provided this exception intentionally because if it were not so, it would be impossible for a minor to even live. The liability of a minor for necessaries supplied to him is only quasi-contractual and not contractual. It should also be noted that if a minor who has been supplied with necessaries suited to his condition in life has no property, the question of liability does not arise. The question as to what constitute necessaries of life depends upon the position and status of the minor in society.

Illustration: *A guardian supplied a minor who was studying in a prestigious college, some extravagant and fashionable clothing. Later the guardian filed a suit to recover the amount spent on the clothing. The court held that clothing comes under the term 'necessaries' but not extravagant and fashionable clothing and hence the guardian cannot recover any amount from the personal asset of the minor.*

(ii) Contract with a Person of Unsound Mind

One of the essential conditions of competency of parties to a contract is that, they should be of sound mind. Sec 12 of the Act lays down a test of soundness of mind, which is as follows:

'A person is said to be of sound mind for the purpose of making a contract if, at the time when he makes it, he is capable of understanding it and of forming a rational judgment as to its effect upon his interest. A person who is usually of unsound mind, but occasionally of sound mind may make a contract when he is of sound mind. A person, who is usually of sound mind, but occasionally of unsound mind, may not make a contract when he is of unsound mind.'

This statement laid down by the section specified that (a) the person making a contract should be capable of understanding it and (b) should be capable of forming a rational judgment as to its effects upon his interest. This section does not totally bar mentally disordered persons from making a contract. The second and third paragraphs of this section clearly permit such persons to make contract when they are of sound mind during lucid intervals. A person who is usually of unsound mind but occasionally of sound mind is presumed to be of unsound mind until the contrary is proved.

With regard to a person who is usually of sound mind, but occasionally of unsound mind, the presumption is that he was of sound mind when he made the contract. As such, any person who tries to show that the contract was entered into at the time of temporary insanity should prove that unsoundness of mind existed at the time of contracting.

1. Contract with a Person Who is a Lunatic

A lunatic is a person who is mentally deranged due to some mental strain or other personal experience. He suffers from intermittent intervals of sanity and insanity. He can enter into contracts during the period when he is of sound mind.

2. Contract with a Person Who is an Idiot

An idiot is a person who has completely lost his mental powers. He does not exhibit understanding of even ordinary matters. Idiocy is permanent whereas lunacy denotes periodical insanity with lucid intervals. An agreement made by an idiot, like that of a minor is void.

3. Contract with a Drunkard or a Person Who is Intoxicated

A drunken or intoxicated person suffers from temporary incapacity to contract; *i.e.*, at a time when he is so drunk or under the influence of drugs that he is incapable of forming a rational judgment. The position of a drunken or intoxicated person is similar to that of a lunatic.

(iii) Contract with a Person Disqualified Under the Act

1. **Contracts With An Alien Enemy:** A person who is not an Indian is an alien. He may be either an (*a*) alien enemy or (*b*) alien friend. Contracts with an alien friend, subject to certain restrictions are valid. Contracts with an alien enemy may be studied under two heads namely:
   (*i*) Contracts during war and
   (*ii*) Contracts made before the outbreak of war

   During the continuance of war, an alien enemy can neither contract with an Indian nor can he be sued in an Indian court. He can do so only after he receives a license from the central government. Contracts made before the war may either be suspended or dissolved. They will be dissolved if they are against public policy or if their performance would benefit the enemy.

2. **Contracts with Foreign Sovereigns, their Diplomatic Staff and Representatives of Foreign States:** These individuals have some privileges and generally cannot be sued unless they, on their own, submit to the jurisdiction of the Indian law courts. The foreign sovereigns, their diplomatic staff and representatives of foreign states can enter into contracts and enforce those contracts in our courts, but an Indian citizen has to obtain a prior sanction of the central government in order to sue them in Indian courts.
3. **Corporations:** A Corporation is an artificial person created by law, having a legal existence apart from its members. It may come into existence by a special act of the legislature or by registration under the Companies Act 1956. The contractual capacity of a Corporate is regulated by the terms of its Memorandum of Association and the provision of the Companies Act. It cannot go beyond what is mentioned in the objects clause of the Memorandum of Association as it would amount to an Ultravires act- an act which is beyond its powers.
4. **Insolvents:** When a debtor is adjudged an insolvent (where a person's liabilities exceed his assets) his property vests in the hands of the official receiver or official assignee. As such the insolvent is deprived of his power to deal in that property and thereby becomes ineligible to enter into a contract.
5. **Convicts:** A convict, when undergoing imprisonment is incapable of entering into a contract. He can, however enter into or sue on a contract if he is lawfully at large under a license called 'ticket of leave'.

(D) Free Consent

Free consent between the parties to an agreement is one of the essential elements of a valid contract. Section 13 states that "*two or more parties are said to consent, when they agree upon the same thing in the same sense*". The parties to the contract should be *ad idem i.e.* agree upon the same thing in the same sense. Their consent too should be free from any pressure. Thus consent involves identity of minds *or consensus-as idem*, that is, agreeing upon the same thing in the same sense. Therefore, if, for whatsoever reason, there is no *consensus-ad-idem,* among the contracting parties, there is no real consent and hence no valid contract. Under Section 14, Consent is said to be free when it is not induced by;

- Coercion,
- Undue Influence,
- Fraud,
- Misrepresentation or
- Mistake.

It may be noted that consent under coercion, undue influence, fraud or misrepresentation, makes the contract voidable. But consent under mistake of both the parties makes the contract void. Even when the parties are under the impression that they have entered into an agreement, the agreement is void from the inception and hence, it is as good as no agreement at all. When there is no consent, there is no contract. According to Salmond, there are two types of flaws in consent, lack of consent and lack of free consent, legally termed as;

(*i*) Error in consensus.

(*ii*) Error in causa.

Error in consensus: When there is no consensus, there is no contract, because the consent in the agreement is caused by the mistake of both the parties.

Illustration: *An illiterate woman made a gift deed in favour of her brother's son (her nephew) under the impression that she was making a deed authorizing her nephew to manage her land and property. However, the nephew took advantage of the old woman being illiterate and drafted an agreement which stated that he was the sole heir to all the property belonging to the old woman. When this matter was brought to the notice of the old woman, she filed a suit. The evidence showed that the woman never intended to make such a gift deed and the deed was not read or explained to her. Held, the deed was void as there was an error in consensus.*

Error in causa: In the case of error in causa, the consent is not altogether missing, but it is not free because, it is caused either by coercion (threat), undue influence, fraud or misrepresentation. When the consent is not free consent, the contract is voidable at the option of the party whose consent is not free.

Illustration: *Mr A is forced to sign a promissory note at gun point. In this case Mr A knows fully well that he is signing a document which he would not have otherwise signed as his consent is not free. The contract is voidable at the option of Mr. A.*

When consent is obtained through unfair means, then the party whose consent was obtained by unfair means can avoid the contract. It is essential to the creation of every contract that there must be a free and genuine consent of the parties to the agreement. Consent of the parties is said to be free when they are of the same mind on all the material terms of the contract.

(i) Flaws in Consent

1. Coercion

When a person is compelled to enter into a contract by the use of force by the other party or under a threat, coercion is said to be employed. Section 15 of the Act defines coercion as "*Coercion is the committing, or threatening to commit, any act forbidden by the Indian Penal Code, or the unlawful detaining or threatening to detain, any property, to the prejudice of any person whatever, with the intention of causing any person to enter into an agreement.*"

Coercion is the committing or threatening to commit any act forbidden by the Indian Penal Code 1860 or the unlawful detaining or threatening to detain any property to the prejudice of any person whatever, with the intention of causing any person to enter into an agreement. In simple terms, coercion is a threat or force used by one party against the other for inducing him to enter into an agreement. Coercion need not proceed from a party to the contract. It may proceed even from a stranger (a third party) to the contract. Coercion includes fear, physical compulsion and menace to goods.

Illustration: *A threatens to kill B, if he does not sell his house to C. B agrees to sell his house to C, under such threat. This type of consent which is obtained is said to be made under coercion.*

(a) Duress

In the English Law, the near equivalent of the term coercion is duress. Duress involves actual or threatened violence over the person of another (his wife, parent or child), with a view to obtaining his consent to the agreement. If the threat is with regard to the goods or property of the other party, it is not duress.

(b) Essentials of Coercion

1. Consent is said to be caused by coercion if it is attained by committing any act forbidden by the IPC- Indian Penal Code.

   Illustration: *A leading case on this point is Ranganayakamma Vs. Alwar Shetty (1889). In this case a young Hindu girl of 13 years, who had just lost her husband, was forced to adopt a boy of their choice by her relatives who refused to remove the dead body of her husband unless she consented to the adoption. It was held that the adoption was not binding on her since her consent was not free but induced by coercion.*

2. Consent is said to be caused by coercion if it is obtained by threatening to do any act forbidden by the Indian Penal Code (IPC).

   Illustration: *(1) In Chikkam Ammairaju Vs. Chikkam Seshamma (1918), a person held out a threat to his wife and son that he would commit suicide if they did not execute a release deed with regard to certain property in favour of his brothers who claimed the property as their own. It was held that the deed was not enforceable against the wife and son as the same was obtained by coercion. Committing suicide is forbidden by The Indian Penal Code. Thus suicide is no crime but an attempt to commit suicide is forbidden by the IPC. As such a threat to commit suicide amounts to coercion.*

   (2) A threatened to shoot B if B does not lend him ₹500. B lends the amount to A. The loan is given under coercion.

3. Consent is said to be caused by coercion when there is unlawful detaining of any property of any person.

   Illustration: *In Muthiah Chettiar Vs. Karuppen Chetty(1927), an agent refused to hand over the account books of a business to the new agent unless the principal released him from liability in respect of all past transactions. It was held that the release deed was voidable at the option of the principal as it was given under coercion.*

4. Consent is said to be caused by coercion when there is threatening to detain any property of any person.

   Illustration: *In Bansraj vs. Secretary of State, the government gave a threat of attachment against the property of P for the recovery of the fine due from T, the son of P. P paid the fine . Held, the contract was induced by coercion and hence voidable.*

5. It does not matter whether the Indian Penal Code is or is not inforce in the place where coercion is employed. If consent is obtained by any of the above mentioned causes, such consent is said to be obtained by coercion and is voidable.

(c) Effect of Coercion

Section 19: When consent to a contract is obtained by coercion , such contract is voidable at the option of the party whose consent was obtained under coercion.

Section 72: A person to whom money has been paid or anything delivered under coercion, must repay or return it.

Illustration: *A railway company refused to deliver certain goods to a party unless a payment of illegal charge of carriage is made. The party (consignee) pays the charge in order to collect the goods. He is entitled to recover the excess charge he paid.*

Difference Between Coercion and Duress

Coercion	Duress
It can be employed against any person, including a third party.	It can be employed only against the contracting party or other immediate members of his family.
It can be employed by any person, even by a third person/party to the contract.	It can be employed only by the contracting party and not by a third party/person.
It may involve un-lawful detaining or threatening to detain any goods.	It does not involve un-lawful detention of goods.
Threat may be against the person or against his property.	Threat is against the person only, not against his property.
It may not cause immediate violence	It causes immediate violence.

2. Undue Influence

Sometimes a party is compelled to enter into an agreement against his will as a result of unfair persuasion by the other party. This happens when a special kind of relationship exists between the parties, such that one party is in a position to exercise undue influence over the other. An agreement entered under undue influence renders such an agreement or contract voidable at the option of the party whose consent was so induced. Undue influence can be described as unfair moral pressure. It is also referred to as equitable fraud.

Section 16(1) defines undue influence as follows: *"a contract is said to be induced by undue influence where the relations subsisting between the parties are such that one of the parties is in a position to dominate the will of the other and uses that position to obtain an unfair advantage over the other"*.

Holland defines undue influences as *"the unconscious use of power over another person, such power being obtained by virtue of a present or previously existing dominating control, arising out of relationship between the parties."*

Sub-section (1) of Section 16 mentions two important elements of undue influence. They are: (*a*) the relationship subsisting between the parties to a contract are such that one of them is in a position to dominate the will of the other, and (*b*) he uses that position to obtain an unfair advantage over the other. A person is deemed to be in a position to dominate the will of another, where;

- He holds a real or apparent authority over the other.

  Illustrations: *(1) master and servant, police officer and the accused, boss and employee, etc.*

  (2) In Mannu Singh Vs. Umdat Pandey (1890), the plaintiff, a Hindu, advanced in years, was induced to gift away the whole of his property under the influence of his spiritual adviser (guru). The only reason for the gift as disclosed in the deed was the donor's desire to secure benefits to his soul in the next world. The Allahabad High Court set aside the gift on the ground that consent was obtained by undue influence.

- He stands in a fiduciary relation (relation based on trust and confidence and a relation which comes into existence for a specific purpose) to the other.

  Illustration: *The relationship between father and son, guardian and ward, advocate and client, doctor and patient, trustee and beneficiary, spiritual adviser and disciple, solicitor and client, trustee and beneficiary, etc.*

- He makes a contract with a person whose mental capacity is temporarily or permanently affected by reason of age, illness or mental or bodily distress.

Illustration: *relation between medical attendant and his patient. In Ranee Annapurni Vs. Swaminath, a Hindu widow was persuaded by a money lender to agree to pay 100% rate of interest on money lent by him to her. She needed the money to establish her right to maintenance. Held, it was a case of undue influence.*

(a) Effect of Undue Influence

When consent to an agreement is obtained by undue influence, the agreement is a contract which is voidable at the option of the party whose consent was so obtained. Any such contract may be set aside either absolutely or if the party who is entitled to avoid it has received any benefit there under, upon such terms and conditions, it should be returned to the other party.

The following are relationships which generally raise presumption of undue influence:

(*i*) Parent and child
(*ii*) Guardian and ward
(*iii*) Trustee and beneficiary
(*iv*) Religious adviser (guru) and discipline
(*v*) Doctor and patient
(*vi*) Solicitor and client

The presumption of undue influence applies whenever the relationship between the parties to the contract is such that one of them is able to take unfair advantage over the other. There is however, no presumption of undue influence in the relationship between (1) landlord and tenant (2) creditor and debtor and (3) husband and wife (*i.e.*, if the wife is not a pardanashin–woman under a veil).

A pardanishin woman is one who, according to the custom of her community, lives in complete seclusion. The law presumes undue influence in the case of a contract with a pardanishin woman. Since, the ordinary presumption that a person understands the document to which he has affixed his name does not apply in the case of a pardanishin woman, a deed of gift by such a woman becomes invalid in the absence of proof that she had independent advice.

It was observed by the Bombay High Court in Shaik Ismail Vs. Amirbibi (1902), that a woman who goes to court to give evidence, who fixes rent with tenants and collects rent, who communicates when necessary in matter of business, with men other than members of her own family, could not be regarded as a pardanishin woman. The burden of proof lies on the other party to show that there was no undue influence, that the party executing the deed has been a free agent, the contents were read out to her, explained to her and she understood the contents and the effects of the document upon her own interests.

Unconscionable of Catching Bargains: When a contract is entered into between parties of unequal bargaining power and the dominant party takes advantage of the ignorance, infirmity and impaired bargaining power of the other party, and the transaction is positively unfair on the face of it, the bargain, which is advantageous to the dominant party, is known as an unconscionable bargain. Such bargains are clearly visible in the case of money lending transactions and gifts.

Illustration: *R a moneylender lends money to Q on terms which appear to be unconscionable. It is on R to prove that the contract was not induce by undue influence.*

In Ranee Annapurni V.s Swaminatha (1910), the plaintiff, a poor Hindu widow, having no financial means, borrowed ₹ 1,500 from a moneylender at 100 percent per annum for the purpose of enabling her to establish her right to maintenance. The Madras High Court decided that the lender could charge an interest only upto 24 percent and not more.

(b) Burden of Proof

In an action to avoid a contract on the ground of undue influence, the plaintiff has to establish that:

(*a*) One party was in a position to dominate the will of the other party. Mere proof of nearness of relationship is not sufficient for the court to assume that one relation was in a position to dominate the will of the other.

(*b*) The other party actually used his influence to obtain the plaintiff's consent to the contract, and

(*c*) The transaction is unreasonable, that is, a contract in which the dominating person may misuse his superior position to get an unfair advantage or huge profit over the other.

It may be noted that, in a moneylending transaction, if the rate of interest is very high, it is not an unreasonable transaction because it is usual for moneylenders to charge high rate of interest from the needy borrowers. However, the government has brought in new amendments to restrict moneylenders from charging exorbitant rates of interest and insisting on moneylenders to secure requisite license from the respective or relevant authorities, in order to protect the rights of the needy borrowers.

Difference Between Coercion and Undue Influence

Both coercion and undue influence vitiate free consent and render a contract voidable at the option of the party whose consent was so caused.

Coercion	Undue Influence
• The consent is given under the threat of an offence (crime). The consent to the agreement is obtained by committing or threatening to commit an offence punishable under the Indian Penal Code (IPC)	• The consent is given under moral influence. The consent is obtained by dominating the will of the other party.
• Coercion is mainly of a physical character. Coercion involves physical force.	• Undue influence is of moral pressure.
• There must be intention of causing any person to enter into an agreement.	• Here the influencing party uses his position to obtain an unfair advantage over the other party.
• It involves a criminal act.	• No criminal act is involved.
• Coercion may proceed from a stranger and may also be directed against a stranger	• Undue influence strictly must come from a party to the contract.

• There is no presumption of coercion by law under any circumstance. The party whose consent is obtained by coercion must prove the fact.	• In the case on undue influence, there is presumption of undue influence by law under certain relationships.
• The act or threat amounting to coercion may be committed outside India (according to the explanation to Sec 15 of the Act).	• Undue influence should be exercised in India.
• Coercion attracts the provision of the Indian Penal Code. As such the party exercising coercion exposes himself to criminal liability, besides an action on contract.	• There is no criminal liability in the case of undue influence.
• In the case of coercion, the contract becomes voidable at the option of the party whose consent was so caused [Sec 19]. The party avoiding the contract has to restore any benefit he has received under the contract, to the other party.	• In the case of undue influence, although the aggrieved party is at liberty to rescind the contract in accordance with [Sec 19A] of the Act, the Court has the discretion to set aside the contract absolutely, or if the aggrieved party has received any benefit, upon such terms and conditions as may appear to be justifiable.

3. *Misrepresentation*

A statement of fact which one party makes in the course of negotiations with a view to inducing the other party to enter into a contract is known as 'representation'. A statement of fact, past or present, is different from a mere statement of opinion or statement of intention or of law. A representation which is false or misleading is known as *misrepresentation*. A representation, when wrongly made, either innocently or intentionally, is a misrepresentation. It must relate to some fact which is material to the contract. It may be expressed by words spoken or written or implied from the acts and conduct of the parties.

In the case of intentional misrepresentation, a fact is represented as being true although it is false or without belief in its truth, with a view to deceiving the other party to the agreement. However, if misrepresentation is made honestly believing it to be true or without knowing that it is false, it becomes known as innocent misrepresentation. Misrepresentation may be:

(*i*) An innocent or unintentional misrepresentation or

(*ii*) An intentional, deliberate or willful misrepresentation with intent to deceive or defraud the other party.

The former is called 'misrepresentation' and the latter is 'fraud'. Misrepresentation is a false statement which the person making it honestly believes to be true or which he does not know to be false. It also includes non-disclosure of a material fact or facts without any intent to deceive the other party.

Section 18 of the Act defines misrepresentation as " *misrepresentation means and includes : (1) the positive assertion, in a manner not warranted by the information of the person making it, of that which is not true, though he believes it to be true; (2) any breach of duty which , without an intent to deceive, gains an advantage to the person committing it, or any one claiming under him, by misleading another to his prejudice or to the prejudice of any one claiming under him; (3) causing, however innocently, a party to an agreement to make a mistake as to the substance of the thing which is the subject of the agreement."*

Illustration: *A says to B that Z's car is a very good and can give a mileage of 25 kilometers per litre. B believes the statement made by A to be true and purchases the car based on the information but it turns out that the car is able to give a mileage of only 15 kilometers per litre. This is a case of misrepresentation. However if A believes that Z's car actually gives a mileage of 25 kilometers to a litre and informs B of the same with no intention to induce B to buy the car then it is innocent misrepresentation.*

According to the definition, under Section 18 of the Act, misrepresentation of facts relating to the subject-matter of the contract may be made by:

(*a*) **Positive assertion of the fact:** If a party to the contract makes a positive statement or assertive statement of fact which he believes it to be true, on the basis of information received from an untrustworthy source, or second-hand information or hearsay, and the statement is not true, he is said to have misrepresented the fact.

Illustration: *In Mohanlal Vs. Sri Gungaji Cotton Mills Co. (1899), A made a positive statement to the plaintiff that C would be a director of a company about to be formed, and the plaintiff, relying on this information, applied for shares in the defendant company. In a suit to set aside the contract, the court held the view that, if A has relied on the second-hand information he derived from D, he was warranted or justified in making the positive assertion that C would be the director.(It may be noted in this context, that a false statement need not be made direct to the plaintiff to become misrepresentation. It is sufficient if it is made to a third party in a manner that the plaintiff will become aware of it.)*

In Babui Panmato Kuer Vs. Ram Agya Singh (1968), the plaintiff , consented to the marriage with the defendant after learning from a talk between her father and another that the proposed bridegroom was a young man with a comfortable livelihood. The court held that the consent by the plaintiff was vitiated by fraud and misrepresentation.

(*b*) **Breach of duty:** Sec 18 (2) states that if a person commits a breach of duty without any intention to deceive the other party, and thereby gains an advantage to himself to the prejudice of the other party, the person committing the breach of duty is said to be guilty of innocent misrepresentation. This includes such cases where a party to the agreement has a duty to disclose all the material facts concerning the subject-matter of the contract known to him, but does not do so, without any intention of deceiving. Even when a statement is true when it was made but subsequently becomes false, should also be disclosed before the contract is entered into. The Act further states that if the change in the circumstances making a true statement untrue is not disclosed to the other party, the person making the statement will also be guilty of misrepresentation under this sub-section.

Illustration: *In Incledon Vs. Watson (1862), the defendant while negotiating for the sale of goodwill of a school to the plaintiff, told him that there were 22 boarders. Although the representation was true when it was made, before the bargain was struck, the number of boarders had fallen to 17, and this fact was known to the defendant. However, he did not inform the fact of the number having fallen. The court held that this breach of duty entitled the plaintiff to rescind the contract.*

(*c*) **Causing mistake about the subject-matter:** Section 18(3) of the Act states that if a party to an agreement induces the other party, although innocently, to commit a mistake as to the nature or quality of the subject-matter of the agreement, he become guilty of misrepresentation.

Illustrations: *(1) In Johnson Vs. Crowe (1874), the defendant agreed to sell and deliver a boiler to the plaintiff at Rajghat. At the time of entering into the agreement, the plaintiff made the representation that there was a road all* *the way to carry the boiler. The representation was innocent. In fact, there was a suspension bridge on the way and the bridge was not strong enough the bear the weight of the boiler. When the defendant came to know of the fact, he abstained from delivering the boiler. In a suit by the plaintiff, it was held that the agreement was voidable at the option of the defendants.*

(2) In The Oceanic Steam Navigation Co. Vs. Soonderdas Dhurumsey (1890), the defendants chartered a ship from the plaintiff's company. The ship was described in the charter party, and the plaintiff company represented that the tonnage of the ship was not more than 2,800. It later turned out that the registered tonnage was 3,045 tonnes. The defendant refused to accept the ship in fulfillment of the charter party. In a suit by the plaintiff company, it was held that the defendants were entitled to avoid the charter party because of the misrepresentation as to the tonnage.

(a) Requisites of misrepresentation

A misrepresentation is relevant if it satisfies the following requirements, namely;

- It must be a representation of a material fact. Mere expression of opinion does not amount to misrepresentation even if it turns out to be wrong.
- It must be made before the conclusion of the contract with a view to inducing the other party to enter into the contract.
- It must be made with an intention that it should be acted upon by the person to whom it is addressed.
- It must be actually have been acted upon and must have induced the contract.
- It must be wrong by the person who made it honestly believed it to be true.
- It must be made without any intention to deceive the other party.
- It need not be made directly to the party entering into such an agreement.

(b) Consequences of misrepresentation

The aggrieved party, in case of misrepresentation by the other party can; (a) avoid or rescind the contract, or, (b) accept the contract but insist that he shall be placed in the position in which he would have been if the representation made had been true.

4. Fraud

Fraud exists when a person makes a misrepresentation of a material fact, known to him to be untrue or made with reckless indifference as to whether it is true or false, with the intention of causing the other party to enter into a contract based on such misrepresentation.

Lord Herschell, in Derry Vs. Peek (1889), defines fraud as *"a false statement made knowingly, or without belief in its truth or recklessly careless whether it to be true or false"*. Therefore, fraud can be defined as an intentional misrepresentation of a material fact which induces another to enter into a contract. According to Section 17 of the Act, Fraud means and includes any of the following acts committed by a party to a contract, or with his connivance, or by his agent or to induce him to enter into a contract:

- The suggestion, as to a fact, of that which is not true by one who does not believe it to be true;
- The active concealment of a fact by one having knowledge or belief of the fact;
- A promise made without any intention of performing it;
- Any other act fitted to deceive;
- Any such act or omission as to law specially declared to be fraudulent.

The act also states that mere silence as to facts likely to affect the willingness of a person to enter into a contract is not fraud, unless the circumstances of the case are such that, regard being had to them, it is the duty of the person keeping silence to speak, or unless his silence is, in itself, equivalent to speech.

Illustrations: *(1) A sells by auction to B a house which A knows needs serious repairs. A says nothing to B about the fault in the building. This is not considered as fraud.*

(2) B says to A, "if you do not deny it, I shall assume that the house is well built and needs no repairs". A says nothing. Here A's silence is equivalent to speech.

(a) Essential Elements of Fraud

1. There must be a representation or assertion and it must be false: Without a representation or assertion, there can be no fraud except in cases where silence may in itself amount to fraud or where there is an effective concealment of a fact. To constitute fraud, there should be a false representation or suggestion by a party to a contract who knows that the suggestion is false. Even a statement made recklessly, without caring for its truth or falseness, is also considered as fraud.

   Illustration: *In Peek Vs. Gurney (1873), the appellant, on the faith of statements appearing in the prospectus of a company, bought some shares from a shareholder of the company. Some of the statements in the prospectus being false, he sued the promoters of the company. The prospectus of a company did not refer to the existence of a document disclosing liabilities. This gave the impression that the company was prosperous. If the existence of the document had been disclosed, the impression would have been quite different. Held, non-disclosure amounted to fraud and anyone who purchased shares on the faith of the prospectus could avoid the contract.*

2. The representation must relate to a material fact which exists now or existed in the past: An exaggerated statement of opinion, not being a statement of fact, affords no basis of fraud. Therefore to constitute fraud, the representation must be one of fact, and not of opinion or intention.

   It is common and usual for a trader to praise his own goods, make a statement as to the value of an article, or a flourishing description of the quality of an article, is merely a puffing statement, and not representation of fact. This is in accordance with the legal maxim, *'simplex commendation non-obligat'*, this means simple commendation does not create an obligation. A mere opinion, a puffing expression or hearsay or flourishing description, is not regarded as representation of fact.

3. The representation must have been made before the conclusion of the contract with the intention of inducing the other party to act upon it. It may sometimes happen that a party to a contract does not make any representation which is false. Instead, he may actively conceal a material fact, which according to him, if stated, would be disadvantageous to him. Active concealment of a fact, which is also known as *'suppressio veri'* is the suppression of truth.

   It should be noted in this context that active concealment does not mean non-disclosure of material facts, since the explanation of Section 17 clearly states that silence is not fraud except under certain circumstances. Active concealment is some positive act on the part of a party to a contract to deliberately conceal a material fact, and thus prevent the other party from knowing the truth.

Illustrations: *(1) The fruit seller may place and arrange fresh fruits on top of the basket in order to conceal the 'not so fresh' and defective fruits in the basket.*

(2) In King vs. Kylsant (1932), the prospectus issued by a company disclosed that the company had paid dividends every year between 1921 and 1927. However, during these years, the company had incurred heavy trading losses, and hence, it could only pay dividends out of such items in the accounts as were not available for dividends. The prospectus did not reveal the fact that the company had suffered substantial trading losses. It was held that, 'the prospectus was false, because it put before intending investors, figures which apparently disclosed the existing position of the company, but in fact hid it, and K, a director, who knew that it was false, was guilty of fraud.'

4. The representation or statement must have been made with a knowledge of its falsity or made recklessly.

   Illustration: *In Shireen Mal Vs. John James Taylor (1952), a man and a woman went through a ceremony of marriage, the husband having no intention of regarding the marriage as a real one. It was held that the consent of the wife was procured by fraud and the marriage was only a pretence.*

5. The other party must have been induced to act upon the representation. This is because, a mere falsehood is not enough to give a right of action.
6. Any fraudulent act must have done with an intention to commit fraud.
7. The party so induced must have acted upon it and suffered some loss. It is common rule of law that '*there is no fraud without damage*'.

Exceptions: Section 17 makes two exceptions to the principle of passive non-disclosure or silence. These are (*a*) circumstances of the case cast a duty upon the person keeping silent to speak and (*b*) silence, in itself is equivalent to speech.

The duty to speak arises when the parties to a contract are in a fiduciary relationship, i.e., when one of them reposes trust and confidence in the other.

(b) Whether Silence Amounts to Fraud?

Section 17 (2) of the Contract Act says that an active concealment of a material fact is fraud, but silence or passive non-disclosure is not fraud. This is because there is no general duty cast upon a party to a contract to disclose to the other party material facts within his knowledge but which are unknown to the other party and which might influence him in coming to a decision about the contract.

Rules

1. Mere silence without any duty to speak does not amount to fraud.
2. Mere silence as to facts likely to affect the willingness of a person to enter into a contract is not fraud.
3. Silence is fraudulent where- (a) the circumstances of the case are such that, regard being had to them, it is the duty of the person keeping silence to speak; or (b) silence in itself is equivalent to speech.
4. In case where there is duty to speak, non-disclosure amounts to breach of duty. If made with intent to deceive, it is fraudulent and if it is made without such intention, it is misrepresentation.

Illustration: *Contracts of 'uberrimae fidei', (which means contracts entered with utmost good faith), where there is legal obligations to disclose all the facts like contracts of insurance, contract for purchase of shares in companies, contracts of insurance, contract of marriage engagements, partnership contracts etc.*

5. There is no duty to disclose facts which are within the knowledge of both the parties. Silence in such cases will not amount to fraud.

(c) Fraud Contracts not Voidable

- Where the defrauded party could discover the truth by ordinary care.

  Illustration: *A by misrepresentation leads B erroneously to believe that 2000 tonnes of sugar is manufactured at A's sugar factory. B examines the accounts of the factory which shows only 1500 tonnes of sugar being manufactured. B later buys the sugar factory from A. B cannot avoid or rescind the contract on account of A's misrepresentation. This is because B could identify or discover the truth by ordinary care.*
- Where the party enters into a contract without knowing the fraud or misrepresentation.
- Where the interest of bonafide third party is affected before the contract is avoided.
- Where affected party cannot be put in the position in which he would have been if the representation made was true.

(d) Effects or Consequences of Fraud

The following remedies are available to the party who has been induced to enter into a contract by fraud.

(*a*) The contract is voidable at the option of the party whose consent was so caused.

(*b*) He may insist that the contract shall be performed and that he shall be put in the position in which he would have been if the representation made had been true.

(*c*) He may rescind the contract within a reasonable time under the Specific Relief Act , 1963.

(*d*) He has a right to sue for damages.

Distinction between Misrepresenatation and Fraud

Misrepresentation	Fraud
• There is no intention to deceive the other party.	• There is an intention to deceive the other party.
• A false innocent statement without any intention to deceive is misrepresentation.	• A false statement deliberately made to deceive is fraud.
• The person making the statement believes it to be true.	• The person making the statement does not believe it to be true.
• It makes the contract voidable at the option of the party injured.	• Besides making the contract voidable at the option of the party injured, it gives right to an independent action in tort.
• The contract cannot be avoided if the party whose consent was so cause, had the means of discovering the truth with ordinary diligence.	• This plea cannot be raised in case of fraud, except in cases when silence amounts to fraud.

5. Mistake

The term mistake is understood to mean misunderstanding or wrong thinking or wrong belief. An erroneous belief about something is called 'mistake'. When an agreement is entered into under a mistake, there is no free consent and hence no contract.

Illustration: *If a person buys an article thinking it is worth ₹200, and it is actually worth ₹50, the contract is good and the person has to bear the loss of his ignorance. Here this person is under a mistake.*

However, if a manufacturer undertakes to manufacture and deliver a certain number of articles by a certain date, and later finds that he mistook the potential capacity of his factory, he cannot say that because of his mistaken notion there was no contract. Mistake may be either (a) mistake of fact or (b) mistake of law.

Mistake of fact: Where both the parties to an agreement are under a mistake as to a matter of fact essential to the agreement, the agreement is void [Sec 20].

Illustration: *A agrees to buy from B a certain property. It turns out that the property was already sold by A's son to somebody else, at the time of A and B making the bargain, though neither party was aware of the fact. This agreement is void.*

In Couturier Vs. Hastie (1856), a contract was entered into for the sale of a cargo of corn, which the parties believed to be en route from Salonica to England. In fact, before the date of sale, the corn had become overheated and had to be sold for what it could fetch at an intermediate port. Neither of the parties was aware of this fact at the time of the contract. The House of Lords held that the buyer was not liable to pay for the corn as the contract was vitiated by mistake. The agreement is void.

(a) Essentials

1. Both the parties must labour under the mistake of fact at the time of formation of the contract to vitiate the contract. Mistake coming into existence subsequently does not make the contract void.
2. The mistake as to matter of fact must be essential to the agreement.
3. Mistake must be one of fact and not of law. (mistake of law is not an excuse).

(b) Types of Mistake of Fact

A mistake of fact may either be (a) Bilateral or mutual mistake or (b) Unilateral mistake.

Bilateral Mistake: When both the parties to an agreement are under a mistake as to essential matter of the agreement, then it is called Bilateral mistake. In such case, the agreement is void [Sec 20]. A Bilateral mistake has to fulfill two conditions, namely;

- Mutual mistake: It means that both the parties should have misunderstood each other.

  Illlustration: *A agreed to purchase B's motor car which was in the garage of B. Both parties did not know that the garage and the car was completely destroyed by fire a day prior to the agreement. There is mutual mistake of fact there is no agreement as it is void.*
- The mistake must be over the essential matter of the agreement: (a false and fundamental assumption).

Illustrations: *(1) In Galloway Vs. Galloway (1914), the plaintiff and the defendant, believing themselves to be lawfully married, entered into a separation agreement by which the defendant agreed to pay the plaintiff £1 a week. There were not, in fact, validly married. In an action by the plaintiff for the arrears of the weekly payment, it* *was held that the agreement was void as there was a mutual mistake of fact which was material to the existence of the agreement.*

(2) In Cooper Vs. Phibbs (1867), an uncle had told his nephew, not intending to misrepresent anything, but being in fact in error, that he (the uncle) was entitled to a fishery; and the nephew, after the uncle's death, acting in the belief of the truth of what the uncle had told him, entered into an agreement to rent the fishery from the uncle's daughters whereas it actually belonged to the nephew himself. Subsequently, he sought to avoid the contract on the ground of mistake in that he ignorantly thought that it belonged to the defendants. The House of Lords set aside the agreement.

Types of Bilateral mistake: Bilateral mistake can be broadly classified into two groups on the basis of (a) mistake as to the subject matter and (b) mistake as to the possibility of performance of the contract.

1. Mistake as to the subject matter:
   (*a*) Mistake as to the existence of the subject matter: When both the parties believe that the subject matter of the contract is existing which in fact is not in existence, then the contract is void.
   (*b*) Mistake as to the identity of the subject matter: When one party to an agreement, intends to deal with one thing and the other intends to deal with another thing, then there is no contract. (no *consensus-ad-idem*, hence no contract).
   (*c*) Mistake as to the quality of the subject matter: If the parties to an agreement have mistaken about the very quality of the subject matter of an agreement then it is void.
   Illustration: *In Nicholson and Venn Vs. Smith Marriott (1947), a quantity of Georgian table linen described as the 'authentic property of Charles I' and as bearing the arms of that unhappy monarch, was sold at an auction. It was held that there was mutual mistake of both the parties as to the quality of the subject- matter, and hence the contract was void.*
   (*d*) Mistake as to the quantity of the subject matter: When both the parties are under a mistake as to the quantity of the subject matter of an agreement then it is void.
   (*e*) Mistake as to the title of the subject matter: If the seller is selling a thing which he is not entitled to sell and both the parties are under a mistake as to the title of the subject matter, then the agreement is void.
   (*f*) Mistake as to the price of the subject matter: If there is a mutual mistake as to the price of the subject matter then the agreement is void.
2. Mistake as to the possibility of performing the contract. When both the parties believe that the contract can be performed but infact it cannot be performed. The contract is void on the ground of impossibility.

Illustration: *In Griffith Vs. Brymer (1903), an agreement for the hire of rooms to watch the Coronation Procession of Edward VII, made in ignorance that the procession has already been cancelled due to the illness of the King. It was held to be void.*

Unilateral Mistake: A unilateral mistake is the mistake of one of the parties to a contract as to a matter of fact. A unilateral mistake is not a valid ground for avoiding the contract. A person is bound by an agreement to which he has expressed a clear assent unless the unilateral mistake is caused by misrepresentation. According to Section 22 of the Act, a contract is not voidable just because of the mistake of one of the parties to it, about the matter of fact. Hence, unilateral mistake is not a defence to avoid a contract.

Illustration: *A buys an article thinking that it is of a particular quality, but actually the quality of the article is of a lower grade. A cannot avoid the contract subsequently.*

Exceptions to unilateral mistake

The following situations make an unilateral mistake a void contract.

1. **Mistake as to the identity of the person contacted with:** It is a fundamental rule of law that if one of the parties represents himself to be some other person than he really is, there is a mistake as to the identity of the person contracted with.

   Illustrations: *(1) If A makes an offer to B, G cannot give himself any rights in respect of the contract by accepting the offer. If he does so, the contract will be void.*

   (2) In Phillips Vs. Brooks (1919), on April 15, 1918, a man called North, entered the plaintiff's shop and saw some pearls and rings. He selected pearls worth £2,550 and a ring of the value of £450. He produced a cheque for £3,000, stating that he was Sir George Bullough and also gave his address, under the same name. The shopkeeper accepted the cheque in good faith believing that the person was George. North later pledged the jewellary with a pawn broker Subsequently the cheque was dishonoured and North was convicted. The shopkeeper demanded the jeweler back from the pawn broker stating that there was never any contract with North but with the mistaken identity of Sir George Bullough. Held that the shopkeeper had contracted to sell and deliver to the person who comes to his ship, even though he believed him as Sir George. The mistake is this case was not about identity but only about the attributes of the buyer.

2. **Mistake as to the nature of the contract:** If a person enters into a contract in the mistaken belief that he is signing a document of a different class and character altogether, there is a mistake as to the nature of contract and the contract is void. He can successfully plead '*non est factum*', which means it is not his document. The very basis of the contract, *i.e.* the consent is missing in this case.

   Illustration: *In Foster Vs. Mackinnon (1869), the defendant has some time previously, signed a guarantee for £3,000 at the request of one Callow, who had been the secretary of a company, in order to enable the company to obtain an advance from their bankers. On 6th November 1867, a bill was drawn by one Cooper on Callow, and was endorsed successively by Cooper, the defendant, and three more persons to the plaintiff, who became the holder for value before it became due, and without notice of any fraud. The defendant, an old man of poor sight sigthed a bill of exchange thinking that it was a guarantee. Held, there was no contract on the ground that the mind of the signer did not accompany the signature.*

(c) Mistake of Law

Mistake of law may be (*i*) mistake of law of the country or (*ii*) mistake of law of a foreign country.

Mistake of law of the country: Section 21 of the Act which enacts the doctrine of the English law, lays down that a contract is not voidable because it was caused by a mistake as to any law in force in India. Accordingly, no relief can be granted on the ground of mistake of law of the land. This is based on the principle '*Ignorantial juris neminum excusat*' which means that ignorance of law is no excuse. Since it is the duty of every citizen to know either by professional advice or otherwise, as concerns him for the matters he is transacting, he cannot avoid the contract on the ground of mistake of law.

Illustration: *A and B make a contract under the wrong belief that particular debt is barred by the Indian law of Limitations. This contract is not voidable.*

Mistake of law of a foreign country: Mistake of law of a foreign country is treated as a mistake of fact and hence the agreement is void [Sec 21].

(E) Lawful Object

The purpose of entering into a contract should be lawful. The object would be unlawful if it is forbidden by law, is of such a nature that, if permitted, would defeat the provisions of any law, is fraudulent and causes injury to the person or property of another or is immoral or opposed to public policy. The agreement entered into should seek to accomplish something which the law deems proper. Only under such situation can the contract be enforced by law. Thus any agreement, if it is illegal, immoral or opposed to public policy, cannot become a valid contract.

A contract must not only be based upon mutual consent of competent parties but must also have a lawful object. If the object of an agreement is the performance of an unlawful act, the agreement is unenforceable. As per Sec 23 of the Contract Act, the object and consideration of an agreement should be lawful. Accordingly the Act states; "*The consideration or object of an agreement is lawful, unless it is forbidden by law; or is of such a nature that, if permitted, it would defeat the provisions of any law, or is fraudulent; or involves or implies injury to the person or property of another; or the Court regards it as immoral, or opposed to public policy.*"

Under the Act, while referring to agreements, the term 'object' and 'consideration' under Sec 23 are not used synonymously. The object indicates the purpose or design of an agreement. The consideration is some act or abstinence or reciprocal of promises.

Illustrations: *(1) A and B enter into an agreement for the division among them of gains acquired, or to be acquired by them by fraud. The agreement is void, as its object is unlawful.*

(2) A promises to obtain for B a license for starting a business illegally if B pays him a bribe of ₹10,000. The agreement is void as the consideration is unlawful.

Consideration is therefore an act, abstinence or promises made at the desire of the promisor whereas, object is the purpose for which the agreement is made. The consideration or object of an agreement is unlawful;

1. **If it is forbidden by law:** If the object or the consideration of an agreement is the doing of an act forbidden by law, the agreement is void. An act is forbidden by law when it is punishable by the criminal law of the country or when it is prohibited by special legislation or regulations made by the competent authority.

   Illustration: *A promises to obtain for B an employment in the public service and B promises to pay ₹1,000 to A. The agreement is void as the consideration for it is unlawful.*
2. If it would defeat the provisions of any law: If the object or consideration of an agreement would defeat the provision of any law then the agreement is void.

   Illustration: *In Napier Vs. National Business Agency Ltd, N agreed to enter a company's service in consideration of a weekly wage of £13 and a weekly expense allowance of £6. Both the parties knew that the expense allowance was a device to evade tax. It was held that the agreement was unlawful.*
3. **If it is fraudulent:** An agreement which is made for a fraudulent purpose is void. Thus an agreement is fraudulent when entered into between parties with a fraudulent purpose or to perpetrate fraud on others, is unlawful.

   Illustration: *A, an agent of B agrees for money, without the knowledge of his principal B, to obtain for K, a lease of land belonging to B the principal. The agreement between A and B is void, as it implies fraud by concealment by A on his principal.*

4. **If it causes injury to the person or his property:** Injury means wrong, harm or damage. Person means one's body and property includes both movable and immovable property.

   Illustration: *In Ram Sarup Vs. Bansi Mandar (1915), a debtor who owed ₹100 executed a bond by which he was required to put forth manual labor until the amount was repaid, and in the case of default, he had to pay exorbitant interest. The court held that 'such a condition is indistinguishable from slavery and as such the contract involved injury to the person of the debtor.*

5. **If the court regards it as immoral:** An agreement, the consideration or object of which is immoral.

   Illustration: *In Bai Vijili Vs. Nansa Nagar (1885), the plaintiff advanced money to the defendant, a married woman, to enable her to obtain a divorce from her husband. The defendant agreed to marry the plaintiff as soon as she could obtain a divorce. In a suit by the plaintiff to recover the money, it was held that the plaintiff was not entitled to recover back the amount, as the agreement had for its object the divorce of the defendant, from her husband and the promise of marriage given under such circumstances was immoral.*

6. **Where the court regards it as opposed to public policy:** A contract made in order to injure the interest of the general public is void. Agreements which are held void on the ground that the consideration or object is opposed to public policy , are

   (a) *Trading with enemy*: Agreements entered into with alien enemies are known as *'detrimental contracts'* since they tend to benefit an enemy country or injure the State in its relations with other states.

   (b) *Stifling prosecution*: An agreement which seeks to absolve an offender of the criminal liability, either by promising not to prosecute him for his offence, or withdraw a criminal case pending against him, is known as an agreement to stifle prosecution.

   (c) *Maintenance and Champerty*: These are agreements that tend to promote speculative litigation. In the case of maintenance, the agreement seeks to provide assistance, financial or otherwise, to bring or defend a law suit, while in the case of champerty, the agreement is for sharing the benefit to be derived from the law suit.

   (d) *Interference with the course of justice*: Any agreement intended to obstruct or prevent legal process or interfere in any manner the course of justice, is void. Agreements for using improper influence of any kind with judges or officers of the court, to bribe witnesses or to promise them payment of money if they give evidence favorable to the party promising or inducing witnesses to gives false evidence, etc are opposed to public policy.

   (e) *Trafficking in Public Officers:* Agreements that interfere with the free exercise of governmental functions include, agreements to influence public officers by promising illegal gratification, to provide money to a member of the Parliament, sale of public offices and appointments to procure a title, honour for reward, etc.

   (f) *Marriage brokerage contracts:* Since it is in the interests of society that reckless or unsuitable marriages should be prevented, third parties are not allowed to make money by bringing about matrimonial unions and therefore such agreements to procure marriages for reward is void.

   Illustration: *An agreement to pay money to the parent or guardian of a minor in consideration of his consenting to give the minor in marriage, has been held to be opposed to public policy by the Full Bench of the Madras High Court in Kalavangunta Venkata Vs. Kalvangunta Lakshmi (1908).*

   (g) *Agreements interfering with parental duties*: Agreements which contemplate an absolute transfer of the rights of parents over their children, as to their custody, education and religious training are void as being opposed to public policy.

***Illustration:** In Giddu Narayanish Vs. Mrs Annie Besant (1907), an agreement whereby a father transferred guardianship of his two minor children in favour of a lady was held to be void, although the father agreed not to revoke the authority of the lady.*

(*h*) *Agreements restraining personal liberty*: An agreement which unduly restricts the liberty of the individual is void.

***Illustration:** It was held in Horwood Vs. Millar's Timber Co. (1917), Where a man agrees with a moneylender not to change his residence or his employment, or to consent to a reduction of his salary, or to part with any of his property, or to incur any obligations on credit, or any obligations legal or moral without the consent of the moneylender, makes the contract void as it is against public policy.*

(F) Agreements not Expressly Declared Void

One of the essential elements of a valid contract states that; *"an agreement become a contract only when it is not hereby expressly declared to be void"*. Void agreements cannot be enforced by law. Enforceability of an agreement even when the parties may be *ad idem* since the Act itself declare them void, the aggrieved party cannot seek any relief from the court. Examples of void agreements are such as those in restraint of trade, in restraint of marriage, in restraint of legal proceedings and wagering agreement. The agreement must not have been expressly declared void by any law inforce in the country.

An agreement is said to be opposed to public policy when it is harmful to the public welfare. Public policy is that principle of law which holds that no subject can lawfully do that which has a mischievous tendency to be injurious to the interest of the public or which is against the public good or public welfare. It is not possible to give a precise or exact definition of the term 'public policy'. The term is quite vague. As new concepts take the place of old, the concept of what is for the public good or in the interest of public or what would be injurious or harmful to the public good or the public interest has varied from time to time.

Some explanations for agreements which are or which have been held to be opposed to public policy and are unlawful are as follows:

1. **Agreements of trading with an alien enemy:** An agreement made with an alien enemy at the time of war is illegal on the ground of 'opposed to public policy'.
2. **Agreement to commit a crime:** Where the consideration in an agreement is to commit a crime, the agreement is opposed to public policy. The court will not enforce such an agreement.

   ***Illustration:** A promises to indemnify B in consideration of him beating C. The agreement is opposed to public policy and hence void.*
3. **Agreements which interfere with administration of justice:** An agreement which obstructs the ordinary process of justice is unlawful and the object of which is to interfere with the administration of justice is unlawful, being opposed to public policy.
4. **Agreements in restraint of legal proceedings:** Sec 28 which deals with these agreements renders two kinds of agreements as void. They are, (*i*) agreements restricting enforcement of rights and (*ii*) agreements curtailing period of limitation.

   (*i*) *Agreements restricting enforcement of rights*: An agreement which wholly or partially prohibits any party from enforcing his rights under or in respect of any contract is void to that extent.

(ii) *Agreements curtailing period of limitation*: Agreements which curtail the period of limitation prescribed by the law of limitation are void because their object is to defeat the provisions of law.

5. **Trafficking in public offices and titles :** Agreements for the sale or transfer of public offices and titles or for the procurement of a public recognition like 'Padma Vibhusan' or 'Param Veer Chakra' , for monetary consideration are unlawful, being opposed to public policy. Similarly, an agreement to pay money to a public servant to induce him to act corruptly is unlawful.
   Illustration: *A promised to obtain an employment to B in a public office and B promised to pay a suitable sum of money for A's help in securing the employment. Held, the agreement was against public policy and illegal. [Pandian Vs. M.M Roy].*
6. **Agreements tending to create interest opposed to duty:** If a person enters into an agreement whereby he is bound to do something which is against his professional duty, the agreement is void on the ground of public policy.
7. **Agreements in restraint of parental rights:** A father, and in his absence the mother, is the legal guardian of his/her minor child. This right of guardianship cannot be exchanged away by any agreement.
8. **Agreements restricting personal liberty:** Agreements which restrict the personal freedom of the parties to it are void on being against public policy.
9. **Agreements in restraint of marriage:** Every agreement in restraint of marriage of any person, other than a minor, is void [Sec 26]. This is because the law regards marriage and married status as the right of every individual.
   Illustration: *In Lowe Vs. Peers, P promised to marry L only and none other person and promised to pay L a sum of £2000 if he married someone else. P however married X. In a suit for recovering the promised sum of money, the court held that L could not recover the sum agreed as the agreement was in restraint of marriage.*
10. Marriage brokerage : An agreement by which a person, for a monetary consideration, promises in return to procure the marriage of another is void.
11. Agreements interfering with marital duties.
12. Agreements to defraud creditors or revenue authorities.
13. Agreement in restraint of trade: An agreement which interferes with the liberty of a person to engage himself in any lawful trade, profession or vocation is called an agreement in restraint of trade. Public policy requires that every man should be at liberty to work for himself and should not be at liberty to deprive himself of the fruit of his labour, skill or talent by any contract that he enters into.

Illustration: *In Sheikh Kalu Vs. Ram Saran Bhagat, out of 30 makers of combs in the city of Patna, 29 agreed to supply their combs only to R and no one else. R was free to reject the goods if he found no market for them. It was held that the agreement was void.*

In England, the law relating to restraint of trade is based on the general principles of law that all restrictions of trade are void. A restraint can however be justified if it is reasonable in the interest of the contracting parties and the public. In India, it is valid if it falls within any of the statutory exceptions.

Exceptions: The following are the two exceptions to the rule that an agreement in restraint of trade is void, namely; (1) Exception created by Statute, and (2) Exceptions arising from judicial interpretation of Sec 27.

1. Exception created by Statute:
   (a) **Sale of goodwill:** A seller of goodwill of a business may be restrained from carrying on;
      (i) A similar business.
      (ii) Within specified local limits.
      (iii) So long as the buyer or any person deriving the title to the goodwill from him, carries on a like business.
      (iv) That such limit appears to the court as reasonable.
   (b) **Partnership agreements:** The Indian Partnership Act 1932, also contains certain exceptions to the general rule, agreements in restraint of trade.
      (i) Under Section 11 of the Partnership Act: All the partners may agree not to carry on a business similar to that of the firm as long as they are partners.
      (ii) Under Section 32 of the Partnership Act: All partners have the right to restrain an outgoing partner from carrying on a similar business within a specified period of time or within local limits of the partnership business.
      (iii) Under Section 54 of the Partnership Act : Partners may in anticipation of dissolution make an agreement that some or all of them will not carry on a business similar to that of the firm for a specified period not exceeding one year or within a specified local area, which might affect the partnership business.
      (iv) Under Section 55(3) of the Partnership Act: A partner may , upon sale of goodwill of a firm, make an agreement that such partner will not carry on business similar to that of the firm within a specified period or within specified local limits , provided the restriction is reasonable.
2. Exception arising from judicial interpretation:
   (a) **Trade combination:** Traders and manufacturers in the same line of business normally form associations to regulate business or to fix prices. The regulations as to the opening and closing of business is a market, licensing of traders, supervision and control of dealers and the mode of dealing are not unlawful even if they are in restraint of trade.

      Illustration: In North Western Salt Co. Vs. Electrolytic Alkali Co. Ltd (1914), a combination to regulate supply and maintain price is not necessarily disadvantageous to the public and as such is not opposed to public policy. But a combination which tends to create monopoly and which is against the public interest is void.
   (b) **Sole selling agreements:** There is a usual practice among manufacturers where they give certain rights to only one agent or distributor to sell goods manufactured by them in a particular area and the agent in turn agrees not to deal in goods of any other manufacturer.
   (c) **Negative stipulations in service agreements:** Sometimes, an employee by the terms of his service agreement is prevented from accepting;
      (i) Any other engagement during his employment and , or,
      (ii) A similar engagement after the termination of his services.
      (iii) Government employees, like doctors , engineers, etc are debarred from taking up private practices during the term of their employment.
      (iv) A chartered accountant appointed by a company may be restricted from private practice during the term of his employment with the company.

Illustration: *Brahmaputra Tea C. Vs. Scarth, it was held that an agreement restraining an employee from taking up service or engaging in any similar business for a period of 5 years after the termination of his service was void as the term period of 5 years was unreasonable.*

If a restraint is intended to protect an employer against an employee making use of trade secrets learned by him in the course of his employment, the restraint is valid, provided , it is not for any other purpose.

Illustration: *In Forster & Sons Ltd vs. Suggett, A was chiefly engaged in making glass bottles. B was working with A as the manager in the company and was instructed in certain confidential methods concerning correct mixture of gas and air in the furnaces. B agreed that during the five years after termination of his services he would not carry on employment or business in the United Kingdom or be interested in glass bottle manufacture. It was held that A was entitled to protection and that the restraint was reasonable.*

However, it should be noted that an employer cannot prevent an employee from earning his living by the exercise of his skill and the use of his knowledge.

(i) Void Agreements

A void agreement is one which is not enforceable by law [Sec. 2(g)]. Such an agreement does not give rise to any legal consequences and is void-ab-initio. Under different sections of the Contract Act, 1872, the following agreements have been expressly declared void:

(*a*) Agreements made with parties having no contractual capacity (minors etc.) Sec 11.
(*b*) Agreement made under mutual mistake of fact. Sec 20
(*c*) Agreements with unlawful consideration or object . Sec 23
(*d*) Agreements where consideration or object is unlawful in part .Sec 24.
(*e*) Agreement without consideration . Sec 25.
(*f*) Agreement in restraint of marriage. Sec 26.
(*g*) Agreement in restraint of trade . Sec 27.
(*h*) Agreement in restraint of legal proceedings Sec 28.
(*i*) Agreement, the meaning of which is uncertain . Sec 29.
(*j*) Agreement by way of wager. Sec 30.
(*k*) Agreements contingent on impossible events. Sec 36.
(*l*) Agreement the performance of which is impossible. Sec 56.
(*m*) Reciprocal promises to do certain things which are legal and certain other things which are illegal. Sec 57.

(ii) Wagering Agreements

A wager is an agreement between two parties by which one promises to pay money or money's worth on the happening of some uncertain event in consideration of the other party's promise to pay if the event does not happen. A Wager is an agreement in which one of the parties to the agreement wins at the expense of the loser, the outcome being determined largely by chance. The word wager means 'a bet' or a betting agreement.

Wagering agreements or wager [Sec. 30]: A wager is an agreement between two parties by which one promises to pay money or money's worth on the happening of some uncertain event in consideration of the other party's promise to pay if the event does not happen.

Sir Williams Anson defines a wager as *'a promise to give money or money's worth upon the determination or ascertainment of an uncertain event'*. This definition was quoted by the Supreme Court in Gherlal Parekh Vs. Mahadeo Das Maiya (1959). The definition of a wagering agreement given by Hawkins.J in Carlill Vs. Carbolic Smoke Ball Co. (1892), which is considered to be the classic definition, and quoted by the Madras High Court in Narayana Ayyangar Vs. Vellachami Ambalam (1927), is as follows: *"A wagering contract is one by which two persons professing to hold opposite views touching the issue of a future uncertain event mutually agree that, dependent upon the determination of that event, one shall win from the other, and that other shall pay or hand over to him a sum of money or other stake; neither of the contracting parties having any other interest in the contract than the sum of stake he will so win or lose, there being no other real consideration for the making of such contract by either of the parties. It is essential to a wagering contract that each party may, under it either win or lose, whether he will win or lose being dependent on the issue of the event, and, therefore, remaining uncertain until that issue is known. If either of the parties may win but cannot lose, or may lose but cannot win, it is not a wagering contract."*

Therefore it can be stated that in a wagering contract, (i) one party stands to win while the other party stands to loose. (ii) The party who does not win, shall loose the stake money of the contract. (iii) Both parties do not have any control over the event on which the contract was entered (iv) Both parties do not have any other interest in the contract other than the stake money.

Wagering agreement is a game of chance, in which the gain or loss is wholly dependent on an uncertain event. However it should be noted that a wagering agreement differs from an insurance contract because, in the case of insurance contracts the parties have an insurable interest, i.e, to protect the life or property of the insured person and hence entered into a contract of insurance.

Illustrations: *(1) A and B mutually agree that if India wins 10 gold medals in the Olympic Games, A will pay B ₹ 1,000 and if India does not win 10 gold medals , B will pay A ₹ 1000.*

(2) A and M mutually agree that if Salman Khan's forthcoming movie becomes a hit, A will pay M ₹5,000 and if the movie flops at the box office, M will pay A ₹ 5,000. These are wagering contracts.

1. *Essentials of a Wagering Agreement*

1. There must be two parties: just as any contract, a wagering contract should consist of two parties.
2. Promise to pay money or money's worth: The wagering agreement must contain a promise to pay money or money's worth.
3. Uncertain event: The grounds on which the wagering contract was entered should be uncertain, (i.e. the event may or may not happen)
4. The promise must be conditional on an event happening or not happening. A wager generally contemplates a future event. It may also relate to a past event provided the parties are not aware of the result or the time of its happening.
5. The parties to the wager must stand to either win or lose: Upon the determination of the contemplated event, each party should stand to either win or lose.
6. No control over the event: Neither party should have control over the happening or non-occurrence of an uncertain event for which the wagering contract was entered into. Neither party should have any other interest in the happening or non-happening of the event other than the sum or stake he will win or lose. Thus, an agreement is not a wager if the party to whom money is promised on the occurrence of an event has an interest in its non-occurrence or vice-versa. That is why a contract of insurance is not a wagering agreement.

2. *Special Cases (Transactions not Considered as Wagers)*

The following transactions are not wagers:

1. Crossword puzzles, picture competitions, literary and athletic competitions in which prizes are awarded on the basis of skill and intelligence are games of skill as opposed to games of chance. A crossword competition involving a good measure of skill for its successful solution. According to the Prize Competition Act, 1955, prize competition in games of skill are not a wager, provided the amount of prize does not exceed ₹ 1,000. However, crossword puzzles, in which prizes depend upon the correspondence of the competitor's solution with a previously prepared solution kept with the editor of a newspaper, is considered a lottery and hence a wagering transaction, according to the view expressed by the Supreme Court in State of Bombay Vs. R.M.D.Chamarbaughwala (1957).
2. Contract of Insurance is not a wager due to the following points of difference between the two: (*i*) an insurance contract (except life assurance) is a contract of indemnity. Its object is to make good the actual loss to the insured. A wagering agreement, on the other hand, is not a contract of indemnity since it results in a profit or loss to one of the parties. (*ii*) In an insurance contract, the insured should have insurable interest in the subject matter, while in a wagering agreement stake is the only interest which the parties will be having. (*iii*) A contract of insurance is a form of social co-operation. As such, it is of immense benefit to the public. A wagering agreement, on the other hand, is not beneficial to the society.
3. Commercial transactions (Share market transactions). Agreements for sale and purchase of any commodity or share market transactions, in which there is a genuine intention to 'do legitimate business i.e., to give and take delivery of goods or shares, are not wagering agreements. If there is no such genuine intention and parties only want to gamble on the rise or fall of the market by paying or receiving the differences in prices only, the transaction would be a wagering agreement and therefore void. *"In order to constitute a wagering contract, neither party should intend to perform the contract itself, but only to pay the differences"*.
4. Lotteries. A lottery is a game of chance. Hence the lottery business is a wagering transaction. Such a transaction is not only void but also illegal because Sec. 294 (A) of the Indian Penal Code declares conducting of lottery a punishable offence. If a lottery is authorized by the Government, the only effect of such permission is that the persons conducting the lottery (*i.e.*, the persons running the lottery and the buyer of lottery ticket) will not be guilty of a criminal offence, but the lottery still remains a wager (Dorabji Tata vs Lance).

3. *Effect of Wagering Agreements*

Wagering agreements have been expressly declared to be void in India. In the State of Maharashtra and Gujarat they have been declared to be illegal. No suit can be brought for recovering anything alleged to be won on any wager, or entrusted to any person to abide by the result of any game or other uncertain event on which any wager is made. (Money deposited with a person called stakeholder, to be paid to the party winning upon a wager cannot be recovered by the winner. On the other hand, the loser can recover his deposit from the stakeholder. But where the stakeholder pays the money to the winner, the loser cannot recover it from him.)

In India wagering agreements are void except in the states of Maharashtra and Gujarat. These states have declared wagering agreements as illegal. Hence suits cannot be filed in the court for recovering anything under wagering agreements. Even collateral transactions are not enforceable in these states.

Illustration: *In Badridas Vs. Meghraj, a promissory note was executed for the payment of liabilities arising out of wagering transactions in shares. Held that the promissory note was not enforceable in a court of law.*

Suit to recover money deposited: Money deposited with a person called the stakeholder, to be paid to the party winning upon a wager cannot be recovered by the winner. On the other hand, the loser can recover his deposit from the stakeholder. In case the stakeholder pays the money to the winner, the loser cannot recover it from the stakeholder or winner. [Bridger Vs. Savage].

4. Collateral Transactions

Since wagering agreements are void, transactions collateral to them are not affected. However, in the states of Maharashtra and Gujarat, the wagering agreements have been declared to be illegal. The rule in England regarding the wagering agreements is also the same. The collateral transactions to such wagering agreements, therefore in these two states (Maharashtra and Gujarat) become illegal. In the rest of India collateral transactions are valid.

5. Restitution

When a contract becomes void, the party who has received any benefit under it must restore it to the other party or must compensate the other party with the value of the benefit. This restoration of the benefit is called 'restitution'. The principle of restitution is that a person who has been unjustly enriched at the expense of another is required to make restitution (make good the loss or restore) to that other. Restitution is not based on loss to the plaintiff, but on benefit which is enjoyed by the defendant at the cost of the plaintiff which is unjust for the defendant to retain.

Illustrations: *A Maharaja sold certain mills without paying overdue municipal taxes. The buyer paid the taxes to save the property from being sold, and then sued the Maharaja for the amount of tax paid. The Privy Council held the view that the Maharaja was bound by law to pay within the meaning of this Section. [Govindram Gordhandas Seksaria Vs. State of Gondal (1950)].*

(G) Possibility of Performance

Agreement to do an act impossible of performance cannot be enforced. The act contemplated in the agreement should be capable of performance. Agreements to do an act impossible of performance cannot be enforced.

Illustrations: *(1) A agrees to bring back to life B's pet dog; B cannot seek redressal of grievance and enforce performance of promise by A in a court of law as the act itself is impossible to perform.*

(2) A promises to make B and his family immortal; B cannot seek redressal of grievance and enforce performance of promise by A in a court of law as the act itself is impossible to perform.

(H) Certainty of Terms of the Contact

The agreement should not be uncertain, vague or impossible. An agreement to do something impossible is void under Section 56. The terms of the agreement should be certain.

Illustration: *A requests for 100 meters of cloth from a cloth merchant. The agreement however does not make certain the type and texture of the cloth required to be purchased. The agreement being vague cannot be enforced.*

(I) Legal Formalities

One aspect of legal formalities is whether the agreement must be written or can it be oral. A contract may be formed in either ways. Agreement made in India may be oral or in writing as per Section 9 of the Act. However, where any other statute requires an agreement to be put in writing or registered, the same should be compiled with; else such an agreement cannot be enforced. But it is in the best interest of both the parties that they must reduce the contract into writing because it could create misunderstanding or confusion at a later stage. However it can be noted that if it is not required under any Act, it depends upon the desire of the parties entering into a contract.

Registration is another aspect of legal formalities. Registration is again optional, though it is compulsory in case of gift and mortgages. Similarly in some cases the documents containing agreements, besides being in writing, need to be stamped and attested also. The Indian Companies Act requires the Memorandum and Articles of Association and the contracts entered into by the company to be put in writing. The Indian Trust act requires the creation of a trust to be reduced to writing. Negotiable Instruments should be in writing according to the Negotiable Instruments Act. Similarly, even a simple contract not supported by consideration should be in writing and registered according to Section 25(i) of the Contract Act. Sale, mortgage and lease of an immovable property can only be done under a written and registered contract as per the provisions of the Transfer of Property Act.

2.6 CONTINGENT CONTRACT

A Contract may be (a) an absolute contract or (b) a contingent contract. An absolute contract is one in which the promisor binds himself to performance in any event without any conditions. Default by one of the parties gives the aggrieved party a cause of action against the defaulting party. Therefore, a contract which must be performed in any event is known as an absolute or unconditional contract.

Illustration: *Radha offers to sell her chain to Geetha for ₹5,000, which is accepted by Geetha. There are no conditions and it is an absolute contract.*

A contingent contract means, a contract which is dependent on the happening or not happening of something. 'Contingent' means that which is dependent on something else. Section 31 of the Act defines a contingent contract as '*a contract to do or not to do something, if some event, collateral to such contract, does or does not happen.*'

Illustrations: *(1) A agrees to take B to watch a movie if B scores 60 or above marks in Sanskrit subject.*

(2) A contracts to pay ₹25,000 to Z if he gets injured in the race. These are contingent contracts.

(A) Essentials of a Contingent Contract

There are three essential characteristics of a contingent contract, namely;

(*a*) Its performance depends upon the happening or non-happening in future of some event.
(*b*) The event must be uncertain otherwise it is not a contingent contract.
(*c*) The event must be collateral (incidental to the contract)

(B) Rules Regarding Contingent Contracts

1. Contingent contracts depend on the happening of an uncertain future event cannot be enforced until the event has happened. If the event becomes impossible, such contracts become void [Sec 32].

   Illustration: *A contracts to pay B a sum of money when B marries G. G dies without being married to B. The contract becomes void.*

2. Where a contingent contract is to be performed if and when a particular event does not happen, its performance can be enforced only when the event becomes impossible. [Sec 33]

   Illustration: *A agrees to pay the school fee of B's son if Z dies. The contract cannot be enforced so long as Z is alive.*

3. If a contract is contingent upon how a person will act at an unspecified time, the event shall be considered to become impossible when such person does anything which renders it impossible that he should so act within any definite time, or otherwise than under further contingencies [Sec 34]

   Illustration: *A agrees to gift his property to B if B marries his daughter Z. However B marries D. The marriage of B to Z must now be considered impossible, although it is possible that D may die and B may later marry Z. This is just a distant possibility.*

4. Contingent contract becomes void if the event does not happen or if the happening of the event becomes impossible before the expiry of that time.

   Illustration: *A promises to gift his car to B, if a certain person becomes the Mayor of the city in the forthcoming corporation elections. The contract cannot be enforced if that certain person becomes the Mayor in the next election.*

5. Contingent agreements to do or not to do anything, if an impossible event happens , are void, whether or not the fact is known to the parties [Sec 36]

Illustrations: *(1) A agrees to give his house on lease to B if he agrees to get his daughter married to A's son. However, unknown to both the parties, A's son is already married to Y. The contract is void.*

(2) A agrees to pay B ₹22000 if B will marry A's daughter to Z. Z was dead at the time of the agreement. The agreement is void.

Contracts of insurance and contracts of indemnity and guarantee are popular instances of contingent contracts. As the performance of a contract is made dependent upon a contingency, contingent contracts are also known as 'conditional' contracts. But in certain cases a contract may look like a 'conditional contract, whereas in fact it may be simply an ordinary absolute contract where the promisor undertakes to perform the contract in all events.

Illustration: *Where A promises to pay ₹5,000 to B, a property broker, if B manages to get a two room accommodation for him at a rental of ₹2,500 per month, it is not a contingent contract, though on the face of it, it appears like a conditional contract. It is an ordinary absolute contract because the uncertain event (namely, managing to get an accommodation) itself forms the consideration of the contract and is not a collateral event.*

Hence, it must be clearly understood that in the case of contingent contracts, the uncertain events must be collateral to such contracts.

Differences between a wagering agreement and a contingent contract:

1. A wagering agreement consists of reciprocal promises whereas a contingent contract may not contain reciprocal promises.

2. A wagering agreement is essentially of a contingent nature, whereas a contingent contract may not be of a wagering nature.
3. A wagering agreement is void whereas a contingent contract is valid.
4. In a wagering agreement, the parties have no other interest in the subject matter of the agreement except the winning or loosing of the amount of the wager. This is not so in case of a contingent contract.
5. In a wagering agreement, the future event is the sole determining factor, while in a contingent contract; the future event is only collateral.

(C) Collateral Events

According to Pollock and Mulla, a collateral event, means an event which is *"neither a performance directly promised as part of the contract, nor the whole of the consideration for a promise."* Thus, where C contracts to pay ₹ 100 to D for whitewashing his house on the terms that no payment shall be made till the completion of the work, it is not collateral to the contract, but is itself a reciprocal promise or is the very thing contracted for, and is thus an integral part of the contract. Similarly, a contract for the sale of goods wherein the seller agrees to give delivery of goods after a week provided the purchaser makes the payment within two days, is an absolute contract and not a contingent contract because the event (making payment by the buyer) is an integral part of the contract (a condition precedent) and not collateral to the contract.

In simple words, the collateral event is one, which does not form part of consideration of the contract, and is independent of it.

Illustration: *A contracts to pay ₹ 50,000 to B, a contractor, for constructing a building, provided the construction is approved by an architect.*

It is a contingent contract because the consideration of the promise to pay ₹ 50,000, for the construction of the building, and the event, namely, approval by an architect, is a collateral event, which is independent of the consideration, and it is on the happening of this collateral event that the contract shall be enforced.

2.7 PERFORMANCE OF A CONTRACT

Performance of a contract implies fulfillment of the terms of the contract by the respective parties to the contract. The Contract Act lays down that *"the parties to a contract must either perform, or offer to perform, their respective promises, unless such performance is dispensed with or excused under the provisions of this Act or of any other law."* This means the performance may be actual performance or attempted performance.

A contract creates rights and obligations between the parties, which continues till the contract has been discharged by actual performance. Performance of a contract consists in doing or causing to be done what the promisor has promised to do. In the case of unilateral contract imposing an obligation on only one of the parties, the contract is discharged when the party bound by the obligation performs the same. In the case of bilateral contract, however, it is necessary that both the parties perform their respective obligations. When the party or parties perform the obligation or obligations undertaken, the contractual relationship subsisting between them comes to an end and the contract is said to be discharged. The performance of the contract in order to be complete must be made in accordance with the terms of the contract.

Offer to performance under the contract by one party to the contract may not be accepted by the other party or one party may refuse to accept the performance the other party. This is called 'tender' or 'attempted performance'. If there is a tender (attempted performance), the promisor does not lose his rights under the contract and the promisor does not become responsible for non-performance. The essentials for a valid tender include; it should be unconditional and made at the proper time and place. Proper time and place depends upon the agreement between the parties and their intention, while entering into the contract.

(A) Effect of Refusal of Performance

When a party to a contract refuses to perform his part of the promise, the other party may terminate the contract, unless he expresses his compliance and acceptance in its continuation.

Illustration: *A enters into a contract with B to tutor his son at his residence and B agrees to pay A ₹200 per day for the tutoring services. A agrees to the offer and starts his service. However after a week A willfully absents himself. B has the right to terminate the contract.*

(B) By Whom Must Contracts be Performed

The nature of the contract itself determines the person by whom the promise undertaken should be performed. The following describes the persons through whom contracts can be performed.

1. **Promisor himself:** If there is something in the contract to show that it was the intention of the parties that the promise should be performed by the promisor himself, such promise must be performed by the promisor. This means contracts, which involve the exercise of personal skill, volition or diligence of the promisor (for instance, a contract to paint a picture or sing), or which are founded on personal confidence between the parties (for instance a contract to marry) must be performed by the promisor himself.
2. **Agent:** Where personal consideration is not the foundation of a contract, the promisor or his representative may employ a competent person to perform it.

   Illustration: *A promises to pay B a sum of money. A may perform this promise, either by personally paying the money to B or by causing it to be paid to B by another person on his behalf.*
3. **Legal representatives:** A contract, which involves the use of personal skill or is founded on personal considerations, comes to an end on the death of the promisor. The rule of law is; *actio personalis, moritur cum persona,* i.e., a personal action dies with the person. As regards any other contract, the legal representatives of the deceased promisor are bound to perform it unless a contrary intention appears from the contract. But their liability under a contract is limited to the value of the property they inherit from the deceased.

   Illustration: *A promises to deliver goods to B on a certain day on payment of ₹1000/. A dies before that day. A's representatives (legal heir or business partner etc) are bound to deliver the goods to B and B is bound to pay ₹1,000 to A's representatives.*
4. **Third persons:** When a promisee accepts performance of the promise from a third person, he cannot afterwards enforce it against the promisor.

   Illustration: *A enters into a contract with B to teach car driving. However, A is transferred by his office to another city and therefore requests Z to teach B car driving. B agrees to the new arrangement. B cannot later enforce A on this issue.*
5. **Joint promisors:** Devolution means passing over from one person to another. When two or more persons have made a joint promise, they are known as joint promisors. Unless a

contrary intention appears from the contract, all joint promisors must jointly fulfill the promise. If any of them dies, his legal representative must, jointly with the surviving promisors, fulfill the promise. If all of them die, the legal representatives of all of them must fulfill the promise jointly.

(C) Contracts Which Need not be Performed

1. When performance of the contract becomes impossible.

   Illustration: *A enters into a contract with B an artist to paint his portrait. After a few days, B meets with an accident and his hands are paralyzed. B who employs his hands for the performance of his promise, however cannot do so and hence the performance of the contract becomes impossible.*
2. When the parties to it agree to substitute a new contract for it or to rescind or alter it.

   Illustration: *A and B enter into a contract for the purchase of a Car manufactured by Maruti Suzuki Company. Later, due to change of mind, A insists that the car he purchases should be manufactured by Tata Motors. A new contract is substituted for the old one.*
3. When the promisee dispenses with or remits, wholly or in part, the performance of the promise made to him or extends the time for such performance or accepts any satisfaction for it.

   Illustration: *A under a contract with B to paint his office building, tells B that he has changed his mind and plans to get his house painted next year.*
4. When the person at whose option it is voidable, rescinds it.

   Illustration: *A enters into a contract with B to sell his Hero Honda motorbike for ₹5000. Later A changes his mind and refuses to sell the motorbike for the said amount.*
5. When the promisee neglects or refuses to afford the promisor reasonable facilities for the performance of his promise.

   Illustration: *A contracts with B to repair B's house. B neglects or refuse to point out to A the places in which his house requires repairs. A is excused for the non performance of the contract, if it is caused by such neglect or refusal.*

2.8 RECIPROCAL PROMISES

Promises, which form the consideration or part of the consideration for each other are called "reciprocal promises". Reciprocal promises are said to be mutual and dependent where the performance by one party depends upon the prior performance of the promises by the other party.

Illustration: *A promises to do or not to do something in consideration of B's promise to do or not to do something, the promises are reciprocal.*

(A) Types of Reciprocal Promises

1. **Mutual and dependent:** In such contracts, the performance of one party decides the performance of the other party. Therefore, if the party on whose prior performance the contract stands does not perform his part of the promise, he cannot claim the performance of the other party. Such a contract is called reciprocal promise.

   Illustration: *A contracts with B to get his house painted for which the colour scheme and the paint is to be furnished by A. However, A does not decide on the colour scheme and furnish the paint required for painting the house to B. Here, B is not bound by his promise to paint the house and he can sue A for compensation for any loss that he might have sustained by the non-performance of the contract.*

2. **Mutual and independent:** In such contracts, each party to the contract are expected to perform their respective promises irrespective of the performance of the other party to the contract.

   Illustration: *A enters into a contract with B on the 1st of May, to design his daughter's wedding gown and also to decorate the wedding hall on 24th of June which is the day of the wedding. B agrees and starts making preparation in lieu of his part of the promise. Here, B's act of making preparations for designing the wedding gown and getting materials ready for decorating the wedding hall is independent of A's promise to pay for his services. If A does not pay for B's services, he can be sued for compensation.*

3. **Mutual and concurrent:** In such contracts the promise between the parties to the contract is simultaneous and coexisting, thereby both the parties. The performance of one party depends on the willingness of the other party to perform his part of the promise concurrently.

   Illustration: *Hiring a taxi to go to a particular destination. In this instance, the person hiring the taxi should be willing to pay the hiring charges to the taxi driver and the taxi driver should be willing to drive his passenger to the destination of his choice.*

(B) Assignment of Contracts

When a party to the contract is not able to fulfill his part of the promise, he may with the consent of the other party, transfer his right, title and interest in the contract to another person. Such an act of transfer of right, title and interest by one party to another is called 'assignment of contract'. Assignment of a contract may happen either by operation of law or by mutual consent of the parties concerned.

Illustration: *A enters into a contract with B a civil contractor, for constructing a house. Later B due to some personal reasons cannot perform his part of the promise and with the consent of A, transfers his right, title and interest to Z, another civil contractor.*

Assignment by operation of law happens due to the insolvency or death of the party to the contract. In case of insolvency, the official receiver or assignee, appointed by the court will be transferred the right, title of the contract. In case of death of one of the parties to the contract, the rights and liabilities of the demised person will devolve upon the legal heirs (wife/husband/children/siblings etc) or representatives (business partners etc) of the deceased person will be transferred the right, title and interest of the contract

(C) Appropriation of Payment

A debtor may borrow from the same creditor at different times and thereby owe several debts to the same creditor. When the time for repayment of the debt arises, the question of which debt has to be cleared first arises. This decision can be appropriation of payment. It should be noted here, the appropriation of payment can arise only when a person has borrowed from a single creditor, at different point in time.

However if the debtor does not express his intimation about appropriation of payment, the creditor may appropriate the payment at his discretion. In case neither of the party appropriates, then the discharge of the debt shall be made according to the oldest debt, i.e, in the order of time and if the debts are equal, the payments shall be applied proportionately.

The rule of appropriating the payment in the order of time comes with the ruling in the Clayton's case. According to this rule, in the absence of any contract to the contrary, receipts can be appropriated against payments according to the order in which the debt was incurred or created.

2.9 DISCHARGE OF A CONTRACT

A contract creates rights and obligations between the parties and it is discharged when the parties who have undertaken the obligations perform those obligations. A contract is said to be discharged when it ceases to operate i.e. when the rights and obligations created by the contract come to an end. Discharge of contract means termination of the contractual relationship between the parties. A contract is said to be discharged when the parties thereto are freed from the task of performing their respective obligations as arising from the contract and the rights and obligations created by the contract come to an end.

Contract may be discharged in any of the following ways:

(*a*) By performance – actual or attempted.

(*b*) By Mutual Consent or agreement.

(*c*) By subsequent of supervening impossibility.

(*d*) By lapse of time.

(*e*) By Operation of law.

(*f*) By breach of contract.

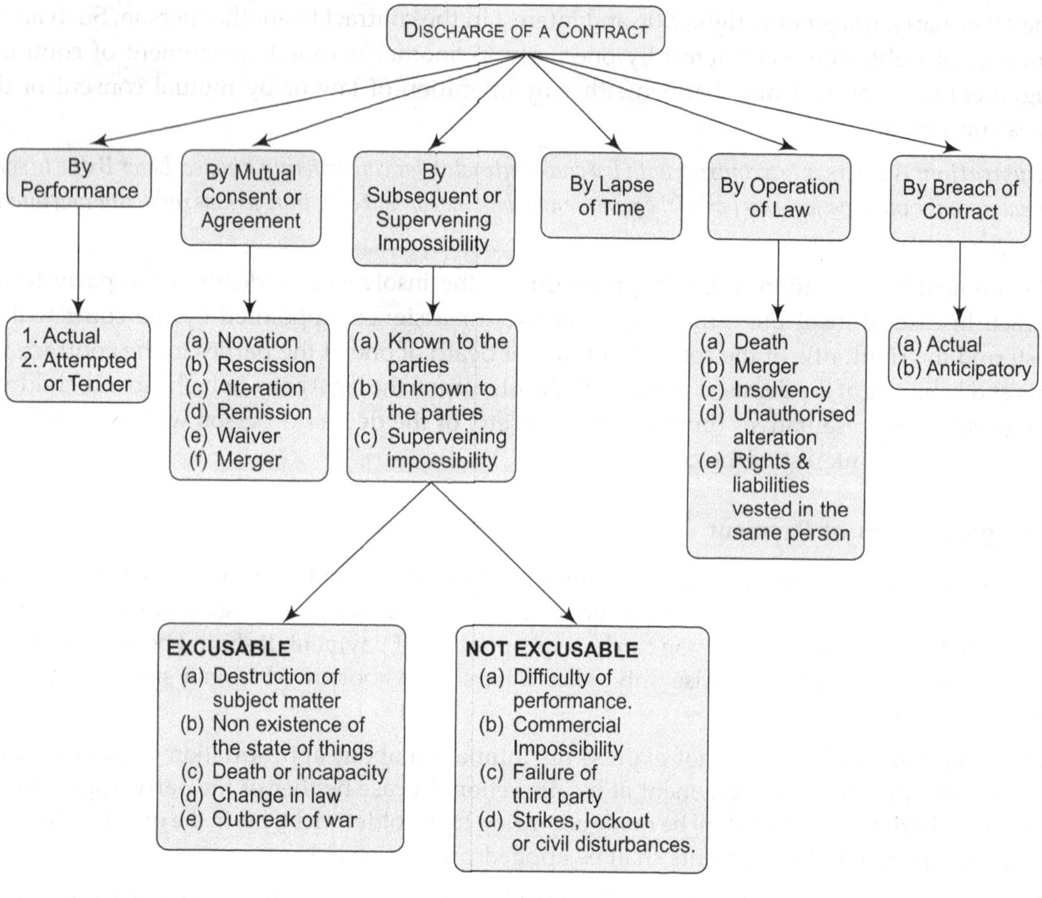

(A) Discharge by Performance

Performance of a contract is the principal and most usual mode of discharge of a contract. Performance means the doing of that which is required by a contract. The contracting parties are bound to perform their respective obligations unless the performance is dispensed with or excused under the provisions of the Contract Act. Discharge of a contract by performance takes place when the parties to the contract fulfill their obligations arising under the contract within the time and in the manner prescribed.

If the promisor dies before performance, his legal representatives are bound to perform the promise, unless a contrary intention appears from the contract. The contract, in such a case, is discharged or terminated by due performance. But if one party only performs his promise, he alone is discharged. Such a party gets a right of action again the other party who is guilty of breach.

Performance may be:

1. Actual performance or
2. Attempted performance or Tender.

1. **Actual Performance:** When both the parties perform their respective promises, according to the terms of the agreement, the contract is discharged. This is termed as discharge of contract by actual performance.

   Illustration: *A enters into a contract with B to buy 100 bags of basmati rice at ₹4000 per quintal. B supplies A with 100 bags of basmati rice and A pays B the agreed price.*

2. **Attempted Performance:** When a promisor offers to perform his promise at the agreed time and place but the promisee refuses to perform his part of the promise, the contract is discharged by attempted performance. However, the promisor has the right to sue the promisor for breach of contract. Offer of performance is also known as attempted performance or tender of performance. If the offer is not accepted by the other party to the contract, the obligation of the party making the tender is extinguished, and he is not liable for non-performance, although his rights still continue.

   Illustration: *A hires B to paint his house. However when B arrives on the stipulated date and time, A does not provide B with the facility and provision to perform his job. Here the contract is discharged by attempted performance.*

(B) Discharge by Mutual Consent or Agreement

Since a contract arises on the basis of an agreement, it follows that a contract can be discharged by mutual agreement. This is in accordance with the legal maxim *"eodem modo quo oritur, eodem modo dissolvitur"*, this means that which is created by agreement may be extinguished by agreement. This may be either through express consent or by implied consent.

When a contract is terminated mutually (through correspondence, action or speech) between the parties to the contract, it is termination of the contract by express consent. Implied consent signifies action between the parties which indicate termination of the contract. Implied consent includes:

(*a*) Novation
(*b*) Rescission
(*c*) Alteration
(*d*) Remission
(*e*) Waiver
(*f*) Merger.

(a) **Novation:** This means substituting a new contract for the existing contract. The new contract may be either between the same parties or between different parties, and the consideration for the new contract is the discharge of the old contract. Novation may be between the same parties or between different parties, by agreement. It cannot be compulsory or by force. Substitution of a new contract may take place even without change of parties. Novation can take place only if the original contract is subsisting. When the parties to a contract agree for "Novation," the original contract is discharged and need not be performed.

Illustrations: *(1) Ram owes money to Shyam, under a contract. However, they mutually agree that henceforth, Gopi shall be the debtor to Shyam instead of Ram. The old debt of Ram to Shyam is discharged and a new contract between Gopi and Shyam is created.*

(2) A owes B ₹2,50,000. A enters into an agreement with B and gives B a mortgage of his (A's) house for ₹1,50,000 in place of the debt of ₹2,50,000. This is a new contract and discharges the old contract.

(b) **Rescission:** Rescission results in the cancellation of the original contract. When the original contract is cancelled or put to an end by mutual agreement, the contract is discharged. A contract may be discharged, before the date of performance, by agreement between the parties to the effect that it shall no longer bind them. Such an agreement amounts to "rescission" or cancellation of the contract.

The consideration for mutual promises being, the abandonment by the respective parties of their rights under the contract. An agreement of rescission releases the parties from their obligations arising out of the contract. Such agreements are to be distinguished from 'agreements in restraint of legal proceedings" which are void as per Section 28. Therefore if, they consent to treat non performance or part performance of a contract equivalent to full performance or discharge of the contract, it is perfectly alright.

Illustrations: *(1) A promises to supply certain goods to B after 6 months. By that time the goods become outdated. A and B may cancel the contract.*

(2) A promises to deliver certain goods to B on a certain date. Before the date of performance, A and B mutually agree that the contract will not be performed. The contract stands discharged by rescission.

(c) **Alteration:** Alteration of a contract means change in one or more of the material term of a contract. If a material alteration in a written contract is done by mutual consent, the original contract is discharged by alteration and the new contract in its altered form takes its place. When the parties to a contract agree mutually to alter one or more of the terms of the contract, then the old contract is discharged. A material alteration is one which alters the legal effect of the contract, *e.g.*, a change in the amount of money to be paid or a change in the rate of interest.

Immaterial alteration, *e.g.*, correcting a clerical error in figures or the spelling of a name, has no effect on the validity of the contract and does not amount to alteration in the technical sense. It is relevant to state that a material alteration made in a written contract by one party without the consent of the other will make the whole contract void and no person can maintain an action upon it. The difference between novation and alteration is that, in case of novation there may be a change of parties also while in case of alteration parties remain the same, only the terms of a contract are altered.

Illustration: *A and B enter into a contract for the supply 100 bags of a certain quality of basmati rice for cash. Later, A decides to change the number of bags from 100 to 75 bags of basmati rice to be paid partly in cash and partly by a post dated cheque. There is material alteration in the contract, however the parties to the contract remain the same.*

(d) **Remission:** It means lesser fulfillment of the promise made. Remission may be defined 'as the acceptance of a lesser sum than what was contracted for or a lesser fulfillment of the promise made.' Section 63 deals with remission of performance and lays down that a promisee may remit or give up wholly or in part, the performance of the promise made to him, and a promise to do so is binding even though there is no consideration for it. The Section further provides that an agreement to extend the time for the performance of a promise also does not require consideration to support it on the ground that it is a partial remission of performance.

Illustrations: *(1) Ram owes ₹5,000 to Bhim. However, Ram is able to repay only ₹3,000 to Bhim. Bhim accepts the amount in full satisfaction of the whole debt. The whole debt is discharged.*

(2) A owes B ₹5,000 payable on 1st June. A is not in a position to meet his liability on the due date and as such makes a request to B to extend the time for payment to the 30th June. No suit can be instituted before the expiry of the extended period of credit although the promise is not supported by any consideration.

(e) **Waiver:** When the parties to a contract agree that they must not be bound by the contract anymore, the contract may be discharged. Waiver means the deliberate abandonment or giving up of 'a right which a person is entitled to under a contract" whereupon, the other party to the contract is released from his obligation. Strictly speaking there is no need of an agreement for a waiver.

Illustration: *Where A promises to stitch a shirt for B if he would sing a song at his birthday party. Accordingly B sang the song but forbids A to stitch the shirt for him to which A consents. The contract is terminated by waiver.*

(f) **Merger :** When an inferior right of a party merges into a superior right accruing to the same party under the same or some other contract, it is called merger.

Illustration: *A takes a property under a lease and then later after a few months, buys the same property. A's right as a lessee merges into his right as the owner of the property.*

(C) Discharge by Subsequent or Supervening Impossibility

A contract is discharged when the performance becomes impossible. If an agreement contemplates doing something which is absolutely impossible, the same becomes void-ab-initio, in accordance with the ruling based on the following legal maxims.

(*a*) *Lex non cogit ad impossibilia. i.e.*, the law does not recognize what is impossible and,

(*b*) *Impossibilium nulla obligatio est. i.e.*, what is impossible does not create an obligation.

The phrase 'impossible in itself', obviously refers to something which is inherently impossible of performance. If the fact of impossibility is unknown to both the parties, the agreement becomes void on the ground of operative mistake. However, if the agreement becomes void-ab-initio on account of impossibility, the question of discharge does not arise since there is no contract to be discharged or terminated.

(a) **Known to the parties:** By virtue of Section 56, Para 1, which provides: "*an agreement to do an act impossible in itself is void.*" There is no question of discharge of a contract which is entered into to perform something that is obviously impossible *e.g.*, an agreement to discover treasure by magic because, in such a case, there is no contract to perform, it being an agreement void-ab-initio.

The contract cannot be performed when there is something which is impossible inherently or by its very nature and which may or may not be known to both the parties at the time when the contract is made. But if the impossibility is not obvious and the promisor alone knows of the impossibility or illegality then existing or the promisor might have known as such after using reasonable diligence, such promisor is bound to compensate the promisee for any loss he may suffer through the non performance of the promise, inspite of the agreement being void-ab-initio.

Illustration: *A contracts to marry B who is already married to C, and being forbidden by the law to which he is subject to practice polygamy A must make compensation to B for the loss caused to her by the non performance of his promise.*

(b) **Unknown to the parties or Subsequent impossibility / Supervening impossibility:** In this connection, Section 56, Para 2, declares: "A contract to do an act which, after the contract is made, becomes impossible, or, by reason of some event which the promisor could not prevent, becomes void when the act becomes impossible or unlawful". Supervening impossibility is also called as *'an act of God'*.

In order that the Section would apply, the following conditions must be fulfilled:

1. That the act should have become impossible
2. That impossibility should be reason of some event which the promisor could not prevent; and
3. That the impossibility should not be self induced by the promisor or due to his negligence.

A contract, which is capable of performance at the time it was entered into, may, owing to some event beyond the control of the promisor, become incapable of performance or render it unlawful. In either case, the contract becomes void. This eventuality is known as subsequent impossibility. This is also termed as the 'Doctrine of frustration'. This doctrine is based on impossibility of performance of the contract. Under Section 56 (Para 2), where an event which could not reasonably have been in the contemplation of the parties when the contract was made renders performances impossible or unlawful, the contract becomes void and stands discharged. This is known as frustration of the contract brought about by supervening impossibility. It is also known as the Doctrine Supervening Impossibility or Doctrine of Frustration. However it should be noted that the frustration should not be self-induced. When a contract cannot be performed as originally intended by the parties, the contract automatically becomes void. Frustration is said to be self-induced if the act or omission which results in frustration is something deliberate and intentional. In other words, frustration should not be due to the default or neglect of the defendant.

Illustration: *A enters into a contract with B for the supply of a certain quality of apples to be imported from another country. However the consignment which was dispatched to A by Z gets destroyed due to natural calamity. The contract between A and B stands cancelled due to frustration and the contract is discharged.*

Excusable-Cases where the doctrine of supervening impossibility applies: A contract will be discharged on the ground of supervening impossibility under the following circumstances. There are six types or methods of discharge of contract by impossibility; namely, (i) destruction of the subject matter of the contract (ii) Non-existence or non-occurrence of a particular event (iii) by death or disablement of the parties to the contract (iv) by subsequent legislation (v) by declaration of war.

1. **Destruction of subject-matter.** When the subject matter of a contract, subsequent to its formation, is destroyed, without the fault of the promisor or promisee, the contract is discharged. It is so only when specific property or goods are destroyed which cannot be regained.

Illustrations: *(1) A music hall was agreed to be let out for a series of concerts on certain days. The hall was destroyed by fire before the date of the first concert. The plaintiff sued the defendant for damages for the breach of contract. It was held that the contract has become void and the defendant was not liable (Taylor Vs. Caldwell).*

(2) The defendant contracted to sell a part of a specific crop of potatoes to be grown on his farms, but failed to supply them as the crop was destroyed by a pest. The contract was held to be discharged (Howell Vs. Compliance).

(3) Similarly, if a factory premises on which a machinery is to be installed are destroyed by fire, or a ship under a charter party is seized by a foreign government, the 'contract is discharged (Tatem Ltd. Vs. Gambocz).

2. **Non existence or non occurrence of a particular event.** When a contract is made by the parties on the basis of a particular event and if that event does not happen, the contract is discharged. Where the ultimate purpose for which the contract was entered into fails, the contract is discharged although there is no destruction of any property affected by the contract and the performance of the contract remains possible in the literal sense.

   Illustration: *The leading case of Krell vs Henry, H hired a room in London from K with the object, as both parties well knew; of using the room to view the intended coronation procession of King Edward on a particular date. By reason of the King's illness the procession was postponed. H consequently could not use the room although he could go there and sit but with no purpose as there was no procession. K filed a suit for the recovery of rent. It was held that H need not pay the rent as the contract was discharged on failure of the ultimate purpose or on postponement of the procession which was the foundation of the contract.*

3. **Death or disablement (personal incapacity of promisor).** Where the performance of a contract depends upon the personal skill or qualification or the existence of a given person, the contract is discharged on the illness or incapacity or the death of that person.

   Illustrations: *(1) A and B contract to marry each other. Before the time fixed for the marriage, A goes mad. The contract becomes void.*

   (2) A contracts to act at a theatre for six months in consideration of a sum paid in advance by B. On several occasions A is too ill to act. The contract to act on those occasions becomes void

   (3) An artist undertook to paint a picture for a certain price but before he could do so, he met with an accident and lost his right arm. Held, the artist was discharged due to disablement.

4. **Change in law (subsequent legislation).** A subsequent change in law, after the contract has been entered, may render the contract illegal and in such cases the contract is deemed discharged. The law may actually forbid the doing of some act undertaken in the contract or it may take from the promisor control of something in respect of which he has contracted to act or not to act in a certain way.

   Illustrations: *(1) A takes some land on lease from B and agrees to construct a good building on the land. However, after the contract was entered, subsequently the land was taken over by the railway company, under its statutory powers for the construction of a railway station. Held, A need not perform the contract.*

   (2) A sold to B 100 bags of wheat at ₹700 per bag. But before delivery the Government rendered the sale and purchase of wheat by private traders' illegal under the Defense of India rules. The contract was discharged by impossibility created by subsequent change in law.

5. **Outbreak of war.** All contracts entered into with an alien enemy during war are illegal, unlawful and void-ab-initio. Contracts entered into before the outbreak of war are suspended during the war and may be revived after the war is over provided they have not already become time barred. However, if war is declared between the countries of the contracting parties then only the contract is suspended during war. If war is declared

between the country of one of the parties to the contract and the hired country, the contract remains binding, and if the party of the country now at war could not perform the contract because of dislocation of transport etc, it will be treated as "difficulty in performance" only and does not discharge the contract. (Tsakiroglou & Co.Ltd. vs. Noble Thorp). The act provides that the parties to such contract may resume their obligations if they deem it necessary after the war is over.

NOT EXCUSABLE- Cases not Covered by Supervening Impossibility

"He that agrees to do an act must do it or pay damages for not doing it", is the general rule of the law of contract. Thus, unless the performance becomes absolutely impossible, a person is bound to perform any obligation which he has undertaken, and cannot claim to be excused by the mere fact that performance has subsequently become unexpectedly burdensome, more difficult or expensive. Exceptions to the rule in some of the cases where impossibility of performance is not an excuse are as follows:

1. **Difficulty of performance.** Increased or unexpected difficulty or higher expense does not, as a rule, excuse the parties from performance.

   Illustration: *(1) A sold to B a certain quantity of Finnish birch timber. A found it impossible to fulfill this contract because of the outbreak of war. The war disorganized transportation and A could not get any supply of timber from Finland. Held, B, was not concerned with the way in which A was going to get timber and therefore there was no frustration. The Court of Appeal observed: "For the contract to be dissolved there must have been a failure of something which was at the basis of the contract in the intention of both parties; and that was not the case here."(Blackburn Bobbin Co., Lid. vs Allen & Sons Ltd.)*

   (2) A contracts with B to supply B 1000 tons of raw silk, by a fixed day for a specified price. A fails to perform his contract with B since he could not procure the required quantity from the market. Held, mere non availability of goods agreed to be sold did not excuse performance (Gwalior Rayon Silk Mfg. Co vs Andavar & Co.)

2. **Commercial impossibility.** When in a transaction profits dwindle to a very low level or actual loss becomes certain, it is said that the performance of the contract has become commercially impossible. Such a situation may arise on account of higher price of the raw material or increase in the wage bill etc. Therefore, commercial impossibility does not discharge a contract.

   Illustrations: *(1) A residing at Delhi contracts to sell 100 embroidered dress suits to B, residing at Bangalore at ₹500 per suit. After the contract has been entered into, A is informed that the government has increased sales tax which has resulted in an increase in the cost of each suit. Considering that selling the embroidered suit at ₹500 would be a loss, A refuses to sell the suits due to commercial impossibility. However, as per the Act, A is bound to supply the goods at the original cost agreed in the contract.*

   (2) X contracted with Y to send certain goods from Bombay to Delhi in September. In August transport companies went on strike and transport was available at very high rates. Held, the increase in freight rates did not excuse performance (Karl Etlinger vs Chagandas & Co.)

3. **Impossibility due to the default of a third person.** The doctrine of supervening impossibility does not cover where the contract could not be performed because of the impossibility created by the failure of a third person on whose work the promisor relied.

   Illustrations: *(1) A, a wholesaler, enters into a contract with B for the sale of certain goods to be produced by Z, a manufacturer of those goods. However, later, Z stops the manufacture of those goods. A is liable to B for damages. The words 'to be produced by Z' simply indicate quality of goods here.*

(2) A, agreed to sell to B 61 bales of cloth to be manufactured by the New Victoria Mills, Kanpur, "as soon as they are supplied" to him by the said Mill. In a suit for damages for non delivery of goods the defendant A pleaded impossibility on the ground that the goods were not supplied to him by the mill. Held that the words "as soon as they are supplied to him by the Mill" simply indicate the process of delivery and did not convey the meaning that delivery was contingent on their being supplied by the mill. Hence the case did not fall within the provisions of Sections 32 and 56 as the default was due to the fault of the defendant. B is therefore, entitled to recover damages from A. (Ganga Saran vs Ram Charan Ram Gopal)

4. **Strikes and lock-outs.** A strike by the workmen or a lockout by the employer also does not excuse performance because the former is manageable (as labour is available otherwise) and the latter is self-induced. Where the impossibility is not absolute or when it is due to the default of the promisor himself, Section 56 would not apply. As such these events also do not discharge a contract.

   Illustration: *The lessor of certain saltpans, failed to repair them according to the terms of the contract, on the ground of a strike of the workmen. Held, a strike by the workmen was not sufficient reason to excuse performance of the contract (Hari Laxman Vs. Secretary of State for India)*

5. **Failure of one of the objects.** When a contract is entered into for several objects, the failure of one of them does not discharge the contract.

   Illustration: *A company agreed to let out a boat to H. (a) for viewing a naval review on the occasion of the coronation of King Edward VII and (b) to sail round the fleet. Due to illness of the King, the naval review was later cancelled but the fleet was assembled. Held, the contract was not discharged because the holding of the review was not the sole basis of the contract. To sail round the fleet which formed an equally basic object of the contract was still capable of attainment (R Steamboat Co vs Hutton).*

(D) Discharge by Lapse of Time

The Limitation Act lays down that in case of breach of a contract legal action should be taken within a specified period called the Period of Limitation, otherwise the promisee is debarred from instituting a suit in a court of law and the contract stands discharged. Thus in certain circumstances lapse of time may also discharge a contract. Where time is of essence in a contract and if the contract is not performed at the fixed time, the contract comes to an end and the party not at fault need not perform his obligation and may sue the other party for damages.

Illustration: *The period of limitation for simple contracts is three years under the Limitation Act and therefore on default by a debtor if the creditor does not file a suit of recovery against him within three years of default, the debt becomes time barred on the expiry of three years and the creditor will be deprived of his remedy at law. This in effect implies discharge of contract.*

(E) Discharge by Operation of Law

A contract terminates by operation of law in the following cases:

A. **DEATH:** Where the contract is of a personal nature, the death of the promisor discharges the contract. In other contracts the rights and liabilities of the deceased person pass on to the legal representatives of the dead man.

B. **INSOLVENCY:** A contract is discharged by the insolvency of one of the parties to it when an Insolvency Court passes an "order of discharge" exonerating the insolvent from liabilities on debts incurred prior to his adjudication.

C. **MERGER:** Where an inferior right contract merges into a superior right contract, the former stands discharged automatically.

Illustrations: *(1) Where a man holding property under a contract of tenancy buys the property, his rights as a tenant are merged into the rights of ownership and the contract of tenancy stands discharged by operation of law.*

(2) Where a part time lecturer is made full time lecturer, the contract of part time lectureship is discharged by merger.

(3) A bill of exchange is discharged if the acceptor becomes the holder of it at or after its maturity in his own right.

D. **UNAUTHORIZED MATERIAL ALTERATION:** A material alteration made in a written document or contract by one party without the consent of the other, will make the whole contract void. Thus, where the amount of money to be received is altered, or an additional signature is forged, on a promissory note by a creditor, he cannot bring a suit on it and the pronote cannot be enforced against the debtor even in its original shape. The effect of making such an alteration is exactly the same as that of canceling the contract (Gour Chunder Vs. Prasanna). However, the document, though altered, can be used as proof of the transaction and the creditor may be allowed to claim refund of money actually advanced by him under Section 65 of the Contract Act which is based on the equitable Doctrine of Restitution (Ananthrao Vs. Kandikanda).

(F) Discharge by Breach of Contract

Breach of contract by a party thereto is also a method of discharge of a contract, because "breach" also brings to an end the obligations created by a contract on the part of each of the parties. Of course the aggrieved party i.e., the party not at fault can sue for damages for breach of contract as per law; but the contract as such stands terminated. Breach of contract may be of two kinds:

1. Anticipatory breach; and
2. Actual breach.

1. **Anticipatory breach:** An anticipatory breach of contract is a breach of contract occurring before the time fixed for performance has arrived. It may take place in two ways:

   (*a*) Expressly by words spoken or written: Here a party to the contract communicates to the other party, before the due date of performance, his intention not to perform it.

   Illustration: *A contracts with B to supply 100 bags of wheat for ₹60,000, on 1st March. However, on 15th February A inform B that he will not be able to supply the wheat. There is express rejection of the contract.*

   (*b*) Impliedly by the conduct of one of the parties: Here a party by his own voluntary act disables himself from performing the contract.

   Illustrations: *(1) A person contracts to sell a particular horse to another on 1stof June and before that date he sells the horse to somebody else;*

   (2) A agrees, to marry B but before the agreed date of marriage she marries C.

In both the above cases there occurs an anticipatory breach of contract brought about by the conduct of one of the parties. Section 39 of the Contract Act deals with anticipatory breach of contract and provides as follows: "When a party to a contract has refused to perform, or disabled himself from performing his promise in its entirety, the promisee may put an end to the contract, unless he has signified, by words, his acquiescence in its continuance.

Effect of an Anticipatory Breach: When there is an anticipatory breach of contract, the promisee is excused from performance or from further performance. Further it gives an option to the promisee (i.e., the aggrieved party) whereby:

- He may either treat the contract as rescinded by the other party for damages for breach of contract immediately without waiting until the due date of performance, or
- He may elect not to rescind but to treat the contract as still operative, and wait for the time of performance and then hold the other party responsible for the consequence of non performance. But in, that case, he will keep the contract alive for the benefit of the other party as well as his own, and the guilty party, if he so decides on reconsideration, may still perform his part of the contract and can also take advantage of any supervening impossibility which may have the effect of discharging the contract.

  Illustrations: *(1) A, agrees to employ B as a clerk in his office from the 1st June. On the 20th of May he informs B that his services will not be required. B is exonerated from his obligation under the contract and may at once sue A for damages for breach of contract without waiting until the time fixed for performance (Mersey Steel and Iron Co. Vs Naylor).*

  (2) A, agrees to sell his house to B for ₹8,50,000 on 1st of March. But on 10th February he changes his mind and writes to B that he will not be able to sell his house. There is an anticipatory breach of contract. Two courses are open to B:

  (i) He may treat the contract as rescinded and at once sue A for damages, or

  (ii) He may wait till 1st of March B adopts the second course.

  On 28th February the house is destroyed by fire. The contract stands discharged by supervening impossibility. A is entitled to take advantage of this supervening impossibility and B cannot recover any damages from him. If the house did, not catch fire, A could have taken back his letter of repudiation and asked B to take possession of the house on payment as per agreement.

2. **Actual Breach:** Actual breach may also discharge a contract. It occurs when a party fails to perform his obligation upon the date fixed for performance by the contract, as for example, where" on the appointed day the seller does not deliver the goods or the buyer refuses to accept the delivery. It is important to note that there can be no actual breach of contract by reason of non performance so long as the time for performance has not yet arrived. Actual breach entitles the party not in default to elect to treat the contract as discharged and to sue the party at fault for damages for breach of contract.

2.10 REMEDIES FOR BREACH OF CONTRACT

A remedy is the means given by law for the enforcement of aright. A 'Right' will be of no value if there were no remedy to enforce that right in the Law Court in the event of its infringement or breach of contract. Whenever, there is breach of contract the injured party is entitled to any one or more of the following remedies against the guilty party:

(*a*) Rescission of the contract.

(*b*) Suit for damages.

(*c*) Suit for quantum meruit.

(*d*) Suit for specific performance of the contract.

(*e*) Suit for injunction.

(A) Recission of Contract

Rescission means the setting aside of the contract. The aggrieved party may be allowed by the court to treat the contract at an end and thereby, terminate all the liabilities under the contract. When there is a breach of contract by one party, the other party may rescind the contract and need not perform his part of the obligations under the contract and may sit quietly at home if he decides not to take any legal action against the guilty party. But in case the aggrieved party intends to sue the guilty party for damages for breach of contract, he has to file a suit for rescission of the contract. Thus the party is absolved of all his obligations under the contract.

Illustration : *P promises Q to supply 15 bags of rice on a certain day. Q agrees to pay the price after the receipt of the goods. P does not supply the goods. Q is discharged from liability to pay the price.*

When the court grants rescission, the aggrieved party is freed from all his obligations under the contract; and becomes entitled to compensation for any damage which he has sustained through the non fulfilment of the contract (Sec. 75). The court may grant rescission-

(*a*) Where the contract is voidable by the plaintiff.

(*b*) Where the contract is unlawful for causes not apparent on its face and the defendant is more to blame than the plaintiff.

The Court may, however, refuse to rescind the contract:

(*a*) Where the plaintiff has expressly or impliedly ratified the contract; or

(*b*) Where, owing to the change of circumstances (not being due to any act of the defendant himself), the parties cannot be restored to their original positions; or

(*c*) Where third parties have, during the subsistence of the contract, acquired rights in good faith and for value; or

(*d*) Where only a part of the contract is sought to be rescinded and such part is not several from the rest of the contract.

Illustration: *A contracts to supply 100 kg of tea leaves for ₹ 8,000 to B on15 April. If A does not supply the tea leaves on the appointed day, B need not pay the price. B may treat the contract as rescinded and may sit quietly at home. B may also file a suit for rescission and claim damages.*

Thus, applying to the court for rescission of the contract' is necessary for claiming damages for breach or for availing any other remedy. In practice a 'suit for rescission' is accompanied by a 'suit for damages,' etc., in the same plaint. It is worth noting that in certain cases a suit for rescission of the contract' may be filed even when no damages are to be claimed.

Illustration: *In case of pledge of movable goods, say gold ornaments, if the pledger does not pay as per the agreement, the pledgee may file a suit for rescission of the contract (of course within the period of limitation which is 3 years), in order to free himself from his obligation to return the ornaments (on payment) and to become entitled to sell the ornaments in order to realise his debt.*

(B) Suit for Damages

Damages are monetary compensation allowed to the injured party for the loss suffered by him as a result of the breach of contract. The fundamental principle underlying damages is not punishment but compensation. By awarding damages the court aims to put the injured party into the position in which he would have been had there been performance and not breach, and not to punish the defaulter party. As a general rule, "compensation must be commensurate with the injury or loss sustained, arising naturally from the breach." If actual loss is not proved, no damages will be awarded . The foundation of modern law of damages, both in India and England, is to be found in the judgment in the case of Hadley Vs. Baxendale (1854).

Illustration: *In Hardley Vs. Baxendale (1854), X's mill was stopped by the breakdown of a shaft. He delivered the shaft to Y a common carrier, to be taken to a manufacturer to copy it and make a new one. X did not make known to Y that delay would result in loss of profits. By some neglect on the part of Y the delivery of the shaft was delayed in transit beyond a reasonable time (so that the mill was idle for a longer period than otherwise would have been the case had there been no breach of the contract of carriage). Held, Y was not liable for loss of profits during the period of delay, as the circumstances communicated to Y did not show that a delay in the delivery of the shaft would entail loss of profits to the mill.*

1. **Types of Damages:**
    1. Ordinary or General or Compensatory damages i.e. Damages arising from the breach.
    2. Special damages i.e. damages in contemplation of the parties at the time of the contract.
    3. Exemplary, Punitive or Vindictive damages.
    4. Nominal damages.
    5. Liquidated damages and penalty.
2. **Assessment of Damages**: The rule in this regard have been laid down by Section 73. Accordingly, an injured party is entitled to receive from the defaulter party:
    A. Such damages which naturally arose in the usual course of things from such breach. No compensation is to be given generally for any remote or indirect loss sustained by reason of the breach (Ordinary Damages).
    B. Such damages which the parties knew, when they entered into the contract, as likely to result from the breach (Special Damages).
    C. In estimating the loss or damage caused to a party by breach, the means which existed of remedying the inconvenience caused by the breach must also be taken into account (Explanation to Sec. 73). (Duty to mitigate damage suffered.)With a view to making the study of the quantum of damages easily comprehensible, the above rules, as enunciated in Section 73 may now be considered in some more details under appropriate heads.
    1. *Ordinary Damages*: When a contract has been broken, the injured party can, as a rule, always recover from the guilty party ordinary or general damages. These are such damages as may fairly and reasonably be considered as arising naturally and directly in the usual course of things from the breach of contract itself. In other words, ordinary damages are restricted to the "direct or proximate consequences" of the breach of contract and remote or indirect losses, which are not the natural and probable consequence of the breach of contract, are generally not regarded.

    Illustrations: *(1) A contracts to pay a sum of money to B on a specified day. A does not pay the money on that day. B, in consequence of not receiving the money on that day, is unable to pay his debts, and is totally ruined. A is not liable to make good to B anything except the principal sum he contracted to pay, together with interest upto the date of payment (If a suit has been filed then A will have also to pay 'cost of the suit' to B.)*

    (2) A contracts to sell and deliver 500 bales of cotton to B on a fixed day. A knows nothing of B's mode of conducting his business. A breaks his promise, and B, having no cotton, is obliged to close his mill.

A is not responsible to B for the loss caused to B by the closing of the mill. (B, however, can claim damages for the breach of contract. He cannot claim the loss of profits caused by the closing of the mill because it cannot be considered to have been in contemplation of both the parties when they made the contract and thus is a remote consequence of the breach.)

In the case of a contract for 'sale and purchase' the general rule as regards measure of damages is that the damages would be assessed on the difference between the contract price and the market price at the date of breach and any subsequent increase or decrease in the market price would not be taken note of. If there is no market price for the subject matter of the contract, the rule is to take the market price as the nearest substitute. If there is no nearest substitute, the market price is to be ascertained by adding to the price at the place of purchase, the conveyance charges to the place of delivery plus the usual profit of the importer (Hajee Ismail & Sons vs Wilson & Co). If the delivery is to be made in instalments, then the due date of each installment is taken as the date of breach and the measure of damages is the sum of the difference of the market value at the several dates of delivery.

Illustrations: *(1) A agrees to sell to B 5 bags of rice at ₹500 per bag, delivery to be given after two months. On the date of delivery the price of rice goes up and the rate is ₹550 per bag. A refuses to deliver the bags to B, B can claim from A ₹ 250, as ordinary damages arising directly from the breach, being the difference between the contract price (i.e.; ₹ 500 per bag) and the market price i,e.," ₹ 550 per bag) on the date of delivery of 5 bags. Notice that if ₹ 250 are paid to B by way of damages, then he will be in the same position as if the contract has been performed.*

(2) A contracts to buy from B, at a stated price, 50 mounds of rice, no time being fixed for delivery: A afterwards informs B that he will not accept the rice if tendered to him. B is entitled to receive from A, by way of compensation, the amount, if any, by which the contract price exceeds that which B can obtain for the rice at the time when A informs B that he will not accept it.

(3) A contracts to buy B's ship for ₹ 60,000, but breaks his promise. As a consequence of breach B sold the ship in the open market and he could only get ₹52,000 for the ship. B can recover by way of compensation ₹8,000, the excess of the contract price over the actual sale price.

Under a contract of 'sale of goods,' if there is a breach of 'warranty,' the seller is liable to pay all damages which the purchaser has to pay to the person to whom the goods are sold by him, whether the seller is aware of such a sale or not. In order that the purchaser should be able to claim such damages and costs it is an overriding requirement that the subcontracts should have been made on the same terms and conditions as the first contract.

Illustration: *A sells certain' merchandise to B, warranting it to be of a particular quality, and B, in reliance upon this warranty, sells it to C with a similar warranty. The goods prove to be not according to the warranty, and B becomes liable to pay C a sum of money by way of compensation. B is entitled to be reimbursed this sum by A.*

2. *Special Damages*: Special damages are those which arise on account of the special or unusual circumstances affecting the plaintiff. In other words, they are such remote losses which are not the natural and probable consequences of the breach of contract. Unlike ordinary damages, special damages cannot be claimed as matter of right. These can be claimed if the special circumstance which would result in a loss in case of breach of contract is brought to the notice of the other party. It is important that such damages must be in contemplation of the parties at the time when the contract is entered into. Subsequent knowledge of the special circumstances will not create any special liability on the guilty party.

Illustrations: *(1) A, having contracted with B to supply B 1,000 tons of iron at ₹100 a ton, to be delivered at a stated time, contracts with C for the purchase of 1,000 tons of iron at ₹80 a ton, telling C that he does so for the purpose of performing his contract with B. C fails to perform his contract with A, and A could not procure other iron, and B, in consequence rescinds the contract. C must pay to A ₹20,000 being the profit which A would have made by the performance of his contract with B. [Illustration to Section 73]. (If C was not told of B's contract then only the difference in contract price and market price, if any, could be claimed.)*

(2) A contracts with B to make and deliver to B, by a fixed day, for a specified price a certain piece of machinery. A does not deliver the piece of machinery at the time specified, and, in consequence of this, B is obliged to procure another at a higher price than that which he was to be paid to A, and is prevented from performing a contract which B had made with a third person at the time of his contract with A, (but which had not been then communicated to A), and is compelled to make compensation for breach of that contract A must pay to B, by way of compensation, the difference between the contract price of the piece of machinery and the sum paid by B for another, but not the sum paid by B to the third person by way of compensation.

(3) A, a builder, contracts to erect and finish a house by the first of January, in order that B may give possession of it at that time to C, to whom B has contracted to 'let it. A is informed of the contract between B and C. A builds the house so badly that, before the first of January, it falls down, and has to be rebuilt by B, who, in consequence loses the rent which he was to have received from C, and is obliged to make compensation for breach of that contract. A must pay to B, by way of compensation, (i) for the cost of rebuilding the house, (ii) for the rent lost, and (iii) for the compensation made to C.

3. *Exemplary or Vindictive Damages:* These are such damages which are awarded with a view to punishing the guilty party for the breach and not by way of compensation for the loss suffered by the aggrieved party. As observed earlier,' the cardinal principle of the taw of damages for a breach of contract is to compensate the injured party for the loss suffered and to punish the guilty party. Hence, obviously exemplary damages have no place in the law of contract and are not recoverable for a breach of contract. There are however, two exceptions to this rule.
   (*a*) **Breach of a contract to marry:** In this case the amount of the damages will depend upon the extent of injury to the party's feelings. One may be ruined, other may not mind so much.
   (b) **Dishonour of a cheque by a banker when there are sufficient funds to the credit of the customer:** In this case the rule of ascertaining damages is, "the smaller the cheque, the greater the damage." Of course, the actual amount of damages will differ according to the status of the party.
4. *Nominal Damages:* Nominal damages are these which are awarded only for name sake. These are neither awarded by way of compensation to the aggrieved party nor by way of punishment to the guilty party. These are awarded to establish the right to decree for breach at contract when the injured party has not actually suffered any real damage and consist of a very small sum of money, say, a rupee or two.

   Illustration : *Where in a contract of sale of goods, if the contract price and the market price is almost the same at the date of breach at the contract, then the aggrieved party is entitled only to nominal damages.*

   Duty to Mitigate Damage Suffered: It is the duty of the injured party to mitigate damage suffered as a result of the breach of contract by the other party. He must use all reasonable means of mitigating the damage, just as a prudent man would, under similar circumstances in his own case. He cannot recover any part of the damage, traceable to his own neglect to mitigate. The onus of proof, however, is on the defendant to show that the plaintiff has failed in his duty of mitigation and the plaintiff is free from the burden of proving that he tried his best to mitigate the loss (Pauzu, Ltd. Vs. Saunders). The rule in regard to mitigation must be applied with discretion and a man who has already put himself in the wrong by breaking his contract has no right to impose new and extraordinary duties on the aggrieved party. Courts should take care to see that they have put the plaintiff in the same position as if the contract had been performed, and have been over generous to the contract breaker by too severe an application of the rule that the plaintiff must take reasonable steps to mitigate damages.

Illustrations: *(1) Where a servant is dismissed, even though wrongfully, it is his duty to mitigate the damages by seeking other employment. He can recover only nominal damages if he refuses a reasonable offer of fresh employment. But if it cannot be proved that he has failed in his duty of mitigation, he will be entitled to the full salary for the whole of the unexpired period of service, if the contract of employment was for a fixed period. If the contract of employment was not for a fixed term, then the principle of awarding damages for a reasonable period of notice comes into play (S S Shetty Vs. Bharat Nidhi Ltd.).*

(2) A took a shop on rent from B and paid one month's rent in advance. B could not give possession of the shop to A. A chose to do no business for 8 months though there were other shops available in the vicinity. A sued B for breach of contract and claimed damages for the loss suffered. Held, he was entitled only to a refund of his advance, and nothing more, as he had failed in his duty to minimize the loss by not taking another shop in the neighborhood (Neki Vs. Pribhu).

5. *Liquidated Damages and Penalty:* 'Liquidated damages' means a sum fixedup in advance, which is a fair and genuine pre-estimate of the probable loss that is likely to result from the breach. 'Penalty' means a sum fixedup in advance, which is extravagant and unconscionable in amount in comparison with the greatest loss that could conceivably be proved to have followed the breach. Thus the essence of a penalty is a payment of money stipulated as per the terms of the offending party. Sometimes the parties fix up at the time of the contract the amount payable as damages in case of breach. In such a case, a distinction is made in English Law as to whether the provision amounts to 'liquidated damages' or a 'penalty'.

   Courts in England usually allow 'liquidated damages' as stipulated in the contract, without any regard to the actual loss sustained.' Penalty' clauses, however, are treated as invalid and the courts in that case calculate damages according to the ordinary principles and allow only reasonable compensation. Under the Indian Law Section 74 does away with the distinction between 'liquidated damages' and 'penalty'. This Section lays down that the Courts are not bound to treat the sum mentioned in the contract, either by way of liquidated damages or penalty, as the sum payable as damages for the breach. Instead the courts are required to allow reasonable compensation so as to cover the actual loss sustained, not exceeding the amount so named in the contract.

   Thus, according to Sec 74, the named sum, regardless whether it is a penalty or not, determines only the maximum limit of liability in case of the breach of contract. The Section does not confer a special benefit upon any party; it merely declares the law that notwithstanding any term in the contract predetermining damages or providing for forfeiture of any property by way of penalty, the Court will award to the party aggrieved only reasonable compensation not exceeding the amount named or penalty stipulated.

Exception: There is, however, one exception provided for by Section 74 to the above rule. When any person enters into any bail, bond, recognizance or other instrument of the same nature, or under the provisions of any law or under the orders of the Government, gives any bond for the performance of any public duty or act in which the public are interested, he shall be liable to pay the whole sum mentioned therein upon breach of the condition of any such instrument.

Illustrations:*(1) A contracts with B to pay ₹1,000 if he fails to pay B ₹500 on a given day, A fails to pay B ₹500 on that day. B is entitled to recover from A such compensation, not exceeding ₹1,000 as the court considers reasonable.*

(2) A undertakes to repay B a loan of ₹1,000 by five equal monthly instalment with a stipulation that, in default of payment of any instalment, the whole shall become due. This stipulation is not by way of penalty and the contract may be forced according to its terms.

(3) A borrows ₹100 from B, and gives him a bond for ₹200 payable by five yearly instalment of ₹40, with a stipulation that, in default of payment of any instalment, the whole shall become due. This is a stipulation by way of penalty.

(C) Suit for Quantum Meruit

'*Quantum Meruit*' means '*as much as merited or as much as is earned*' or '*In proportion to the work done*'. This remedy may be availed of either without claiming damages or in addition to claiming damages for breach. This principle of law provides for payment of compensation under certain circumstances, to a person who has rendered goods or services to another person under a contract, which could not or has not been fully performed. An action based on the *Doctrine of Quantum Meruit* arises where the plaintiff claims a reasonable remuneration for his services, when there is no enforceable contract or express promise as to the amount of remuneration.

According to this Doctrine, a person who has done some work for another, or rendered some service to him, or delivered goods to him, not intending to do so gratuitously but at the request of the latter, and no specific sum is owing to him, is entitled to recover a reasonable sum from the person who has enjoyed the benefit thereof.

The third remedy for a breach of contract available to an injured party against the guilty party is to file a suit upon Quantum Meruit Sections 65 to 70. The phrase *quantum meruit* literally means 'as much as is earned' or 'in proportion to the work done.' A right to sue upon quantum meruit usually arises where after part performance of the contract by one party, there is a breach of contract, or the contract is discovered void or becomes void.

This remedy may be availed of either without claiming damages (*i.e.*, claiming reasonable compensation only for the work done) or in addition to claiming damages for breach (*i.e.*, claiming reasonable compensation for part performance and damages for the remaining unperformed part). Therefore, when a person has done some work under a contract and the other party refuses to perform the contract or if the contract could not be continued due to happening of some event, then, the party who has performed the work (or promise) has a right to be reimbursed for the work already done. This right does not arise out of the contract but arises out of a claim of the quasi contractual obligation.

Quasi contracts are implied contracts because they are 'such obligations' which resemble those created by contracts. They are called 'construction contracts' under English Law. A claim based on the doctrine of quantum meruit, may either be contractual or quasi-contractual. Where there is a breach of contract, the party complaining of the breach, is entitled not only to bring an action for damages, but also to payment for what he has done under the contract.

The aggrieved party may file a suit upon quantum meruit and may claim payment in proportion to work done or goods supplied in the following cases:

1. Where work has been done in pursuance of a contract, which has been discharged by the default of the defendant.

   ***Illustrations** (1). P agreed to write a volume on ancient armour to be published in a magazine owned by C. For this he was to receive £100 on completion. When he had completed part, but not the whole, of his volume, C abandoned the magazine. P was held entitled to get damages for breach of contract and payment quantum meruit for the part already completed (Planche Vs. Colburn).*

   (2). A, engages B, a contractor, to build a three storied house. After a part is constructed A prevents B from working anymore. B, the contractor, is entitled to get reasonable compensation for work done under the Doctrine of Quantum Meruit in addition to the damages for breach of contract. Notice that in both the above cases the contract was wrongfully terminated by the defendant, and both damages as well as payment quantum meruit have been allowed. It is important that in the case of a wrongful breach of contract the injured party can always claim payment quantum meruit, whether the contract is divisible or indivisible.

2. Where work has been done in pursuance of a contract which is discovered void' or 'becomes void,' provided the contract is divisible.

   ***Illustrations:** (1). C was appointed as managing director of a company by the board of directors under a written contract which provided for his remuneration. The contract was found void because the directors who constituted the 'Board' were not qualified to make the appointment. C nevertheless, purporting to act under the agreement, rendered services to the company and sued for the sums specified in the agreement, or, alternatively, for a reasonable, remuneration on a quantum meruit. Held, C could recover on a quantum meruit. (CravenEllis Vs. Canons Ltd.).*

   (2). A contracts with B to repair his' house at a piece rate. After a part of the repairs were carried out, the house is destroyed by lightning. Although the contract becomes void and stands discharged because of destruction of the house, A can claim payment for the work done on 'quantum meruit'. Note that if under the contract a lump sum is to be paid for the repair job as a whole, then A cannot claim quantum meruit because no money is due till the whole job is done.

3. When a person enjoys benefit of non-gratuitous act although there exists no express agreement between the parties. One of such cases is provided in Section 70. Section 70 lays' down that when services are rendered or goods are supplied by a person, (i) without any intention of doing so gratuitously, and (ii) the benefit of the same is enjoyed by the other party, the latter must compensate the former or restore the thing so delivered.

   ***Illustrations:** (1). A, a trader, leaves certain goods at B's house by mistake. B treats the goods as his own. He is bound to pay A for them.*

   (2). Where A ploughed the field of B with a tractor to the satisfaction of B in B's presence, it was held that A was entitled to payment as the work was 'not intended to be gratuitous and the other party has enjoyed the benefit of the same. (Ram Krishna vs Rangoobed).

4. A party who is guilty of breach of contract may also sue on a quantum meruit provided both the following conditions are fulfilled:

   - the contract must be divisible, and
   - the other party must have enjoyed the benefit of the part which has been performed, although he had an option of declining it.

Illustrations: *(1) Where a common carrier fails to take a complete consignment to the agreed destination, he may recover pro-rata freight. (He will, of course, be liable for breach of the contract.)*

(2) S had agreed to erect upon H's land two houses and stables for £565. S did part of the work and then abandoned the contract. H himself completed the buildings using some materials left on his land by S. In an action by S for the value of work done and of the materials used by H, it was held that S could recover the value of the materials (for H had the option to accept or to reject these) but he' could not recover the value of the work done (for H had no option with regard to the partly erected building, but to accept that). The court observed, 'The mere fact that a defendant is in possession of what he cannot help keeping, or even has done work upon it, affords no ground for such an inference. He is not bound to keep unfinished a building which in an incomplete state would be a nuisance on his land.' (Sumpter Vs. Hedges).

5. When an agreement is discovered to be void [Sec 65] : When an agreement is discovered to be void, or when a contract becomes void, any person who has received any advantage under such agreement or contract is bound to restore it, or to make compensation for it, to the person from whom he received it.
6. When something is done without any intension to do so gratuitously [Sec 70]: When a thing is lawfully done or goods are supplied by a person without any intension to do so gratuitously to another person and such other person enjoys the benefit thereof, he is bound to make compensation to the former in respect of, or to restore the thing so done or delivered.
7. When there is an express or implied contract to render services but there is no agreement as to remuneration. In such a situation, reasonable remuneration is payable. What is reasonable remuneration is determined by the court. This reasonable remuneration is based on quantum meruit.

   Illustration: *In Upton Rural District Council Vs. Powell, there was an implied agreement between P and a fire brigade for the services provided by the brigade beyond their jurisdiction. Held, reasonable remuneration was payable by P for the services received by him.*
8. When the completion of the contract has been prevented by the act of the other party to the contract.

   Illustration: *In Planche Vs Colburn, G engaged P to write a book on ancient armoury to be published by instalments in a periodical called 'The Juvenile Library', for the fee of £100. After a few issues of the periodical had appeared, it was abandoned. It was held that P could recover on quantum meruit for the work he had done under the contract.*
9. When a contract is divisible. When a contract is divisible and the party not in default has enjoyed the benefit of the past performance, the party in default may sue on '*quantum meruit*'.
10. When an indivisible contract is completely performed but badly. In the above case, the person who has performed the contract can claim the lump sum, but the other party can make a deduction for bad work.

(D) Suit for Specific Performance

In certain cases of breach of a contract, damages are not an adequate remedy. The Court may, in such cases, direct the party in breach to carry out his promise according to the terms of the contract. This is a direction by the Court for specific performance of the contract at the suit of the party not in breach. Specific performance means the actual carrying out of the contract as agreed. Under certain circumstances an aggrieved party may file a suit for specific performance, *i.e.*, for a decree by the court directing the defendant to actually perform the promise that he has made. Such a suit may be filed either instead of or in addition to a suit for damages.

A decree for specific performance is not granted for contracts of every description. It is only where it is just and equitable so to do, *i.e.*, where the legal remedy is inadequate or defective, that the Courts issue a decree for specific performance. It is usually granted in contracts connected with land, buildings, articles and unique goods having some special value to the party suing because of family association. In all these contracts monetary compensation is not an adequate relief because the injured party will not be able to get an exact substitute in the market.

Some of the cases in which specific performance of a contract may, in the discretion of the Court, be enforced are as follows:

- When the act agreed to be done is such that compensation in money for its non performance is not an adequate relief.
- When there exists no standard for ascertaining the actual damage caused by the non performance of the act agreed to be done.
- When it is probable that the compensation in money cannot be got for the non performance of the act agreed to be done.

Specific performance is not granted, as a rule, in the following cases:

1. Where monetary compensation is an adequate relief. Thus the Courts refuse specific performance of contract to lend or to borrow money or where the contract is for the sale of goods easily procurable elsewhere.
2. The contract is not certain, or is inequitable to either party.
3. Where the Court cannot supervise the actual execution of the contract, e.g., a building construction contract. Moreover, in most cases damages afford an adequate remedy.
4. Damages are an adequate remedy.
5. Where the contract is for personal services, e.g., a contract to marry or to paint a picture. In such contracts 'injunction' (*i.e.*, an order which forbids the defendant to perform a like personal service for other persons) is granted in place of specific performance.
6. The Court cannot supervise its carrying out, e.g., a building contract.
7. The contract is made by a company in excess of its powers as laid down in its Memorandum of Association.
8. The contract is of a personal nature, e.g., a contract to marry.
9. The contract is made by trustees in beach of their trust.
10. The contract is in its nature revocable.

(E) Suit for Injunction

Where a party is in breach of a negative term of a contract (where he is doing something which he promised not to do), the Court may, by issuing an order, restrain him from doing what he promised not to do. Such an order of the Court is known as an 'injunction'. 'Injunction' is an order of a Court restraining a person from doing a particular act. It is a mode of securing the specific performance of the negative terms of the contract. To put it differently, where a party is in breach of negative term of the contract (that is, where he is doing something which he promised not to do), the court may, by issuing an injunction, restrain him from doing, what he promised not to do.

Thus 'injunction' is a preventive relief. It is particularly appropriate in cases of anticipatory breach of contract where damages would not be an adequate relief. The grant of an injunction by the Court is normally discretionary, but there seems no reason why the Court should refuse the grant of an injunction to restrain the breach of a contract

(*a*) Whereby a promisor undertakes not to do something, *e.g.*, not to carry on a certain trade or

(*b*) Which is negative in substance though not in form..

Illustrations: *(1). A, agreed to sing at B's theatre for three months from 1st April and to sing for no one else during that period. Subsequently she contracted to sing at C's theatre and refused to sing at B's theatre. On a suit by B, the Court refused to order specific performance of her positive engagement to sing at the plaintiff's theatre, but granted an injunction restraining A from singing elsewhere and awarded damages to B to compensate him for the loss caused by A's refusal.(Lumley Vs. Wagnerl)*

(2). G agreed to take the whole of his supply of electricity from a certain company. The agreement was held to import a negative promise that he would take none from elsewhere. He was, therefore, restrained by an injunction from buying electricity from any other company. (Metropolitan Electric Supply Company Vs. Ginder).

(3). G agreed to take all the electric energy required by his premises from M. Held, this was in substance an agreement not to take energy from any other person and it could be enforced by injunction (Metropolitan Electric Supply Co. Vs. Ginder(1901)

(i) Stipulation Regarding Payment of Interest

The Explanation added to Section 74 states, "a stipulation for increased interest from the date of default may be a stipulation by way of penalty." It implies that such a stipulation may be considered a penalty clause and disallowed by the courts, if the enhanced rate is exorbitant.

Illustration: *A gives B a bond for the repayment of ₹1,000 with interest at12 percent per annum at the end of six months, with a stipulation that in case of default interest shall be payable at the rate of 75 per cent per annum from the date of default. This is a stipulation by way of penalty and B is only entitled to recover from A such compensation as the Court considers reasonable.*

The following rules must also be noted in connection with payment of interest :

(*a*) Unless the parties have made a stipulation for the payment of interest or there is a usage to that effect, interest cannot be recovered legally as damages, generally speaking (Mahabir Prasad Vs. Durga Datt).

(*b*) Where a contract provides that the amount should be paid without interest by a particular date and on default it will be payable with interest, such a stipulation may be allowed if the interest is reasonable. If the interest is exorbitant, the courts will give relief.

(*c*) Payment of compound interest on default is allowed, only if it is not at an enhanced rate (Bhushan Rao Vs. Subayyal).

(ii) Earnest Money

Money deposited as security for the due performance of a contract is known as earnest money. Forfeiture of earnest money is allowed if the amount is reasonable. But where it is in the nature of penalty, the Court has jurisdiction toward such sum only as it considers reasonable but not exceeding the amount so agreed (Fateh Chand vs Balkishen Dass).The proportion the amount bears to the total sale price, the nature of the contract and other circumstances have to be taken into account in ascertaining the reasonableness of the amount.

(iii) Cost of Suit

The aggrieved party is entitled, in addition to the damages, to get the costs of getting the decree for damages. The cost of suit for damages is in the discretion of the Court.

(F) Summary of the Rules Regarding the Measure of Damages

1. The damages are awarded by way of compensation for the loss suffered by the aggrieved party and not for the purpose of punishing the guilty party for the breach.
2. The injured party is to be placed in the same position, so far as money can do, as if the contract had been performed.
3. The aggrieved party can recover by way of compensation only the actual loss suffered by him, arising naturally in the usual course of things.
4. Special or remote damages, i.e., damages which are not the natural and probable consequence of the breach are usually not allowed until they are in the knowledge of both the parties at the time of entering into the contract.
5. The fact that damages are difficult to assess does not prevent the injured party from recovering them.
6. When no real loss arises from the breach of contract, only nominal damages are awarded.
7. If the parties fix up in advance the sum payable as damages in case of breach of contract, the Court will allow only reasonable compensation so as to cover' the actual loss sustained, not exceeding the amount so named in the contract.
8. Exemplary damages cannot be awarded for breach of contract except in case of breach of contract of marriage or wrongful refusal by the bank to honor the customer's cheque.
9. It is the duty of the injured party to minimize the damage suffered.
10. The injured party is entitled to get the costs of getting the decree for damages from the defaulter party.

2.11 QUASI CONTRACT

These contracts are also called implied contracts or constructive contracts created by law on the ground of equitable consideration. *i.e.*, on the principle, that a person shall not become rich unjustly, at the expense of another. Hence Quasi Contracts are created by law and not by the intention of parties. Under certain special circumstances obligations resembling those created by a contract are imposed by law although the parties have never entered into a contract. Such obligations imposed by law are referred to as 'Quasi Contracts' or 'Constructive Contracts' under the English law, and 'certain relations resembling those created by contracts' under the Indian law.

Under certain circumstances, a person may receive a benefit to which the law regards another person as better entitled or for which the law considers he should pay to the other person, even though there is no contract between the parties. Relationships thus created are called as Quasi Contracts. Such relationships are termed quasi contracts, because, although there is no contract or agreement between the parties, they are put in the same position as if there were a contract between them.

The term 'Quasi Contract' has been used because such a contract resembles a contract so far as result or effect is concerned but it has little or no affinity with a contract in respect of mode of creation- like offer and acceptance etc. These are termed quasi contracts or constructive contracts under the English law and certain relations resembling those created by contracts under the Indian Law. A quasi contract rests on the ground of equity that a person shall not be allowed to enrich himself unjustly at the expense of another. The principle of unjust enrichment requires:

- That the defendant has been 'enriched' by the receipt of a 'benefit'.
- That this enrichment is at the expense of another.
- That the retention of the enrichment is unjust.

(A) Kinds of Quasi-contractual Obligations

There are five kinds of quasi-contractual obligations:

1. **Supply of necessaries [Sec 68]:** If a person, incapable of entering into a contract, or anyone whom he is legally bound to support, is supplied by another with necessaries suited to his condition in life, the person who has furnished such supplies is entitled to be reimbursed from the property of such incapable person. "If a person, incapable of entering into a contract or anyone whom he is legally bound to support, is supplied by another person with necessaries suited to his condition in life, the person who has furnished such supplies is entitled to be reimbursed from the property of such incapable person."

   Although agreements by minors, idiots, lunatics, etc., are void-ab-initio, but Section 68 makes an exception to this rule by providing that their estates are liable to reimburse the supplier who supplies them or to someone whom they are legally bound to support with 'necessaries' of life. The following points need to be emphasized:

   (*a*) The Section does not create any personal liability but only the estates are liable.

   (*b*) The things supplied must come within the category of '*necessaries*'. The word '*necessaries*' here covers not only bare necessities of existence, *e.g.*, food and clothes, but all things which are reasonably necessary to the incompetent person, having regard to his status in society, *e.g.*, a watch, a radio, a bicycle may be included therein.

   (*c*) Necessaries should be supplied only to such incompetent person or to someone whom he is legally bound to support such as his wife and children.

   (*d*) Incompetent person's property is liable to pay only reasonable price for the goods or services supplied and not the price which the incompetent person might have agreed to pay (legally speaking an incompetent person cannot agree to anything).

   Illustrations: *(1) X supplies the wife and children of B, a lunatic with necessaries suitable to their condition in life. X is entitled to be reimbursed from B's property.*

   (2) A supplies B, a lunatic, with necessaries suitable to his condition in life. A is entitled to be reimbursed from B's property.

2. **Reimbursement of person paying money due by another, the payment of which he is interested. Payment by an interested person [Sec 69]:** A person, who is interested in the payment of money which another is bound by law to pay, and who therefore pays it, is entitled to be reimbursed by the other.

   Illustrations: *(1) P left his carriage on D's premises. D's landlord seized the carriage as distress for rent. P paid the rent to obtain the release of his carriage. Held, P could recover the amount from D [Exall Vs. Partridge (1799)].*

   (2) B holds land in Bengal, on a lease granted by A, the Zamindar. The revenue payable by A to the Government being in arrear, his land is advertised for sale by the Government. Under the revenue law the consequences of

such sale will be annulment of B's lease. B to prevent the sale and the consequent annulment of his own lease, pays to the Government the sum due from a. A is bound to make good to B the amount so paid.

In order to make Section 69 applicable, the following conditions must be satisfied:

1. The plaintiff should be interested in making the payment in order to protect his own interest and the payment should not be voluntary one. Moreover, the payment must have been done in good faith and not to manufacture evidence of title to land or any other thing.

   Illustrations: *(1) A subtenant pays the arrears of rent due by the tenant the landlord, in order to save the tenancy from forfeiture. The subtenant is entitled to recover from the tenant, the amount paid by him to the landlord, although there is no contract between the two.*

   (2) A, pays the arrears of rent of his neighbor B, just to avoid a struggle between B and his landlord. A cannot recover from B as he acted voluntarily and had no interest of his own in the payment. [But if B should agree to reimburse A, this would be a good contract under Section 25(2).]

   (3) P left his carriage in D's premises. D's landlord seized the carriage for rent. P paid the rent to obtain the release of his carriage. Held, P could recover the amount from D ([Exall Vs. Partrige]

2. The payment must be such as the other party was bound by law to pay.

   Illustrations: *(1) In Abid Hussain vs Ganga Sahai, A's goods were wrongfully attached to realize the arrears of Government revenue due by B. A pays the dues to save the goods from being sold. He is entitled to recover the amount from B .*

   (2) In Brook's Wharf Ltd. Vs. Goodman Bros, W was the owner of a warehouse. G imported certain goods and kept them in the warehouse. The goods were stolen without any negligence on the part of W. The authorities made a demand on W for the payment of the customs duty which W paid. Held, W could recover the amount from G.

3. The payment should not be a voluntary one. The payment must not be such as the plaintiff himself was bound to pay. He should only be interested in making the payment. In other words, a suit under this section is maintainable only for reimbursement and not for contribution. Thus, where there is a joint liability on joint wrong doers and only one of them discharges the liability, no suit for contribution from the other would be maintainable under this Section (Ramkrishna Vs. Radhakrishana). [A suit for contribution from the other joint promisor would be maintainable under Section 43.]

   Illustration: *A and B have been fined jointly ₹500 for selling adulterated ghee. A alone pays the amount of fine in good faith, A cannot later claim contribution from B under Section 69. Although B was bound by law to pay and A has paid B's share in good faith, yet A cannot recover as he himself was bound to make the payment, being jointly liable with B and was not simply interested in making the payment. [A can, however, claim contribution from B under Section 43.]*

3. **Obligation to pay for non-gratuitous acts [70]:** When a person lawfully does anything for another person or delivers anything to him not intending to do so gratuitously, and such other person enjoys the benefit thereof, the latter is bound to make compensation to the former in respect of, or to restore, the thing so done ore delivered. This is the third type of quasi contract provided in the Contract Act.

   Section 70 lays down thus, "Where a person lawfully does anything for another person, or delivers anything to him, not intending to do so gratuitously, and such other person enjoys the benefit thereof, the latter is bound to make compensation to the former in respect of, or to restore, the thing so done or delivered." However before any right of action arises, three conditions must be satisfied, namely:

(*i*) The thing must have been done lawfully in good faith. This means that the act done must be in pursuance of the implied wishes (because there should not be any request in the case of a quasi contract) and in the presence of the other party, giving him the full choice to reject the thing or service.

(*ii*) The thing must have been done by a person not intending to act gratuitous i.e., it must have been done with the intention of being paid for.

(*iii*) The person for whom the act is done must have enjoyed the benefit of the act.

Illustrations: *(1)A, a tradesman leaves goods at B's house by mistake. B treats the goods as his own. He is bound to pay A for them. [Illustration to Section 70].*

(2) A saves B's property from fire. A is not entitled to compensation from B if the circumstances show that he intended to act gratuitously. [Illustration to Section 70]

(3) Where a coolie takes the luggage at the railway station without being asked by the passenger or a shoe shiner starts shining shoes of the passenger without being asked to do so, and if the passenger does not object to that, then he is bound to pay reasonably for the same as the work was not intended to be gratuitous.

(4) In Damodar Mudaliar Vs. Secretary of State of India (1894), eleven villages were irrigated by a certain tank. Some of them were zamindari villages while others were held under direct State tenancy. The Government effected some repairs to the tank for its preservation, and the same was not done gratuitously. The zamindars also enjoyed the benefit of the repairs. It was held that they were liable to contribute proportionately towards the expenses of repairs.

4. **Responsibility of finder of goods [71]:** A person, who finds goods belonging to another and takes them into his custody, is subject to the same responsibility as a bailee. He is bound to take as much care of the goods as a man of ordinary prudence work, under similar circumstances, take of his own goods of the same bulk, quality and value. He must also take all necessary measures to trace its owner. If he does not, he will be guilty of wrongful conversion of the property. Till the owner is found out, the property in goods will vest in the finder and he can retain the goods as his own against the whole world, except the owner.

   Section 71 lays down another circumstance in which also a quasi contractual obligation is to be presumed. It says: "A person who finds goods belonging to another and takes them into his custody, is subject to the same responsibility as a bailee". Thus law between the owner and finder of the goods also implies an agreement and the latter is deemed to be a bailee.

   Duties of finder of goods: He must try to find out the real, owner of the goods and must not appropriate the property to his own use. If the real owner is traced, he must restore the goods to him on demand. If he does not take these measures, he will be guilty of criminal misappropriation of the property under Section 403 of Indian Penal Code. Further, till the goods are in possession of the finder, he must take as much care of the goods as a man of ordinary prudence would, under similar circumstances, take of his own goods of the same bulk, quality and value (Sec.151).

   Rights of finder of goods: Till the true owner is found out, he can retain possession of the goods against everybody in the world. He is entitled to receive from the true owner, all expenses incurred by him for preserving the goods or finding the true owner. He has a lien on the goods for the money so spent i.e., he can refuse to redeem the goods to the true owner until these moneys are paid. He is not entitled to file a suit for the recovery of such sums. But he can file a suit against the owner to recover any reward, which was offered by the owner for the return of the goods, provided he came to know of the offer of reward before actually finding out the goods. The finder of goods is entitled to sell the goods if the owner cannot be found out or if he refuses to pay the lawful charges incurred the finder, in the following two situations only:

(*a*) When the thing is in danger of perishing or of losing the greater part of its value, or by when the lawful charges of the finder amount to two thirds of the value of the goods found.

(*b*) The true owner is entitled to get the balance of sale proceeds, if there is surplus after meeting the lawful charges. It is to be noted that no one except the real owner can claim possession of goods from the finder. If anybody deprives him of the possession of the goods, he can file a suit for damages for trespass.

Illustration: *H picked up a diamond on the floor of F's shop and handed it over to F to keep it till the owner appeared. In spite of best efforts the true owner could not be searched. After the lapse of some weeks, H tendered to F the lawful expenses incurred by him for finding the true owner and an indemnity bond and requested him to return the diamond to him (i.e., H). F refused to do so. Held, F must return the diamond to H as he was entitled to retain the goods as against everybody except the true owner (Hollins Vs. Fowler S).*

The finder can sell the goods in the following cases:

(*a*) When the thing found is in danger of perishing.

(*b*) When the owner cannot, with reasonable diligence be found out.

(*c*) When the owner is found out, but he refuses to pay the lawful charges of the finder.

(*d*) When the lawful charges of the finder, in respect of the thing found, amount to two thirds of the value of the thing found.

5. **Mistake or Coercion [72]:** A person to whom money has been paid, or anything delivered, by mistake or under coercion, must repay or return it to the person who paid it by mistake or under coercion. This is the fifth and the last kind of quasi contract mentioned in the Act Section 72 declares thus, "A person to whom money has been paid, or anything delivered, by mistake or under coercion, must repay or return it." Accordingly, if one party under a mistake pays money to another party, which is not due by contract or otherwise, that money must be repaid.

The term 'mistake' has been used in the Section without any qualification or limitation whatever and comprises within its scope a mistake of law as well as a mistake of fact (Sales Tax Officer vs Kanhaiyalal Mukund). The term 'coercion' has been used in its ordinary sense and not as defined in Section 157. Here 'coercion' means 'under pressure'.

Illustrations: *(1) A pays some money to B by mistake. It is really due to C. B must refund the money to A. C, however, cannot recover the amount from B as there is no privity of contract between B and C.*

(2). A and B jointly owe ₹100 to C. A alone pays the amount to C, and B, not knowing this fact, pays ₹100 over again to C. C is bound to repay the amount to B.

(3) A pays some money to B by mistake. It is really due to C. B must refund the money to A. C, however, cannot recover the amount from B in the absence of privities of contract between B and C.

(4) A fruit parcel is delivered under a mistake to R who consumes the fruits thinking them as birthday present; R must return the parcel or pay for the fruits. Although there is no agreement between R and the true owner, yet he is bound to pay as the law regards it a quasi contract.

It is to be noted, that this Section does not cover a base where money has been paid in payment of a natural obligation. Thus, where one has paid up a time barred debt, he cannot recover it. Similarly, the Section does not apply when there is a deliberate disregard of law *e.g.*, where moneys are paid voluntarily knowing fully well that the contract has become void, it cannot be recovered under the Section (Ananth Bandhu Vs. Union of India).

2.12 E-COMMERCE CONTRACTS

When a contract is entered through the electronic media, *i.e.*, the internet, such contracts are termed as E-contracts. The advent of the electronic media, particularly the internet has expanded the area of operation in commercial transactions in the business arena. The internet has created a revolution in business and economics. The trend of almost all business is expansion of business activities and the internet is the most suited mode for business growth. The internet not only helps in creating demand for new business but also helps in improved distribution channels , innovations and networking. The internet is found to be more affordable, faster and a cheaper method of business development process. It is also being used as an informational and communication tool for mass advertising, marketing and improving customer relations. Moreover, the internet has its hold all over the world and as such vendors will have the opportunity to target customers for their products or services worldwide.

The method of online of internet contract involves the seller advertising his products or services on the internet through specific or general web pages. The buyer who wishes to avail of the services or buy the products that he sees, on the web page may play an order either online (through the internet itself) or through telephone. Once the order is accepted, a contract is formed. In many instances, payment instructions will follow by telephone and the delivery of the product by traditional methods. Such a contract created, through the internet are called E-commerce contracts.

It has been observed by business houses that the infrastructure for electronic commerce is expanding even in a developing country like India. The attractive mode of presentation, offers for customers and the ease of connectivity is increasing the number of users of the facility. Electronic Data Interchange- EDI is currently the primary electronic commerce medium for business to business transactions. In contrast to the Internet, EDI-Electronic Data Interchange is a closed environment governed by standardized trading agreements, association rules and standards. Though the system is costly to establish, but it is more secure and there is ease of use by the customer who wishes to buy products online in the comfort of his home or office. Another advantage is that business transactions can be made from any part of the world, wherever the internet can be accessed.

Many vendors are being attracted by the virtual mall space and the business ideas of Amazon.com, (one of the first online store) and several others, who are doing very good business online. Though these type of online transactions have its own advantages and disadvantages, the software engineers and the legal experts are finding ways and means of blocking the loopholes and making it safe for internet users worldwide. The advent of 'digital signatures' is a step towards this direction. Digital signatures facilitate certain elements of legal proof in the event of a dispute, however though they are not the only ways of forming a contract. The interest in commercial activity through the internet has focused attention on the contractual issues raised by the electronic medium itself.

Examples:

1. A agreed to construct a building for B for ₹ 2 lakh, on the terms that no payment shall be made till the completion of the work. Is this a contingent contract?

   [**Hint**. No, this is not a contingent contract because the uncertain event (*i.e.*, A's completing the work) is not collateral to the contract but is the very thing contracted for, and is thus an integral part of the contract.]

2. A agrees to sell land to B at a price to be fixed by C. C refuses to fix the price, the contract enforceable?

   [Hint. No, the contract is not enforceable because by C's refusal to fix the price the agreement becomes void for uncertainty in terms.]

3. A promises to pay B for his services whatever A himself will think right or reasonable. Later, being dissatisfied with the payment made, B sues A. Decide.

   [Hint. B's suit will not be admitted by the Court because if the performance of a promise is contingent upon the mere will and pleasure of the promisor, certain or capable of being made certain, are void (Sec. 29).]

4. A agreed to construct a building for B for ₹ 2 lakhs, on the terms that no payment shall be made till the completion of the work. Is this a contingent contract?

   [Hint. No, this is not a contingent contract because the uncertain event (*i.e.*, A's completing the work) is not collateral to the contract but is the very thing contracted for, and is thus an integral part of the contract.]

5. A agrees to sell land to B at a price to be fixed by C. C refuses to fix the price is the contract enforceable?

   [Hint. No, the contract is not enforceable because by C's refusal to fix the price the agreement becomes void for uncertainty in terms.]

QUESTIONS

Section 2.1

1. Write a note on the Indian Contract Act 1872.
2. What purpose does the study of the Indian Contract Act serve ?

Section 2.2

1. Define 'Agreement'.
2. Explain the importance of '*consensus-ad-idem*' in an agreement between two parties.

Section 2.3

1. How does '*vinculum juris*' affect the parties to a contract ?
2. Distinguish between a social obligation and a legal obligation.
3. What requisites make a person eligible to enter into a contract ?

Section 2.4

1. On what basis are contracts classified under ? Explain.
2. Distinguish between void agreement and voidable agreements.
3. Write short notes with examples, on:
   (*a*) Unilateral contract and Bilateral contract
   (*b*) Executed contract and Executory contract
   (*c*) Implied contract and Express contract
   (*d*) Valid, void and voidable contracts.

Section 2.5

1. What are the elements necessary to make an agreement enforceable in a Court of Law ?
2. Explain different kinds of offer.
3. Explain the legal rules as to offer.
4. When and how does an offer terminate ?
5. What are the legal rules as to acceptance ?
6. What is the role of communication in a contract ? When is communication of acceptance said to be compete ?
7. Write a note on:
   (*a*) revocation of proposal
   (*b*) revocation of acceptance.
8. What is consideration and what are the rules set by the Indian Contract Act regarding consideration ?
9. Write a note on the 'Doctrine of Privity of Contract'.
10. Explain, exception to the rule 'stranger to a contract cannot sue', with an illustration.
11. What are the exceptions to the statement 'a contract without consideration is void' ?
12. Which categories of individuals, according to the Contract Act are considered as incompetent to enter into a contract ?
13. Explain the implications of entering into contracts with
    (*a*) a minor
    (*b*) persons of unsound mind
    (*c*) foreign sovereigns and representatives of foreign states
    (*d*) insolvents and convicts.
14. When is consent considered to be free ?
15. Write an note will illustrations on:
    (*a*) Coercion
    (*b*) Undue Influence
    (*c*) Fraud
    (*d*) Misrepresentation
    (*e*) Mistake.
16. Explain the term 'burden of proof', under Undue Influence.
17. Elucidate the differences between
    (*a*) Coercion and Undue Influence
    (*b*) Fraud and Misrepresentation.
18. Does silence amount to fraud. Explain with illustrations.
19. Write a note on the different types of mistake of fact.
20. Write a note on agreements which are held void on the ground that consideration or object is opposed to public policy.

21. Explain the benefits of having a written agreement while entering into a contract.
22. Explain the term 'possibility of performance' with an illustration.
23. What are the essentials of a wagering agreement ? How would you identify a wagering agreement ?
24. Write a note on 'agreements not expressly declared to be void' under the Indian Contract Act.
25. Write a note on collateral transitions.
26. What is restitution under the Contract Act ?

Section 2.6

1. What is meant by contingent contract ? What are the essentials of a contingent contract ?
2. What is meant by a collateral event ?
3. What are the rules regarding contingent contracts ?

Section 2.7

1. What are the repercussions when there is refusal of performance ?
2. Distinguish between actual performance and attempted performance.
3. Who can perform the contract ?
4. What are the instances when a contract need not be performed ?

Section 2.8

1. What is meant by reciprocal promises ?
2. Write a note on the types of reciprocal promises.
3. What is meant by assignment of a contract ?
4. Explain appropriation of payment according to the Contract Act.

Section 2.9

1. Explain the methods in which a contract entered into between the parties may be discharged.
2. What are the different methods by which a contract can be discharged by performance ?
3. What does implied consent to discharging a contract include, under the Contract Act ?
4. What is meant by 'supervening impossibility' ? When is supervening impossibility excusable and when is it not excusable, under the Act ?
5. Write a note on Period of Limitation.
6. When can a contract be terminated by operation of law ?
7. Explain the difference and outcomes of Actual Breach and Anticipatory Breach of Contract. Explain with an illustration.

Section 2.10

1. What are the remedies available to the aggrieved party when there is breach of contract ?
2. When does the Court grant Recession of a contract ?
3. When and under what circumstances can a party file a suit for damages ?

4. Explain types of damages and how are they awarded ?
5. Write a note on a Suit for Quantum Meruit. Under what circumstances can an aggrieved party file a suit for Quantum Meruit ?
6. Under what circumstances can the aggrieved party file a suit for specific performance ?
7. When is specific performance not granted as a rule ?
8. When can an aggrieved part file a suit for injunction ? What are circumstances when the court may refuse a grant for injunction ?
9. Explain Earnest Money.

Section 2.11

1. Explain the term 'Quasi Contracts'.
2. Write a note of kinds of quasi contractual obligations.
3. What are the duties and rights of a finder of goods ?

Section 2.12

1. Write a note on E-Commerce. Explain its advantages and disadvantages.

OBJECTIVE TYPE QUESTIONS

1. The contract must be
   (*a*) Restricted by law (*b*) Unenforceable by law
   (*c*) Enforceable by law (*d*) None of the above.
2. Agreements which are not enforceable by law are
   (*a*) Valid agreements (*b*) Void agreements
   (*c*) Agreements (*d*) None of the above.
3. An agreement consists of:
   (*a*) Offer (*b*) Acceptance
   (*c*) Both a and b (*d*) None of the above.
4. If an agreement is capable of being enforced by law then it is called as:
   (*a*) Agreement only (*b*) Novatio
   (*c*) Void agreements (*d*) Contract.
5. "Every promise and every set of promises forming consideration for each other" is a definition of an:
   (*a*) Agreement (*b*) Promise
   (*c*) Contract (*d*) Proposal.
6. A enters into a contract with B who was born on 1st June 1997 to sell the house for an undisclosed amount. As on 2012, such a contract is said to be:
   (*a*) Voidable contract (*b*) Valid contract
   (*c*) Valid promise (*d*) Void ab initio.

7. Quid Pro Quo means:
   (*a*) Consideration (*b*) Promise
   (*c*) Something in return (*d*) Something unfavorable.
8. Ananth agreed to purchase gold from Babul stolen from some shop. But, later Ananth doesn't purchase the gold from Babul, the agreement is said to be:
   (*a*) Babul can sue Ananth for non-performance of his promise
   (*b*) The contract is valid
   (*c*) The contract is void
   (*d*) Void ab initio.
9. A contract is said to be void when,
   (*a*) Both the parties to an agreement are under a mistake of the fact
   (*b*) Consideration is unlawful
   (*c*) An agreement is without consideration
   (*d*) All of the above.
10. An voidable contract is enforceable by:
    (*a*) Only the promisor
    (*b*) Only by the promisee
    (*c*) Any one of the two
    (*d*) By the third party who is not concerned with the agreement.
11. Void-ab-initio means:
    (*a*) Void from the very beginning (*b*) Void at any moment
    (*c*) Void at the option of the party (*d*) Voidable.
12. If the proposal is made in words then the contract is said to be:
    (*a*) Implied contract (*b*) Executed contract
    (*c*) Executory contract (*d*) Express contract.
13. Where consideration consists of performance, it is called
    (*a*) Executed consideration (*b*) Executory contract
    (*c*) Implied contract (*d*) None of the above.
14. Tacit contract means
    (*a*) No party is considered for the agreement
    (*b*) Only the promisor is entered in the contract
    (*c*) One of the party doesn't agree to the contract
    (*d*) When the behaviour of the party shows his assent to the contract.
15. Rakesh agrees to sell his house to Naveen for a certain amount, this kind of offer is:
    (*a*) Cross offer (*b*) Counter offer
    (*c*) Special offer (*d*) General offer.
16. Invitation of sealed tenders for the supply of spare parts from Company M is an example of:
    (*a*) Open offer (*b*) General offer
    (*c*) Counter offer (*d*) Cross offer.

17. Open offer is also called:

(*a*) Sitting offer (*b*) Standing offer
(*c*) Walking offer (*d*) Cross offer.

18. The Indian Contract Act extends to the whole of India except the State of:

(*a*) Andaman and Nicobar islands (*b*) Jammu and Kashmir
(*c*) Central government ruled states (*d*) Bihar.

19. If a person signifies his willingness to do or abstain from doing anything, (as a return promise) it is :

(*a*) Consideration (*b*) Vocation
(*c*) Novatio (*d*) Agreement.

20. What happens to an offer if it is not being accepted in the mode prescribed

(*a*) An offer lapses (*b*) An offer is accepted
(*c*) An offer is kept untouched (*d*) An offer is accepted by default.

21. An offer lapses by

(*a*) Acceptance is not communicated
(*b*) Not being accepted in the mode prescribed
(*c*) By rejection
(*d*) All of the above.

22. Consideration could be given by

(*a*) Third party also (*b*) Only by the parties to the contract
(*c*) Only by the promisor (*d*) Only by the promisee.

23. Consideration need not be adequate. This statement is

(*a*) True (*b*) False
(*c*) Cant say (*d*) None of the above.

24. Consideration moves at the instance of the

(*a*) Promisor (*b*) Promise
(*c*) Parties to the contract (*d*) All the above.

25. Gratuitous mean:

(*a*) Without expecting any return
(*b*) No express agreement between the parties
(*c*) Where a person enjoys the benefit
(*d*) The person enters into the contract.

26. Consideration which consists of a performance is known as:

(*a*) A promise (*b*) A performance
(*c*) An act (*d*) A contract.

27. Consideration which consists of non performance is known as:

(*a*) Gratuitous (*b*) An abstinence
(*c*) Quid pro quo (*d*) An agreement.

28. Inadequate consideration would not ___________ an agreement:
   (*a*) Validate (*b*) Inform
   (*c*) Invalidate (*d*) Void.
29. Agreement without consideration is:
   (*a*) Valid at the option of the parties (*b*) Void
   (*c*) Valid by default by the law (*d*) Voidable.
30. Consideration need not be adequate
   (*a*) True (*b*) False
   (*c*) Cant say (*d*) All of the above.
31. Consideration may also mean:
   (*a*) Turnover of the business (*b*) Price of the transaction
   (*c*) Price paid for an obligation (*d*) Consent of the parties.
32. Consideration is therefore the evidence of
   (*a*) Mutual obligations (*b*) Promisor obligation
   (*c*) Promisee obligation (*d*) Third party obligation.
33. Consideration made at the desire of the third party is:
   (*a*) Valid (*b*) Invalid
   (*c*) Void (*d*) Voidable.
34. Consideration moving from a third party is:
   (*a*) Perfectly void (*b*) Perfectly valid
   (*c*) Perfectly voidable (*d*) Voidable at the option of parties.
35. Which of the following doesn't require consideration:
   (*a*) Agreement made between parties out of natural love
   (*b*) Agreement made by the government
   (*c*) Agreement made by the government on behalf of departments
   (*d*) Agreement made by the citizens of India.
36. A promise without consideration is not
   (*a*) Agreement (*b*) Contract
   (*c*) Proposal (*d*) Legally enforceable.
37. Proposal or acceptance is made otherwise than in words, the promise is said to be
   (*a*) Implied (*b*) Explicit
   (*c*) Implicit (*d*) Tacit.
38. If there is a fiduciary relationship between Mr. A and B and Mr. A is paying very high rate of interest to Mr. B, then this is the classic example for:
   (*a*) Undue Influence (*b*) Misrepresentation
   (*c*) Mistake (*d*) Coercion.
39. If a person is in a position to dominate the will of the other to obtain the unfair advantage of the other is,
   (*a*) Mistake (*b*) Misrepresentation
   (*c*) Coercion (*d*) Undue Influence.

40. An insurance agent concealing the terms and conditions of life insurance is a matter of:

(*a*) Fraud as he conceals the matter
(*b*) Not a Fraud
(*c*) Misrepresentation
(*d*) Undue influence.

41. A person making the statement believes it to be true which might later turn out to be untrue is known as:

(*a*) Misrepresentation
(*b*) Mistake
(*c*) Fraud
(*d*) Coercion.

42. If a guarantee is obtained by misrepresentation then the contract becomes:

(*a*) Valid at the option of the parties
(*b*) Invalid
(*c*) Valid by the nature of agreement
(*d*) Voidable.

43. Coercion, Fraud, Misrepresentation, Undue Influence and Mistake are covered under :

(*a*) Consideration
(*b*) Essential elements of a contract
(*c*) Free Consent.
(*d*) Quasi Contract.

44. If both the parties are under a mistake as to a matter of fact which is essential to the contract is:

(*a*) Void
(*b*) Voidable
(*c*) Valid
(*d*) Invalid.

45. The consideration is said to be void, only when

(*a*) When both the persons are not happy with the contract
(*b*) Unlawful
(*c*) The value assigned for a thing is higher than its actual value
(*d*) The government bans it.

46. A and B are partners in a firm. They agree to defraud the government department by submitting a tender in their individual names and not in the name of the Firm. The above is an example of:

(*a*) Legal activity
(*b*) Illegal activities
(*c*) Voidable activity
(*d*) Void activity.

47. A jeweller sells the ornaments imported from another country along with that of the one which are smuggled. Then the agreement will be :

(*a*) Valid only for the imported ornaments
(*b*) Valid for the whole ornaments imported
(*c*) Void for both the imported and smuggled ornaments
(*d*) Void for the imported ornaments.

48. If the agreement entered is not of specific nature, then the contract would be:

(*a*) Voidable
(*b*) Valid
(*c*) Void
(*d*) Invalid.

49. Betting or gambling is a type of:

(*a*) Speculation
(*b*) Wagering agreement
(*c*) Wagering and speculation both
(*d*) None of the above.

50. Wagering contract is ______________:

(*a*) Void ab initio (*b*) Not enforceable in a court of law

(*c*) Can be enforced in a court of law (*d*) Both A and B.

51. Payment of certain sum of money for an uncertain event is called

(*a*) Wagering (*b*) Investment

(*c*) Speculation (*d*) Speculative investment.

52. Primary tenet in a contract means:

(*a*) The two parties of the contract must perform their part of the promise

(*b*) The parties enter into a contract with an intention of creating a legal relationship

(*c*) One who occupies the house of the owner

(*d*) None of the above.

53. Who is bound to perform the contract (promise) if all the joint promisors die?

(*a*) The persons who are made as liable

(*b*) The persons who act as third party to the contract

(*c*) Legal representatives of all joint promisors

(*d*) None of the above.

54. In the event of death of joint promisors, the legal representatives ________ the promise made by the deceased promisor.

(*a*) Fulfill

(*b*) Need not fulfill

(*c*) It is left to the option of the other joint promisors

(*d*) None of the above.

55. A, B and C jointly borrows ₹ 10000 from X, A being majority shareholder of the company, from whom can X recover the amount?

(*a*) Either A (*b*) Either B

(*c*) Either C (*d*) A, B and C jointly.

56. Joint and several liability does apply to:

(*a*) Joint parties of the contract (*b*) Legal heirs

(*c*) One of the parties among the contract (*d*) Assignment.

57. Joint and several liability does not apply to

(*a*) Legal hiers (*b*) Assignment

(*c*) Joint parties (*d*) Promisee or promisor.

58. The difference between assignment and succession is

(*a*) Only benefit and risk follows benefit (*b*) Only benefit

(*c*) Only risk (*d*) Both benefit and risk.

59. When Ram sells 500 quintals of rice at ₹ 100 per quintal to Shyam, and Shyam promises to pay ₹ 50000 on the delivery of goods. This kind of promise is known as

(*a*) Reciprocal promise (*b*) Implied promise

(*c*) Actual promise (*d*) Alternative promise.

60. In case of reciprocal promise, if one party prevents the other from performing his promise, the contract becomes __________ at the option of the other party.

(*a*) Valid (*b*) Void

(*c*) Invalid (*d*) Voidable.

61. An agreement to do an act impossible in itself is known as

(*a*) Void (*b*) Voidable

(*c*) Invalid (*d*) Valid.

62. Company A enters into a contract with its distributors to manufacture and distribute distillery but the law subsequently changed and banned it. Then, the contract becomes.

(*a*) Valid as the contract was entered before the ban on liquor

(*b*) Exception to the law

(*c*) Void

(*d*) Voidable.

63. In India, "Doctrine of frustration" is known as

(*a*) Supervening impossibility

(*b*) When a person becomes depressed

(*c*) When the Court cannot interfere between the parties

(*d*) None of the above.

64. If the contract is substituted by a new contract, then it is known as

(*a*) Novatio (*b*) Substituted law

(*c*) Modified law (*d*) Alternative law.

65. In an attempted performance the __________ offers to perform his part but __________ refuses to accept his part.

(*a*) Promisor, Promisee (*b*) Promisee, Promisor

(*c*) Owner, Tenent (*d*) Manufacturer, Consumer.

66. The contract is discharged by operation of law only when

(*a*) There is a war declared

(*b*) When a war is declared between the countries where the promisor and promise reside

(*c*) Both A and B

(*d*) None of the above.

67. The contract is discharged by operation of law only when

(*a*) The Promisor dies (*b*) Becomes insolvent

(*c*) Both A and B (*d*) None of the above.

68. Performance which form the consideration for each other are called as

(*a*) Mutual promise (*b*) Reciprocal promise

(*c*) Incidental promise (*d*) Anticipated promise.

69. Mutual promise is also called as

(*a*) Implied promise (*b*) Actual promise

(*c*) Reciprocal promise (*d*) Anticipated promise.

70. If the Promisor refuses to perform his obligation before the specified time, then it is called:
   (a) Actual breach (b) Anticipatory breach
   (c) Both a and b (d) None of the above.

71. If the Promisor refuses to perform his obligation on the due date, then it is said to be;
   (a) Actual breach (b) Anticipatory breach
   (c) None of the above (d) No breach as the promise is fulfilled.

72. The compensation for breach of contract are:
   (a) Compensation not applicable (b) Penalty
   (c) Liquidated damage and penalty (d) Liquidated damages.

73. Liquidated damages are recognized as:
   (a) Compensation (b) Punishment
   (c) Penalty (d) Price paid.

74. Quantum meruit means:
   (a) Promise fulfilled (b) Promise unfulfilled
   (c) Work done in full (d) As per the quantum of work done.

75. Liquidated damages are reassessed amount of loss based on __________.
   (a) Probable loss sustained and as per the circumstances
   (b) Probable profit earned and as per the circumstances
   (c) Profit earned by the person from the contract
   (d) Turnover.

76. Special damages can be claimed only:
   (a) For special contracts (b) As previously notified in the contract
   (c) For special products / services (d) For special people.

77. "A contracts to pay B ₹ 10,000 if B's house is burnt" is an example of:
   (a) Contingent contract (b) Wagering contract
   (c) Implied contract (d) Explicit contract.

78. Which contract can be enforced if the happening of the event becomes impossible.
   (a) Void (b) Valid
   (c) Voidable (d) Invalid.

79. In contingent contract the event is:
   (a) Contingent (b) Void
   (c) Voidable (d) Collateral.

80. A contingent contract is________, whereas the wagering contract is void.
   (a) Void (b) Invalid
   (c) Valid (d) Voidable.

81. Certain specific obligation to be performed by certain persons. This is known as:
   (a) Quasi contract (b) Illegal contract
   (c) Express contract (d) Unilateral contract.

82. General Insurance is a kind of:
(*a*) Wagering contract (*b*) Speculation contract
(*c*) Implied contract (*d*) Contingent contract.

83. Quasi contract is also known as
(*a*) Implied in law contract (*b*) Contingent contract
(*c*) Quasi contract (*d*) Implicit contract.

84. Quasi contract is a __________ for formed to impose equity between two parties.
(*a*) Legal substitute (*b*) Compensation
(*c*) Penalty (*d*) Both B and C.

85. Supply of necessaries is a type of
(*a*) Quasi contract (*b*) Mandatory supplies
(*c*) Legal contract (*d*) Essential supplies contract.

86. An agreement by a minor is absolutely
(*a*) Void (*b*) Void ab initio
(*c*) Invalid (*d*) Valid by court.

87. Rule of estoppels does not apply to
(*a*) Persons of Indian origin
(*b*) NRIs Non Resident of India
(*c*) Minor
(*d*) Person who are competent to contract.

88. One person dominates the willingness of the other is called
(*a*) Fraud (*b*) Coercion
(*c*) Misrepresentation (*d*) Undue influence.

89. Discharge of contract done by deliberate abandonment of a right is called
(*a*) Discharge by novatio (*b*) Discharge by waiver
(*c*) Discharge by alteration (*d*) Discharge by rescission.

90. A contract to do an act, which, after the contract is made, becomes impossible or unlawful is known as
(*a*) Subsequent impossibility
(*b*) Impossible act
(*c*) Impossibility at the time of contract
(*d*) Valid contract.

91. Where an inferior right contract merges into a superior right contract, the former stands discharged automatically, the contract is discharged by
(*a*) Operation of law material alteration
(*b*) Operation of law by merger
(*c*) Operation of law by death
(*d*) Operation of law by insolvency.

ANSWERS

1. (*c*)	**2.** (*b*)	**3.** (*c*)	**4.** (*d*)
5. (*a*)	**6.** (*d*)	**7.** (*c*)	**8.** (*c*)
9. (*d*)	**10.** (*c*)	**11.** (*a*)	**12.** (*d*)
13. (*a*)	**14.** (*d*)	**15.** (*c*)	**16.** (*a*)
17. (*b*)	**18.** (*b*)	**19.** (*a*)	**20.** (*a*)
21. (*d*)	**22.** (*a*)	**23.** (*a*)	**24.** (*a*)
25. (*a*)	**26.** (*c*)	**27.** (*b*)	**28.** (*c*)
29. (*b*)	**30.** (*a*)	**31.** (*c*)	**32.** (*a*)
33. (*b*)	**34.** (*b*)	**35.** (*a*)	**36.** (*a*)
37. (*a*)	**38.** (*a*)	**39.** (*d*)	**40.** (*b*)
41. (*a*)	**42.** (*b*)	**43.** (*c*)	**44.** (*a*)
45. (*b*)	**46.** (*b*)	**47.** (*a*)	**48.** (*a*)
49. (*b*)	**50.** (*d*)	**51.** (*a*)	**52.** (*b*)
53. (*c*)	**54.** (*a*)	**55.** (*d*)	**56.** (*b*)
57. (*b*)	**58.** (*a*)	**59.** (*a*)	**60.** (*d*)
61. (*a*)	**62.** (*c*)	**63.** (*a*)	**64.** (*a*)
65. (*a*)	**66.** (*b*)	**67.** (*c*)	**68.** (*a*)
69. (*c*)	**70.** (*b*)	**71.** (*a*)	**72.** (*c*)
73. (*a*)	**74.** (*d*)	**75.** (*a*)	**76.** (*b*)
77. (*a*)	**78.** (*a*)	**79.** (*d*)	**80.** (*c*)
81. (*a*)	**82.** (*d*)	**83.** (*a*)	**84.** (*a*)
85. (*a*)	**86.** (*a*)	**87.** (*c*)	**88.** (*d*)
89. (*b*)	**90.** (*a*)	**91.** (*b*)	

3

The Sale of Goods Act, 1930

3.1 INTRODUCTION TO THE SALE OF GOODS ACT, 1930

The Sale of Goods is the most common of all commercial transactions. A knowledge of the main principles is of this Act is of utmost importance to all concerned. The law relating to the Sale of Goods is contained in the Sale of Goods Act 1930. Prior to this Act, the law of Sale of Goods was contained in Chapter VII of the Indian Contract Act, 1872. The Act covers topics such as the concept of sale of goods, delivery of goods and passing of ownership. The Act also covers the field of documents of title to goods and the transfer of ownership on the basis of the transactions and documents, between the buyer and the seller, warranties and conditions arising out of sale and other obligations of the buyer and the seller.

(A) Scheme of the Act

The Act came into force on the 1st of July , 1930 and extends to the whole of India, except the State of Jammu and Kashmir. It is to be noted that the sections quoted in this chapter refer to the Sale of Goods Act, 1930, unless otherwise stated. The Sale of Goods Act, recognises freedom of contract, similar to the Indian Contract Act 1872 , and the parties are free to make their terms and conditions.

(B) Definition

0 of the Act defines the term 'goods' as *'goods means every kind of movable property other than actionable claims and money; and includes stock and shares, growing crops, grass, and things attached to or forming part of the land which are agreed to be severed before sale or under the contract of sale.'*

Under Section 4(1) of the Sale of Goods Act, 1930, defines a Contract of Sale as follows: *'A contract of sale of goods is a contract whereby the seller transfers or agrees to transfer the property in goods to the buyer for a price.'*

3.2 MEANING OF THE TERM 'GOODS'

Section 2(7) of the Act has defined the term 'goods' as *'Goods means every kind of movable property other than actionable claims and money; and includes stock and shares, growing crops, grass and things attached to or forming part of the land which are agreed to be severed before sale or under the contract of sale.'* The term 'Goods' also include, goodwill, patents, trademarks, copyrights, cooking gas, water, electricity. However, according to the English Law, stocks and shares are not goods, but under the Indian Law, they are considered as goods. The sale of immovable property is dealt with in the Transfer of Property Act 1882.

In the case of grass which forms part of the land, the grass has to be separated, severed or detached from the land to constitute it as goods. Similarly in the case of trees sold, in Kursell Vs. Timber Operators & Contractors Ltd., it was held that there was a contract of sale of movable property or goods. However, contracts for the sale of things forming part of the land itself are not contracts for sale of goods.

Illustration: *A contract for the sale of coalmine or building stone quarry is not a contract of Sale of Goods.*

According to Section 3 of the Transfer of Property Act, 1882, "immovable property" does not include standing timber, growing crops or grass. These things therefore are movable property and thus goods. Standing timber has to be distinguished from trees, the former being movable and the latter being immovable property.

(A) Water, Electricity and Cooking Gas (Constitute Goods)

While defining goods, the Sale of Goods Act does not make any mention about water, electricity and gas. This matter attracted the attention of the Law Commission of India and it has stated in its report on the Sale of Goods Act that: "In view of the fact that contracts with regard to the supply of electrical energy, and water are common, we think that the matter should be placed beyond doubt and amendment should be made in Section 2(7) so as to include power in the shape of electrical energy water and gas within the definition of "goods". Consequent on the recommendations of the Law Commission some amendments were made in the Sales of Goods Act in1963

Illustration: *In The Commissioner of Sales Tax, Madhya Pradesh Vs. Madhya Pradesh Electricity Board, the Supreme Court has held that although electric energy is not tangible or cannot be retouched like a piece of wood or book, it is still "goods" as it can be transmitted, transferred, delivered, stored, possessed in the same way as any other movable property.*

(B) Does Actionable Claims and Money Constitute Goods

Actionable Claims means claims which can be enforced by a legal action or a suit, example, a book debt. A book debt is not goods because it can only be assigned as per Transfer of Property Act but cannot be sold. Same is case with a bill of exchange, promissory note, etc. Negotiable Instruments like promissory note can be transferred under Negotiable Instruments Act by mere delivery or, endorsement and delivery. Such instruments cannot be sold.

The Transfer of Property Act defines actionable claim as under: an 'actionable claim' means a claim to any debt, other than a debt secured by mortgage of immovable property or by hypothecation or pledge of movable property, or to any beneficial interest in movable property not in the possession, either actual or constructive, of the claimant, which the Civil Courts recognize as affording grounds for relief, whether such debt or beneficial interest be existent, accruing, conditional or contingent. An actionable claim therefore means either:

- Any unsecured debt, or
- Any beneficial interest in movable property, not in the possession of the claimant.

'Money' means current money. It is not regarded as goods because it is the medium of exchange through which goods can be bought. Money means the recognized currency in circulation and for obvious reasons it is not the subject matter of Sale of Goods. Money constitutes consideration for the sale of goods, rather than itself being Goods. Old and rare coins however, are goods, and they can be sold or purchased as such. The special feature of a contract of sale is:

1. Contract of sale of goods is in every case a contract of sale of movable property.
2. The consideration for the contract of sale in every case is money paid or agreed to be paid as a price.

(C) Classification of Goods

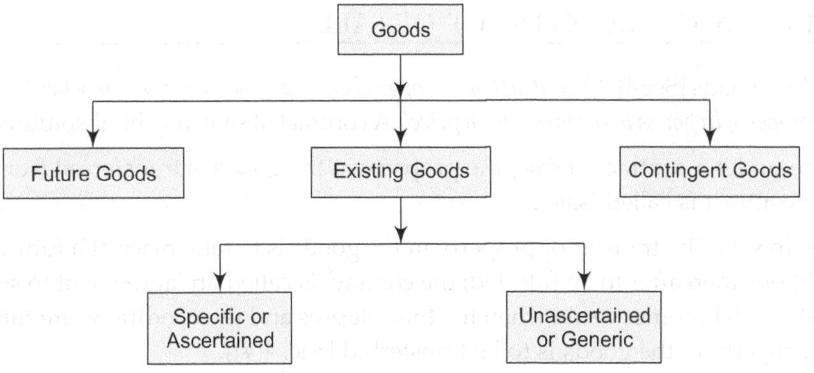

Section 6 of the Sale of Goods Act classifies goods into (a) Future goods (b) Existing goods and (c) Contingent goods.

1. **Future goods:** Future goods are those goods that do not exist at the time of the contract of sale and it is yet to be acquired or manufactured by the seller. According to the Act, Future Goods are *'goods to be manufactured or produced or acquired by the seller after the making of the contract of sale.'* However, it should be noted that a present sale of Future Goods operates only as an agreement to sell but does not amount to a sale.
2. **Existing goods:** Existing goods are those that are owned or possessed by the seller at the time of sale. The Existing Goods may be:
   (*a*) *Specific goods*: These are goods which are identified and agreed upon at the time a contract of sale is made. Sec 2(14).

   Ascertained goods: Though commonly used as similar in meaning to specific goods, these are goods which become ascertained subsequent to the formation of a contract of sale.

   Illustration: *When A enters an electronic shop to purchase a Sony TV set, it is ascertained goods and when he chooses one TV set from a range of Sony TV sets, it becomes specific goods.*

   (*b*) *Unascertained goods*: These are goods which are not identified and agreed upon at the time of the contract of sale. They are defined only by description. It may form part of a lot.

   Illustration: *When goods are not specified from an assembly of goods, such goods are called unascertained goods.*

3. **Contingent goods:** When the acquisition of good depends upon a contingency or an event which may or may not happen, are known as contingency goods.

Illustration: *A agrees to sell specific goods in a particular ship to be delivered on the arrival of the ship. If the ship arrives but with no such goods on board, the seller is not liable for the contract. A is however liable to deliver the goods only when the ship arrives with the goods.*

(D) Document of Title to Goods

Section 2(4) of the Sale of Goods Act recognises the following as documents of title to goods; bill of lading, dock warrant, ware-housekeeper's certificate, wharf certificate, railway receipt, warrant or order for the delivery of goods and any other document used in the ordinary course of business. A document of title to goods may be described as any document used as proof of the possession or control of goods, authorising or purporting to authorise, either by endorsement or by delivery, the possessor of the document to transfer or receive goods thereby represented.

3.3 FORMATION OF A CONTRACT OF SALE

Contract of sale of goods [Sec 4]: *'A contract of sale of goods is a contract whereby the seller transfers or agrees to transfer the property in goods to the buyer for a price'*. A contract of sale may be absolute or conditional.

Sale: Where under a contract of sale, the property in the goods is transferred from the seller to the buyer, the contract is called 'sale'.

Agreement to sell: The transfer of property in the goods is to take place at a future time subject to some conditions thereafter to be fulfilled; the contract is called an 'agreement to sell'. [Sec 4(3)]. An agreement to sell becomes a sale when the time elapses and the conditions are fulfilled, subject to which the property in the goods is to be transferred [Sec. 4(4)].

Illustrations: *(1) X agrees to buy A's car for ₹ 5 Lakhs, only if Q, an automobile engineer approves of the car. This is an agreement to sell for A and an agreement to buy for X.*

(2) A agrees to buy a refrigerator belonging to B in two monthly instalments, the ownership to pass to A after the payment of the second instalment. This is an agreement to sell.

Property: Property means the right of ownership. When we say that the property in goods has passed from the seller to the buyer, it means that the seller ceases to be, and the buyer becomes the owner of the goods.

(A) Essentials of a Contract of Sale

1. *There must be at least two parties (Bilateral contract):* Section 5(1) of the Sale of Goods Act states that *'A contract of sale is made by an offer to buy or sell goods for a price and the acceptance of such offer.'* A contract of sale is much similar to the formation of a valid contract (refer requisites of the elements of a contract). There must be two distinct parties, *i.e.*, a buyer and a seller, to affect a contract of sale and they must be competent to contract. The seller means a person who sells or agrees to sell and the buyer means a person who buys or agrees to buy the goods. The seller and the buyer should be two different persons; if a person purchases his own goods, it is no sale. A sale has to be bilateral because the property in goods has to pass from the seller to the buyer. However, a part-owner may sell to another part-owner.

However, there may be a contract or sale between one part owner and another, which means, that a partner may sell his goods to the firm in which he is partner and the firm may also sell goods to a partner. In the same way, when a person's goods are being sold in execution of a decree, he himself may purchase them. In the case of sale by auction, the Sale of Goods Act permits a seller of goods to reserve a right to himself of making a bid at the auction and purchasing his own goods. Although the general rule is that a person cannot buy his own goods, there is an exemption where a person's gods are sold in execution of a decree by the court, he himself may participate in the auction and buy them.

Illustration: *In, the State of Gujarat Vs.Raman Lal and Co,(1965), a partnership firm was dissolved and the surplus assets, including the stock in trade, were divided among the partners in the same proportion. The sales –tax officials sought to tax this transaction. Held, this transaction did not amount to a sale as the partners themselves were the joint owners of the goods and they could not be both sellers and buyers. Secondly, no money consideration was promised or paid by any partner to the firm as consideration for the goods allotted to them.*

2. *The subject matter of the contract must necessarily be goods:* There must be some goods, the property in which is or is to be transferred from the seller to the buyer. The goods which form the subject matter of the contract of sale must be movable. Transfer of immovable property is not regulated by the Sale of Goods Act 1930.

   Illustration: *In, The Associated Hotels of India Vs. Excise & Taxation Officer, a Hotel company provided residence and food, making a consolidated charge for both the services. No rebate was allowed if food was not taken by the customers. Held, supply of food was not sale of goods but simply a service and did not involve any sale of food.*

3. *The consideration in a contract of sale should be Price.* The consideration for the contract of sale, called price, must be money (legal tender money). When goods are exchanged for goods, it is not a sale but barter. However, it may be partly in money and partly in goods. Such a contract of sale is called part-exchange contracts. The Act is not applicable where the buyer has to perform some act in order to purchase the goods. If there is no price for the exchange of ownership of the goods, it amounts to gift and not a contract of sale. Price includes cash, cheque, credit card, debit card, demand draft, etc.

   Illustrations: *(1) In Aldridge Vs. Johnson (1857), a contract for the sale of 52 bullocks valued at £6 each against 100 quarters of barley valued at £2 per quarter, the difference to be paid in cash, was treated as sale of goods.*

   (2) 500 shirts , valued at ₹ 120 each were exchanged for 20 bags containing 50 kilos of basmathi rice, each at ₹50 per kilo, the difference to be made up in cash. This is a contract of sale.

4. *Transfer of general property:* There must be a transfer of general property as distinguished from special property in goods from the seller to the buyer. Property means ownership. A mere transfer of possession of the goods cannot be termed as sale. To constitute a contract of sale the seller must either transfer or agree to transfer the property in the goods to the buyer. The expression 'transfer of property' refers to transfer of ownership of the goods from the seller to the buyer.

   According to the definition in the Act, *'property' means general property in the goods rather than mere 'special property'*. The term general property means ownership and special property means only some of the rights, *e.g.*, the rights of possession and use. Therefore, property in the goods is different from possession. If, under a contract the ownership in the goods is transferred from one person to another, it may be a contract of sale, but when mere right of possession is transferred the transaction may be by way of hire or pledge. Therefore a contract of sale of goods is a contract whereby the seller either transfers the property (ownership) or agrees to transfer the property in the goods to the buyer and this forms the essence of the contract.

Illustrations: *(1) If A owns certain goods, he has general property in the goods. If he pledges them with B, then B has special property in the goods.*

(2) In United India Ins. Co. Vs. O. Jameela Beevi, there was sale of a motor vehicle (jeep). The price stipulated in the agreement was ₹10,000 out of which ₹2,000 had been paid by the buyer immediately and the document containing the agreement of sale stipulated registration in the name of the buyer, after the advance of ₹ 8,000 was paid. It was also agreed that: (a) until the entire price is paid the ownership in the vehicle shall not pass to the buyer and (b) the seller was to execute the requisite papers after the payment of the balance of the price. However before the conditions were fulfilled, the vehicle met with an accident and the question arose as to who was the true owner of the vehicle for the purpose of liability of the insurance company. It was held that since the requisite conditions necessary for the transfer of property had not yet been fulfilled, the seller was still the owner of the vehicle at the time of the accident.

The rights and obligations between the seller and the buyer is dependent on the transfer of property and the time of transfer of ownership is of paramount importance with regard to :

(I) As soon as the property in the goods passes to the buyer, risk also follows. The buyer thereafter becomes responsible for the loss or destruction of the goods if the property is transferred, even though the possession is not transferred.

(II) When the ownership in goods gets transferred to the buyer, the seller gets the right to sue the buyer for the price.

(III) A third party can be sued for damage or destruction of the goods only after ascertaining transfer of property.

(IV) The buyer has the right to re-sell the goods to any other person only after the ownership in the property has passed to him.

(V) Mere transfer of property does not give the buyer a right of possession unless delivery and payment, which are concurrent conditions, are agreed upon.

(VI) Though property is transferred, sale by a non-owner in possession of the goods confers a good title to a third party who receives in good faith and without notice of the earlier sale.

(VII) The right of the Official Receiver to take over the goods in the event of insolvency of either the buyer or seller depends upon whether property in the goods is transferred.

Illustrations: *(1) In Rugg Vs Minett (1809), the contract was for the sale of 24 lots of turpentine to be filled into casks and then delivered to the buyer. Some casks were filled in the presence of the buyer. Even before the remaining casks could be filled, and the casks filled with the oil could be delivered, a fire broke out and the entire quantity of oil was destroyed. When the question, who should bear the loss and in whom property vested arose, it was held that the buyer should bear the loss with respect to the casks already filled in and the loss in respect of the oil not filled in, the loss should be borne by the seller.*

(2) In Elphick Vs. Barnes (1880), a horse was delivered to be tried for eight days, and to be returned , if the buyer did not like it. The horse died within the period stipulated without the defendant's fault. In a suit by the plaintiff for the price of the horse, it was held that he could not recover the price since the property in the horse still vested with him.

5. *Essential elements of a valid contract:* All the essential elements of a valid contract must be present in the contract of sale. A contract of sale is specie of contract and therefore a contract of sale must conform to all the essential elements of a valid contract.

(B) Sale and an Agreement to Sell

A sale is an executed contract. Under a contract of sale, the goods are considered to be sold only when the ownership is transferred from the seller to the buyer. The definition of a contract of sale, under Section 4(1) of the Sale of Goods Act 1930, includes a Sale as well as an Agreement to Sell. Section 4(3) states '*Where under a contract of sale, the property in the goods is transferred from the seller to the buyer, the contract is called a sale, but where the transfer of the property in the goods is to take place at a future time or subject to some condition thereafter to be fulfilled, the contract is called an agreement to sell.*' In a sale there is immediate transfer of property and it is an executed contract. Whereas in case of an agreement to sell, the transfer of property takes place at a future time or subject to some condition thereafter to be fulfilled and it is an executory contract.

Illustration: *Girish sells his Yamaha Motorbike to Suresh for ₹30,000. If all the essential elements of a valid contract are present, this contract become a valid contract of sale and the ownership of the motorbike stands transferred from Girish to Suresh.*

If Suresh offers to pay the price after a week of taking possession of the Yamaha Motorbike, or in case Girish postpones the delivery of the Motorbike after receiving the price, it is considered as a contract of sale and the ownership is transferred .

1. *Transfer of property:* In a Sale, the property in the goods passes from the seller to the buyer immediately. In an Agreement to Sell, the transfer of property in goods is to take place at a later stage or future time. The ownership does not pass to the buyer at the time of the contract so that the seller continues to be the owner until the agreement to sell becomes an actual sale by the expiry of a certain time or the fulfilment of some condition.
2. *Type of Contract:* A Sale is an executed contract while an Agreement to Sell is an executory contract.
3. *Type of goods:* A Sale can only be in case of existing and specific goods only. An Agreement to Sell is mostly in case of future and contingent goods. It may also (in some cases) refer to unascertained existing goods.
4. *Risk of loss:* In a Sale, if the goods are destroyed, the loss falls on the buyer even though the goods are in the possession of the seller. In an Agreement to Sell, if the goods are destroyed, the loss falls on the seller, even though the goods are in the possession of the buyer. The general rule of the law is that unless otherwise agreed upon , the risk of loss prima facie passes with property. Therefore, in the case of Sale, if the goods are destroyed, the loss falls on the buyer even though the goods may never have come into his hand. Whereas in an Agreement to Sell, where the ownership in the goods is yet to pass from the seller to the buyer, such loss has to be borne by the seller even though the goods are in the possession of the buyer.
5. *Consequences of breach:* In a Sale, if the buyer fails to pay the price of the goods, the seller can sue for the price even though the goods are still in his possession. In an Agreement to Sell, the seller can only sue for damages and not for the price even though the goods are in the possession of the buyer.
6. *Right to re-sell:* In a Sale, the seller cannot re-sell the goods except the sale by an unpaid seller under Sec 54. In case of an Agreement to Sell, the original buyer can only sue the seller for damages. In a contract of Sale , the seller cannot resell the goods except in certain cases. But in the case of an Agreement to Sell, especially in the case of resale, the buyer who buys the goods for consideration and without notice of the prior Agreement gets a good title. Further, goods forming the subject matter of an Agreement to Sell can also be attached in execution of a decree of the court against the seller.

7. *General and particular property:* A Sale is a contract plus conveyance, and creates *'jus in rem' i.e.,* gives right to the buyer to enjoy the goods as against the world at large including the seller. An Agreement to Sell is only a contract, pure and simple, and creates *'jus in personam' i.e.,* gives a right to the buyer against the seller to sue for damages.
8. *Insolvency of buyer:* In a contract of Sale, if the buyer becomes an insolvent before he pays for the goods, the seller , in the absence of a lien over the goods, must return them to the official receiver or assignee. He can only claim a rateable dividend for the price of the goods. In an Agreement to Sell, if the buyer becomes insolvent and has not yet paid the price, the seller is not bound to part with the goods until he is paid for the goods.
9. *Insolvency of the Seller when the buyer has already paid the price:* In a Sale, if the seller becomes an insolvent, the buyer, being the owner , is entitled to recover the goods from the official receiver or assignee as the goods rests with the buyer. In an Agreement to Sell, if the buyer, who has paid the price, finds that the seller has become insolvent, he (buyer) can only claim a rateable dividend and not the goods because property in them has not yet passed to him.

Illustration: *On the 14th of June, Raju agrees to sell his car to Reena on the 24th of June, for a sum of ₹ 2 Lakhs. This is an agreement to sell, as Raju agrees to transfer ownership of the car to Reena at a future date.*

(C) Distinction between Sale and Hire Purchase Agreement

Sale	Hire-Purchase Agreement
Ownership is transferred from the seller to the buyer as soon as the contract is entered into	Ownership is transferred from the seller to the hire-purchaser only when a certain agreed number of instalments is paid.
The position of the buyer is that of the owner	The position of the hire-purchaser is that of the bailee
The buyer cannot terminate the contract and as such is bound to pay the price of the goods.	The hire purchaser has an option to terminate the contract at any stage and cannot be forced to pay further instalments.
If the payment is made by the buyer in instalments, the amount payable by the buyer to the seller is reduced, for the payment made by the buyer is towards the price of the goods.	The instalments paid by the hire purchaser are regarded as hire charges and not as payment towards the price of the goods till option to purchase the goods is exercised.

(D) Sale and Bailment

1. In a Sale, the property in goods is transferred from the seller to the buyer. In a Bailment, there is only transfer of possession from the bailor to the bailee. The objects may be for safe custody, personal use carriage from one place to another, etc.
2. In a Sale, the buyer can deal with the goods in any way he likes. The bailee can deal with the goods according to the directions of the bailor.
3. In Sale the reason of transfer of ownership is sale itself, while in Bailment, it may either by for safe custody, use or carriage from one place to another.
4. The consideration in Sale is always in terms of money, but in Bailment, it is not necessary as it may be the understanding to return of goods bailed on the accomplishment of a purpose.

5. In a Contract of Sale, there is no return of goods from the buyer to the seller unless there is a breach between the parties on the terms of sale, etc. In Bailment, the goods are necessarily to be returned after a specified time or accomplishment of the purpose.
6. In a Contract of Sale, any profit accrued in goods sold is the property of the buyer, while in case of Bailment, such accrual is to be returned by the bailee to the bailor.
7. If the goods sold is lost or damaged, the loss or damage so caused is to be borne by the buyer (if ownership is transferred to the buyer). However in the case of Bailment, the bailee will have to bear the cost if he is guilty of negligence and carelessness in taking care of the goods bailed.
8. In a Contract of Sale, there is no charge to be paid by the seller to the buyer. But in the case of Bailment, the bailer has to pay the charges which the bailee has incurred in keeping the goods in safe condition or for maintenance of the goods bailed.

(E) Sale and Mortgage

1. In a Contract of Sale, ownership of goods as a whole is transferred from the seller to the buyer; but in the case of Mortgage, only the possession is transferred and ownership transfer is limited to the payment of interest on the amount loaned.
2. In the case of Sale, the buyer becomes the absolute owner of goods, whereas in the case of Mortgage, ownership remains with the mortgagor.
3. In a Contract of Sale, the consideration is the price while in Mortgage, it is the surety for an advance of loan along with interest.

(F) Sale and Contract for Work and Materials

A Contract of Sale contemplates the delivery of goods whereas a Contract for Work and Materials, involves exercise of skill and labour by one party in respect of materials supplied by another, the delivery of goods being only subsidiary or incidental.

Illustrations: *(1) In Lee Vs. Griffin, (1861), a dentist agreed to supply two sets of artificial teeth for a (deceased) lady, of whom the defendant was the successor. The denture was made from the materials of the plaintiff. In an action by the plaintiff to recover £21, it was held that the contract was one for the sale of goods.*

(2) In Myers & Co. Vs. Brent Cross Service Co. A contract involved the repair of a car and the supply of parts for that purpose. Held, it was a contract for work and materials.

(3) In Clay Vs. Yates (1856), the plaintiff, a printer, contracted to print for the defendant, a second edition of the book, making use of his own materials. The contract was held to be one of work and labour.

(G) Effect of Destruction of Goods

According to Section 7 of the Act, *'Where there is a contract for the sale of specific goods, the contract is void if the goods without the knowledge of the seller have, at the time when the contract was made perished or become so damaged as no longer to answer to their description in the contract.'*

1. Goods perishing before making of contract [Sec 7]: A contract for the sale of specific goods is void if at the time when the contract was made, the goods have, without the knowledge of the seller, perished. This rule is based on the ground of mutual mistake of impossibility of performance.

Illustration: *A agrees to sell his motorbike to B who informs A that he is buying the motorbike to ride to Bangalore immediately. The motorbike is not in good condition at the time of the agreement. Both A and B are ignorant of this fact. The agreement is void.*

The contract is also void in the case of indivisible lot of specific goods if only a part of the goods has perished at the time when the contract was made. However, this Section is not applicable to unascertained goods. Therefore if the contract is for the sale of unascertained goods, the perishing of the same does not render the contract void. The seller is bound to procure the goods and supply the same. Secondly, if the seller has to obtain from the producer or manufacturer the goods which are not ascertained, and the manufacturer makes default in supplying the goods, the seller cannot plead excuse for non-performance due to the default by the manufacturer or producer.

Illustrations: *(1) In Barrow, Lane and Ballard Ltd. Vs. Phillip Phillios & Co. (1929), there was a contract for the sale of 700 bags of Chinese groundnuts stored in a warehouse. Subsequently it was discovered that at the time of the contract 109 bags had been stolen. The seller delivered the remaining bags and the buyer refused to take delivery. In an action by the seller for the price, it was held that the contract was indivisible for 700 bags and hence, the buyer was not bound to accept the remaining bags.*

(2) A sold to B 500 bags of special Basmathi rice, identified by a certain brand mark and lying in a particular warehouse. Unknown to A, 65 bags had been stolen at the time of the sale. A tendered delivery of only 435 bags. Held, the sale was void and B could not be compelled to take the remainder.

2. Goods perishing after the agreement to sell but before the sale is effected [Sec 8]: According to this section '*Where there is an agreement to sell specific goods, and subsequently the goods, without any fault on the part of the seller or buyer, perish or become so damaged as no longer to answer their description in the agreement before the risk passes to the buyer, the agreement is thereby avoided.*'

An agreement to sell specific goods becomes void if subsequently the goods, without any fault on the part of the seller or buyer, perish or become so damaged as no longer to answer to the description in the agreement before the risk passes to the buyer. Fault means wrongful act or default. This rule is based on the ground of impossibility of performance. Again this Section has no application to unascertained goods.

Illustrations: *(1) In Howell Vs. Coupland, A agrees to sell to B 10 bales of Egyptian cotton out of 100 bales lying in his godown. The godown had been destroyed by fire at the time of the contract. Both A and B are unaware of this fact. The contract is not void as the sale here is not of specific goods, but of a certain quantity of unascertained goods. A must supply 10 bales of cotton or pay damages for the breach.*

(2) In Elphick Vs. Barnes (1880), there was an agreement to buy a horse on the condition that the price would be paid after a week's trial. The horse died on the third day without the fault of either of the parties. It was held that the contract to buy the horse and to pay the price had been averted because the property had not passed and the horse died after the contract was made. The seller had to bear the loss since the horse remained his property.

3.4 PRICE

The Price in a Contract of Sale means the money consideration for the sale of goods [Sec 2(10)]. It forms an essential part of the contract. It must be expressed in money. It is the consideration for the transfer or agreement to transfer the property in goods from the seller to the buyer. It is not essential that the price should be fixed at the time of sale. It must, however be payable, though it may not have been fixed. If price is not fixed or is not capable of being fixed, the contract is void-ab-initio.

(A) Determination of Price

The price is an essential element in every contract of sale of goods. Ascertainment of price [Sec 9(1)]. Price in a contract of sale may be fixed by one of the following modes.

1. The price may be fixed by the contract itself. This is the most usual way of fixing the price.
2. It may be fixed in accordance with an agreement. The parties may not themselves fix the price but may leave it to be determined according to the manner agreed upon. It may, for example, agreed that the market price prevailing on the date of the supply of goods will be the price to be paid or the price as determined by a third party will be price for the goods.
3. It may also be determined by a course of dealing between the parties. When the parties have neither themselves fixed the price nor agreed upon some manner for determining the same, we may have to look at their course of dealing.

   Illustrations: *(1) If the buyer has previously been paying a particular price to a particular seller, the price prevailing on the day of the supply of goods shall apply.*

   (2) In a particular trade, there is a usage to deduct discount in determining the price. The usage is implied by the course of dealings between the parties.

   In the same way if the agreement envisages fixation of the price by the buyer corporation, the price fixed by a committee of such corporation will be the price payable by the buyer, and the seller has to accept the same. Where the price is not determined in accordance to any of the above stated manner, the buyer shall pay a reasonable price to the seller. It is to be noted that it may not be necessary that the prevailing market price always be considered as reasonable price. This may sometimes be considered unreasonable also.
4. By the valuation of a third party who agrees to value and fix the price. Section 10(1) provides that if a third party who is supposed to make valuation cannot or does not make such valuation, the agreement is thereby avoided. However, in such a case, if the parties maintain an action for damages and the buyer has already received the goods or part thereof and appropriated them, then he is bound to pay reasonable price for the same. In case the third party, who is to make the valuation, is prevented from doing so by the fault of either the seller or the buyer, the party not in fault may, against the party in fault bring an action for damages.

In case, the price is not capable of being fixed in any of the above mentioned methods, the buyer may pay to the seller a reasonable price (Sec 9). What is reasonable price will vary from case to case. Usually, the market price prevailing is treated as reasonable price. Section 10 of the Sale of Goods Act lays down that in case price is left to be fixed by the valuer and he fails to fix the same, the agreement becomes void except as to that part of goods delivered and accepted regarding which the buyer is bound to pay a reasonable price. And if one of the parties prevent the valuer from making the valuation for the goods, such party shall be liable to pay damages to the other contracting party.

(B) Mode of Payment of Price

The seller decides the kind of payment. However, the seller is not bound to accept any kind of payment except in legal tender money unless there is an agreement express or implied (to the contrary) or unless the seller is stopped from disputing the mode of payment. The seller is not bound to accept payment by cheque or any other method unless he wishes it to be so.

(C) Earnest

It is the tangible thing given by the buyer as a token of good-faith and as a security for the proper performance of the contract by the seller. If the contract is duly performed, the earnest is returned to the buyer. If it is in the form of money paid by the buyer, then it may be deducted from the purchase price. Earnest money is also known as deposit and is paid by the buyer in advance, as a security for the due performance of his part of the contract. Earnest money is not paid as part payment of price. If the transaction is completed, the earnest money is adjusted against the price, but if the sale goes off through buyer's fault, the deposit or earnest money gets forfeited and the seller need not return it back to the buyer. However, if the contract of sale is not completed due to the sellers default, he is bound to return the earnest money or deposit to the buyer.

It may be noted that in case of breach by the buyer and the seller resells the goods, but sues the buyer for the breach of agreement to buy, and for loss arising on such resale, the seller can forfeit the earnest money, which will be taken into account before deciding on the amount of damages to be paid.

Illustration: *A advertises his house for sale. B approaches A and they mutually agree on a contract for a fixed price. To ensure that the sale is finalised between them, and to guarantee the sale, B, the buyer hands over to A, ₹5,000 as earnest. This amount paid as a token will be the earnest. This amount may be deducted from the final amount of the cost of sale price.*

(D) Tax Revisions

If there is revision of tax by the government , and a new tax policy is implemented on the goods, before the sale of contract can be performed, the parties to the contract of sale would become entitled to readjust the price of the goods accordingly. Revision of tax could mean an increase or decrease or remission in customs, or excise duty, or any tax on the sale of purchase of goods imposed or increased or decreased or remitted after the contract for sale of goods was made. This clause is also determined according to the terms in the agreement of sale between the seller and the buyer.

(E) Time

Stipulation as to Time in a contract of sale may be:

1. *Stipulation relating to time of payment:* These are not of the essence of a contract of sale, unless a different intention appears from the contract.
2. *Stipulation not relating to time of payment (delivery of goods, etc):* As regards these stipulations, time may be of the essence of the contract but this essentially depends on the terms of the contract. In a contract of sale, stipulations other than those relating to the time of payment are regarded an essence of the contract. Thus, if a time is fixed for the delivery of goods, the delivery must be made at the fixed time; otherwise the other party is entitled to put an end to the contract.

3.5 CONDITIONS AND WARRANTIES

Stipulations

Section 4(2) of the Act states that '*A contract of sale may be absolute or conditional.*' An absolute contract of sale is one without any conditions. For example, buying things across the counter in a shop, wherein the buyer asks for specific goods by paying cash, and the seller delivers the goods to the buyer.

Usually a contract of sale may either be with a condition precedent or condition subsequent. Conditions precedent are those that must be fulfilled before an agreement to sell becomes a sale and conditions subsequent are inserted in a contract of sale. Every contract of sale has a number of stipulations regarding the nature and quality of goods. Such stipulations may either be conditions or warranties. However, all stipulations cannot be treated as the same. Some stipulations may be intended by the parties to be of a fundamental nature, *e.g.*, quality of the goods to be supplied, the breach of which will be regarded as a breach of contract.

In a contract of Sale of Goods, there may be various terms or stipulations. Stipulations regarding quality of the goods, price, mode of payment, delivery of goods, etc., are very important and are identified as Conditions and Warranties. There is a difference between Conditions and Warranties. While some of them may not be very important, but some stipulations may be major terms which go to the very foundation on which the contract was formed and a breach of a stipulation can make the contract void or voidable. Such major terms which are identified are called 'Conditions'. However, in certain other cases, there may be minor stipulations which are not very vital and their breach may not make the contract void. These minor terms identified are called 'Warranties'.

Illustration: *Sheela places an order for a particular sari from a Sari dealer to be delivered to her by the 2nd of April, to enable her to wear the sari on her wedding to be held on the 6th of April. Here the stipulations with regard to the design of the sari, the colour and the date of delivery are essential to the main purpose of the contract and therefore are CONDITIONS, whereas stipulations regarding the time of payment of the price and the mode of delivery of the sari are not specifically essential to the main purpose of the contract. They are only collateral to the contract and are WARRANTIES.*

It is also necessary to distinguish mere statements or expressions made by the seller with reference to the goods he sells. Such statements made by the seller are neither Conditions nor Warranties. They do not form part of the contract and give no right of action.

Illustration: *When a car dealer, while praising his car states that the car proves very lucky to the person who buys it and would make the owner win in any car race that he would participate in; the sellers statement is only commendatory, in other words, the seller is praising his goods to ensure its immediate sale. Such statements made by the seller does not form part of the contract and its breach, (i.e., if the one who purchases the car does not actually win any race later), does not give rise to any legal consequences or make the contract void.*

Secondly, there is no specific rule to identify a condition and warranty in a contract of sale. The stipulation mentioned in a contract of sale identifies and distinguishes between a condition and a warranty (depending on the specific contract of sale and the construction of the contract of sale). Slater has pointed out 'There are many cases in which it is difficult to determine exactly whether a stipulation is a condition or a warranty'. It is precisely for this reason that Sec 12(4) has laid down that, *'Whether a stipulation in a contract of sale is a condition or a warranty depends in each case on the construction of the contract. A stipulation may be a condition, though called a warranty in the contract.'*

Illustration: *If A enters into a contract with B for the supply of a particular brand of rice for his son's wedding party to be held on a particular date, the time of the delivery and the brand of rice chosen for the delivery becomes a CONDITION. However, if A enters into a contract with B for the supply of a particular brand of rice for keeping the rice in stock , on a particular day, the time of delivery is a WARRANTY.*

If a suit is filed for breach of Condition, the court has to look into the intention of the parties who have entered into the contract of sale by referring to the terms of the contract and the circumstances under which such contract was entered, in order to judge whether the stipulation amounts to a Condition or Warranty. A stipulation in a Contract of Sale with reference to goods which are the subject thereof, may be a Condition or a Warranty [Sec 12(1)].

Illustration: *In Dettini Vs. Gye (1876), the plaintiff, a musician agreed to sing at concerts under the direction of the defendant. A term in the contract was that the plaintiff should be in London at least six days before the commencement of the engagement for the purpose of rehearsals. The plaintiff actually arrived only two days before the performance. The defendant repudiated the contract and the plaintiff sued him. It was held that the stipulation was only ancillary to the contract, and hence, was only a warranty.*

(A) Condition

A condition is a stipulation which is essential to the main purpose of the contract. It goes to the root of the contract. Its non-fulfilment upsets the very basis of the contract. If there is a breach of condition, the aggrieved party can treat the contract as repudiated.

Illustration: *In Behn Vs. Burness, through a charter party (contract entered between the owner of the ship and the hirers of the ship), it was agreed that the particular ship , with a capacity of 420 tonnes, 'Now in the port of Amsterdam', should proceed directly to Newport to load a cargo. In fact, at the time of the contract, the ship was not in the port of Amsterdam and when ultimately the ship reached Newport, the charterer refused to load the cargo. It was held that the words 'now in the port of Amsterdam', amounted to a condition and the breach of the condition entitled the charterer to repudiate the contract.*

(B) Warranty

A Warranty is a stipulation which is collateral to the main purpose of the contract. It is not of such vital importance as a Condition. If there is a breach of warranty, the aggrieved party can only claim damages but it has not right to treat the contract as repudiated.

Therefore, it may be established, according to the definition in the Act that a Condition forms the very basis of a contract of sale, the breach of which entitles the aggrieved party to repudiate the contract. Whereas, a breach of warranty is only of secondary importance, the breach of which give rise to the aggrieved party to claim damages as a compensation but not leading to repudiation of the contract.

Illustration: *A approaches B a dealer in washing machines and says 'I want to purchase a washing machine which has the provision of washing and also spin drying'. B, points to a particular washing machine in his showroom and says that it can perform both washing and spin drying . A buys the washing machine but when he uses it, finds that the washing machine can only wash but does not have any provision for spin drying. There is a breach of condition because the stipulation made by the seller is essential to the main purpose of the contract of sale. Hence the contract can be repudiated.*

(C) Difference between Condition and Warranty

1. *Difference as to value* — A condition is a stipulation which is essential to the main purpose of the contract. A warranty is a stipulation which is collateral to the main purpose of the contract.
2. *Differences as to breach* — If there is a breach of condition, the aggrieved party can repudiate the contract of sale; in case of breach of warranty, the aggrieved party can claim damages only.

3. *Differences as to treatment* — A breach of a Condition may be treated as a breach of Warranty. This would happen where the aggrieved party is contented with payment of damages only. A breach of a Warranty, however, cannot be treated as a breach of a Condition.

(D) When a Condition should be Treated as a Warranty

1. *Voluntary waiver of Condition*: Where a contract of sale is subject to any condition to be fulfilled by the seller, the buyer may either (a) waive the Condition or (b) elect to treat the breach of the Condition as a breach of Warranty. If the buyer once decides to waive the condition, he cannot afterwards insist on its fulfilment.
2. *Acceptance of goods by the buyer*: Where a contract of sale is not severable and the buyer has accepted the goods or part thereof, the breach of any Condition to be fulfilled by the seller can only be treated as a breach of Warranty, unless there is a term of the contract, express or implied, to the contrary.
3. *Express and implied Conditions and Warranties*: In a contract of sale of goods, Conditions and Warranties may be express or implied. Express Conditions and Warranties are those which are expressly provided in the contract. Implied Conditions and Warranties are those which the law implies into the contract unless the parties stipulate to the contrary.

(E) Implied Condition

1. *Condition as to title [Sec 14(a)]*: In a contract of sale, unless the circumstances of the contract are such as to show a different intention, there is an implied condition on the part of the seller that:
   (*a*) In the case of a sale, he has a right to sell the goods , and
   (*b*) In the case of an agreement to sell, he will have a right to sell the goods at the time when the property is to pass.

   Illustration: *In Rowland Vs. Divall, (1923), The plaintiff bought a second-hand car from the defendant and used it for four months. He then discovered that the car had been stolen and the defendant had no title to it. On being compelled to restore the car to the true owner, the plaintiff sued the defendant to recover the purchase money. Held, that the buyer was entitled to recover the whole purchase price, and that the seller was not entitled to set-off anything for the four months use of the car which the buyer had enjoyed. R could recover the price paid.*

   A seller cannot have a right to sell the goods by infringing a trade mark

   Illustration: *In Niblett Ltd. Vs. Confectioneries Materials Co., (1921), the defendants sold to the plaintiff 3,000 tins of condensed milk. On their arrival in London from New York, it was found that 1,000 tins were labelled 'Nissly brand'. Another manufacturer of condensed milk under the name of 'Nestle brand' claimed that it was an infringement of his trade mark. The plaintiff had to remove all the labels and sell the tins at a loss. He sued the defendants for breach of the condition as to title. It was held that , the plaintiff had the right to reject the goods or to recover compensation for the loss suffered by him.*
2. *Sale by description:* When there is a contract for the sale of goods by description, there is an implied condition that the goods shall correspond with the description. The rule of law contained in Sec 15 is summarised in the following maxim: *'if you contract to sell peas, you cannot oblige a party to take beans'*. Sale of goods by description, may include the following situations:

(a) Where the buyer has not seen the goods and relies on their description given by the seller.

Illustrations: *(1) Shepherd Vs. Kain, a ship was contracted to be sold on a 'copper fastened vessel', to be taken with all faults, without any allowance for any defects whatsoever. The ship turned out to be 'partially copper fastened'. It was held that the buyer was entitled to reject the contract.*

(2) In Varley Vs. Whipp (1900), W bought a reaping machine which he had never seen and which V, the seller describes 'to have been new the previous year and used to cut only 50 or 60 acres'. W found the machine to be extremely old. Held, W could return the machine as it did not correspond with the description.

(b) Where the buyer has seen the goods but he relies not on what he has seen but what was stated to him and the deviation of the goods from the description is not apparent.

Illustration: *In Nicholas & Venn Vs. Smith Marriott, in an auction sale of a set of napkins and table cloth, they were described as 'dating from the seventh century'. The buyer bought the set after seeing it. Subsequently he found the set to be an eighteenth century set. Held, he could reject the set.*

(c) Packing of goods may sometimes be a part of the description.

Illustration: *In Moore & Co. Vs. Landauer & Co.,(1921), the plaintiffs sold 3,000 cases of Australian canned fruit, each case to contain 30 tins. When the cases were delivered, it was discovered that about half the cases contained only 24 tins. Although the total number of tins was the same, and the arbitrator had found that there was no difference in value between the tins as they were packed and as they should have been packed, it was held by the Court of Appeal that the defendants were entitled to reject the whole consignment on the ground that the goods delivered did not correspond with the description of those ordered.*

3. *Condition as to quality or fitness [Sec 16(1)]:* Normally, in a contract of sale , there is no implied condition as to quality or fitness of the goods for a particular purpose. The buyer must examine the goods thoroughly before he buys them in order to satisfy himself that the goods will by suitable for the purpose for which he is buying them. The following points should however be noted in this regard:

(a) Where the buyer, expressly or by implication, makes known to the seller the particular purpose for which he needs the goods and depends upon the skill and judgement of the seller whose business it is to supply goods of that description, there is an implied condition that the goods shall be reasonable fit for that purpose.

(b) If the buyer purchasing an article for a particular use is suffering from an abnormality and it is not make known to the seller at the time of sale, implied condition of fitness does not apply.

Illustration: *In Griffiths Vs. Peter Conway, Ltd (1939), the plaintiff, Mrs. Griffiths, bought a Harris Tweed coat from the defendants. Her skin was abnormally sensitive but she did not make this fact known to the defendants. She contracted dermatitis after wearing the coat. Consequently, she sued the seller claiming damages for breach of the implied condition. It was held that the seller was not liable. The main grounds for the judgment was (a) the coat was reasonable fit for the purpose of being worn by a normal person, and (b) the plaintiff had not disclosed the fact that she was an abnormal buyer with sensitive skin.*

(c) If the buyer purchases an article under its patent or other trade name, the implied condition that articles are fit for a particular purpose shall not apply, unless the buyer relies on the sellers skill and judgement and makes known to the seller that he so relies on him.

Illustration: *In Baldry Vs. Marshall (1925), B told M, a motor car dealer, that he wanted a comfortable car suitable for touring purposes. M recommended a 'Bugatti car' and B thereupon bought one. The car was unsuitable for touring purposes. Held, B could reject the car and recover the price.*

(*d*) In case the goods can be used for a number of purposes, the buyer must tell the seller the particular purpose for which he requires the goods. If he does not, he cannot hold the seller liable if the goods do not suit the particular purpose for which he buys the goods.

4. *Condition as to merchantability [Sec 16(2)]:* Where goods are bought by description from a seller who deals in goods of that description (whether he is the manufacturer or producer of the goods or otherwise), there is an implied condition that the goods are of merchantable quality. This means goods should be such as are commercially saleable at their full value under the description by which they are known in the market.

   Illustration: *In Jones Vs. Just (1868), a London merchant sold to a firm of Liverpool merchants, a certain number of bales of Manilla hemp to arrive from Singapore. The goods had been damaged by sea-water in the course of transit. Consequently, they could not be sold in the market in their original condition as Manilla hemp, but only at 5% of the original price. In a suit by the buyers for damages, it was held that they were entitled to recover the loss as the goods were not merchantable.*

   If the goods are of such a quality and in such a condition that a reasonable person acting reasonably would accept them after having examined them thoroughly, they are of merchantable quality. Thus, a watch that will not keep time, a pen that will not write and tobacco that will not smoke, cannot be regarded as merchantable under such names.

   Illustrations: *(1) In R.S.Thakur Vs. H.G.E.Corporation, A radio set was sold to a layman. The set was defective from the beginning and it did not work inspite of repairs. Held, the buyer could return the set and claim refund.*

   (2) In Evans Vs. Stella Benjamin (1951), a refrigerator sold, performed all the functions which a refrigerator usually does, except making ice. In a suit by the buyer, it was held that it amounted to breach of an implied condition.

   Packing of the goods is an equally important consideration in judging their merchantability.

   Illustration: *In Moreth Vs. Fitch & Gibbons, M asked for a bottle of Stone's Ginger wine at F's shop, which was licensed for the sale of wines. While M was drawing the cork, the bottle broke and M was injured. Held the sale was by description and M was entitled to recover damages as the bottle was not of merchantable quality.*

5. *Condition implied by custom:* An implied condition as to quality or fitness for a particular purpose may be decided by the usage of trade [Sec 16(3)].

   Illustrations: *(1) If a perambulator or a bottle of milk is purchased, the purpose for which it is purchased is implied in the thing itself. In such a case the buyer need not tell the seller the purpose for which he buys the goods.*

   (2) In Dr. Baretto Vs. T.R.Price, A bought a set of false teeth from a dentist. The set did not fit into A's mouth. Held, he could reject the set as the purpose for which anybody would buy it was implicitly known to the seller, i.e., the dentist.

6. *Sale by sample [Sec 17]:* When a contract of sale includes a contract of sale by sample, where there is a term in the contract, express or implied, to that effect (in the case of a contract for sale by sample), there is an implied condition that:

   (*a*) The bulk shall correspond with the sample in quality.

   (*b*) The buyer shall have a reasonable opportunity of comparing the bulk with the sample.

   (*c*) The goods shall be free from any defect, rendering them unmerchantable . The defect should not however be apparent on a reasonable examination of the sample [Sec. 17(2)].

7. *Condition as to wholesomeness:* In the case of eatables and provisions, in addition to the implied condition as to merchantability, there is another implied condition that the goods shall be wholesome.

Illustration: *In Frost Vs. Aylesbory Diary Co. Ltd. (1905), The defendant supplied to the plaintiff milk for family use. The milk was consumed by the plaintiff and the members of his family. The milk contained typhoid germs and the plaintiff's wife was infected thereby and died. Since the purpose for which the milk was required having been made known to the seller, there was an implied condition that the milk was reasonably fit for consumption, and as such the defendant was held liable in damages for breach of the implied condition and could recover damages.*

(F) Implied Warranty

The implied warranties in a contract of sale are as follows:

1. *Warranty of quiet possession [Sec 14(b)]:* In a contract of sale, unless there is a contrary intention, there is an implied warranty that the buyer shall have and enjoy quiet possession of goods. If the buyer is in any way disturbed in the enjoyment of the goods in consequence of the seller's defective title to sell, he can claim damages from the seller.
2. *Warranty of freedom from encumbrances [Sec 14(c)]:* The buyer is entitled to a further warranty that the goods are not subject to any charge or right in favour of a third party. If his possession is in any way disturbed by reason of the existence of any charge or encumbrances on the goods in favour of any third party, he shall have a right to claim damages for breach of this warranty.
3. *Warranty as to quality or fitness by image of trade [Sec 16(4):* An implied warranty as to quality or fitness for a particular purpose may be annexed by image of trade. (Particular brand of rice, particular brand of shoes, particular electronics brand, etc).
4. *Warranty to disclose dangerous nature of goods:* Where a person sells goods, knowing that the goods are inherently dangerous or they are likely to be dangerous to the buyer and that the buyer is ignorant of the danger, the seller must warn the buyer of the probable danger, otherwise he will be liable in damages.

(G) Caveat Emptor

The term 'Caveat Emptor' means 'let the buyer beware'. In a contract of sale of goods, the seller is under no obligation to reveal unflattering truths about the goods sold by him. Therefore, when a person buys some goods, he (the buyer) must examine them thoroughly. If the goods turn out to be defective or do not suit his purpose or if he depends upon his own skill and judgement and makes a bad selection, the buyer cannot blame anybody except himself.

Illustration: *In Ward Vs. Hobbs (1878), the plaintiff bought some pigs from the defendant who knew that the pigs were suffering from swine fever. He did not disclose this fact to the plaintiff, and the pigs were sold 'with all faults'. Subsequently, to the purchase, all the pigs except one died of fever. In a suit by the plaintiff for breach of warranty, it was held that the defendant was not liable in damages because the defendant under the doctrine of caveat emptor, was not bound to disclose every defect of which he may be aware of, although his silence may operate virtually to deceive the vendee. There was no implied warranty by H and the sale was good and H was not liable in damages.*

Exceptions to the rule

1. Section 16 of the Sale of Goods Act recognises the following exceptions to the Doctrine of *Caveat Emptor*. Accordingly, there is an implied condition as to quality or fitness of the goods

for a particular purpose. Clause(1) lays down that, *'Where the buyer, expressly or by implication, makes known to the seller, the particular purpose for which the goods are required, so as to show that the buyer relies on the seller's skill and judgment, and the goods are of a description which it is the course of the seller's business to supply (whether he is the manufacturer or producer or not), there is an implied condition that the goods shall be reasonably fit for such purpose.'* Therefore, according to this exception, to make the seller liable for breach of the implied condition as to quality or fitness of the goods, it is necessary that (1) the buyer has made known to the seller expressly or by implication the purpose for which the goods are required (2) has relied on the skill or judgment of the seller, and (3) the business of the seller is to sell such goods whether or not he is a manufacturer or producer.

Illustration: *In Priest Vs. Last (1903), the plaintiff went to the defendant, a retail chemist, and asked for a 'hot water bottle'. Having no knowledge of hot water bottles, he enquired before buying, whether the bottle exhibited would stand boiling water. In reply, he was told that it was meant for hot but not boiling water. He thereupon bought it. After only five days, it burst while being used and injured his wife. In an action against the seller for breach of warranty, it was held that there was an implied condition that the bottle was fit for holding hot water and since the bottle , when sold, was not fit for use as a hot water bottle, the seller was liable in damages to the buyer.*

2. The second exception to the Doctrine of *Caveat Emptor* as stated in Section 16(2) of the Act states; *'Where goods are bought by description from a seller who deals in goods of that description (whether he is the manufacturer or producer or not), there is an implied condition that the goods shall be of merchantable quality; provided that, if the buyer has examined the goods, there shall be no implied condition as regards defects which such examination ought to have revealed.'* Therefore, according to this sub-section, two conditions need to be satisfied for this exception provided by the Act, to operate. (1) The sale should be by description and (2) The seller should be a dealer in goods of that description. If these conditions are satisfied, the law implies a condition as to merchantability.

   (*i*) *Fitness for buyers purpose:* Where the buyer expressly or by implication, makes known to the seller, the particular purpose for which he requires the goods and relies on the seller's skill or judgement and the goods are of a description which it is in the course of the seller's business to supply, the seller must supply the goods which shall be fit for the buyer's purpose [Sec 16(1)].

   Illustration: *In Frost Vs. Aylesbury Diary Co. (1905), [case already explained], the defendant supplied milk to the plaintiff for his personal use. However the milk contained typhoid germs and affected the plaintiff's wife and led to her death. The milk was not fit for the buyers purpose and hence the defendant was held liable in damages for breach of the implied condition- fitness for buyers purpose.*

   (*ii*) *Sale under a patent or trade name:* In the case of a contract for the sale of a specified article under its patent or other trade name, there is no implied condition that the goods shall be reasonably fit for any particular purpose.

Illustration: *In Chanter Vs. Hopkins (1838), the buyer ordered for the defendant's patented smoke consuming furnace for using the same in his brewery. After buying, it was found that the apparatus was found not fit for the brewery. It was held that sale being on the basis of the seller's patent, there was no implied condition or warranty as to the fitness of the goods for a particular purpose and the seller was entitled to recover the price from the buyer.*

3. Merchantable quality: Where goods are bought by description from a seller who deals in goods of that description, there is an implied condition that the goods shall be of merchantable quality.

Illustrations: *(1) In Moorelli vs. Fitch and Gibbons (1928), the plaintiff asked for a bottle of Stone's Ginger wine at the defendant's shop, which was licenced for the sale of wines. While the plaintiff was drawing the cork with a corkscrew, the bottle broke at the neck and injured him. The Court held that the sale was one by description and that the bottle was not of merchantable quality, and consequently the plaintiff was entitled to damages.*

(2) In Jackson Vs. Rotax Motor and Cycle Co. Ltd, (1910), the sellers who were manufacturers of motor horns, sold 609 horns to the defendant. Of these, 364 were defective for various reasons. Some were dented, but could have been made of merchantable quality at a very low cost. The buyers rejected them on the ground that they were not of merchantable quality. In a suit by the plaintiffs for the price, the Court of Appeal held that the defendants were entitled to reject the whole consignment as it was not of merchantable quality.

4. Usage of Trade: An implied warranty or condition as to quality or fitness for a particular purpose may be annexed by the image of trade [Sec 16(3)].

   Illustration: *In Wren Vs. Holt (1903), the plaintiff went to the defendant's beer-house and asked for and was served with beer made by a particular firm, and was injured by reason of the fact that the beer contained arsenic. The defendant was held liable for damages for breach of warranty, as examination by the plaintiff would not have revealed the defect.*

5. Consent by fraud: Where consent of the buyer, in a contract of sale, is obtained by the seller by fraud or where the seller knowingly conceals a defect which could not be discovered by the buyer on a reasonable examination, the Doctrine of *Caveat Emptor* does not apply.

Illustration: *In Mody Vs. Gregson (1868), the defendants, manufacturers of grey shirtings, contracted to supply to the plaintiffs, a quantity of shirtings according to sample, each piece to weigh 7lbs. The goods were delivered and accepted as being according to sample and of the agreed weight. After the plaintiffs accepted the goods and shipped them to Calcutta, it was discovered that the weight was made up by introducing into the fabric china clay. This rendered the goods unmerchantable, but the introduction of china clay could not be discovered by a reasonable examination of the sample. Held, the sellers were liable for breach .*

3.6 TRANSFER OF PROPERTY

There are three stages in the performance of a contract of sale of goods by a seller, they are:

(*a*) The transfer of property in the goods.

(*b*) The transfer of possession of goods, and

(*c*) The passing of the risk

Transfer of property in goods from the seller to the buyer is the main object of a contract of sale. The term 'property in goods' means, custody or control of goods. When or time at which the property (ownership) in goods passes from the seller to the buyer.

1. The risk passes with ownership: The rule is that the risk passes with ownership. If the goods are destroyed by accident, the loss falls on the owner.

   Illustration: *In Daneby Hamilton and Co. Vs. Barden, B contracted to purchase 30 tonnes of apple juice from D. D crushed the apple, put them into casks and kept them ready for delivery. However, B delayed in taking delivery of the casks and the juice became putrid and had to be thrown away. It was held that B was liable to pay for the price.*

2. Action against the third party: Only the owner of the goods can take action against the third party if and when the goods are destroyed by the actions of the third party.

3. Insolvency of the seller or buyer: In case of insolvency of the seller or buyer, the question whether the goods can be taken over by the official receiver depends upon whether the insolvent party is the owner of the goods or not.
4. Suit for the price: The seller can sue the buyer for the price only if the buyer becomes the owner of the goods.

(A) Rules Relating to Passing of Property or Transfer of Ownership

1. *Goods must be ascertained [Sec. 18]:* In a contract of sale of unascertained goods, the property in the goods is transferred to the buyer only after the goods are ascertained (the goods identified and set apart).
2. *Intention of the parties [Sec.19]:* In the contract of sale of specific or ascertained goods, the ownership in the goods passes to the buyer at the time when the parties intend to pass it. The intention of the parties may be ascertained from the terms of the contract, the contract of the parties and the circumstances of the case.

Illustration: *In Chidambaram Chettiar Vs. Steel Bros, in a mixed contract for storage of paddy and the sale of the same thereafter, the paddy was delivered by S to B for storage. B had the option to name a particular day on which he was to buy the paddy. Held, the property in the paddy did not pass to B until B named the particular day on which he was to buy the paddy.*

Section 20, 21 and 22 of the Act states the procedure to be adopted when the intention of the parties cannot be ascertained.

1 . **Specific goods**

Section 20: When there is an unconditional contract for the sale of specific goods in a deliverable state, (it is that state of the goods in which, the buyer is bound to take delivery of the goods under the contract (Sec 2(3)), the ownership in goods passes to the buyer when the contract is made.

Illustration: *In Tarling Vs. Baxter, there was a contract for the sale of certain trees on the seller's land on the 4th of January and the price to be paid by the 4th of February. The trees were destroyed before they were cut. Held, that the ownership had passed to the buyer on the making of the contract and he was liable for the loss.*

Section 21: When there is a contract for the sale of specific goods not in a deliverable state, the property (ownership) passes to the buyer only after the seller puts them in deliverable state and the buyer is informed.

Illustration: *In Underwood Ltd. Vs. Cement Syndicate, there was a contract for sale of a machine weighing 30 tonnes and fixed on a concrete floor. A part of the machine was destroyed while being detached from the floor. Held, that the buyer was not liable for the loss. He can refuse to take delivery of the machine as it was not in a deliverable state.*

Section 22: When there is a contract for the sale of specific goods in a deliverable state, but the seller has to weigh, measure or test the goods for ascertaining the price, the property does not pass until such thing is done and the buyer is informed.

2. **Unascertained goods [Sec 23]**

In a contract of sale of unascertained goods, the property in the goods is transferred to the buyer, only after the goods are ascertained, *i.e.*, identified and set apart.

3. **Goods sent on approval or on sale or return [Sec 24(3)]**

When the goods are delivered to the buyer on approval or on sale or return or other similar terms, the property therein passes to the buyer:

(i) When he signifies his approval or acceptance to the seller.

(ii) When he does any other act adopting the transaction.

Illustration: *In Kirkham Vs. Attenborough, K delivered some jewellery to W on sale or return. W pledged the jewellery with A. Held, the pledge was an act by W adopting the transaction. As such, the property in the jewellery had passed to W therefore, K could not recover it from A.*

(iii) If he does not signify his approval or acceptance to the seller but retains the goods without giving notice of rejection, beyond the time fixed for the return of the goods, or if no time has been fixed, beyond a reasonable time. The question as to what is a reasonable time is a question of fact and is dependent on the type of transaction [Sec 63].

Illustration: *In Hoogly Chinsurah Municipality Vs. Spence Ltd., S Ltd, agreed to sell a tractor to HG Municipality on the condition that if the latter was not satisfied, it could reject the tractor. The municipality used the tractor for a month and a half and then wanted to reject the tractor. Held, a reasonable time to reject having elapsed, the property in the tractor had passed to the municipality and therefore the Municipality could not reject the tractor.*

(B) Sale by Non-owners

'Nemodat quod non habet', which means, *'no one can give what one has not got'*. According to this maxim, a non-owner with no title or having a defective title to the goods , cannot convey a better title to the buyer although he may be an innocent buyer. Under the Indian law, the general rule is expressed in Section 27 of the Sale of Goods Act which states *'subject to the provisions of the Act and of any other law for the time being in force, where goods are sold by a person who is not the owner thereof and who does not sell them under the authority or with the consent of the owner, the buyer acquires no better title to the goods than the seller had, unless the goods is by his conduct precluded from denying the seller's authority to sell.'* Therefore, if a person who is not the true owner or not acting under the authority of the owner, sells goods, the buyer cannot acquire a better title to them than the seller had. However, if the buyer bought the goods in good faith, not knowing the defective title of the seller, his only remedy is a suit against the immediate transferor for damages for breach of the implied condition as to title.

Illustrations: *(1) A steals an article and sells it to B, B does not become the owner of the article. This is because A does not have a good title to the goods and hence B too does not acquire a good title over the goods even though B bought the goods in good faith (as an innocent buyer) . Hence it is only the owner of the goods or a person authorised by him who can sell the goods.*

(2) In Farquharson Bros. Vs. King & Co. (1902), the appellants, timber merchants, instructed their agents who were stocking timber to accept all delivery orders signed by their clerk, who had authority to make limited sales. The clerk sold timber to the respondents under an assumed name. The respondents acted in good faith and knew nothing of the appellants or of the clerk under his real name. The clerk also fraudulently transferred some of the timber to himself under the assumed name. In an action for conversion, it was held that the appellants were entitled to recover the value of the timber from the respondents since the clerk having no title or apparent authority himself, could not give the respondents any title.

Section 27 of the Act states that where the goods are sold by a person who is not the true owner of the goods and who does not sell them without authority or without the consent of the owner, the buyer gets no better title to the goods than the seller. But the following are the exceptions to this rule:

1. **Estoppel:** Sale by a person not the owner [Sec 28] : when the true owner, by his conduct or by an act makes the buyer to believe that the seller has the authority to sell and makes the buyer to buy the goods, the true owner cannot later deny or refuse such a fact. In such a case the

buyer gets a better title than the seller. According to this rule of evidence, estoppels may be either (1) by words (2) by conduct, or (3) negligent omission.

Illustrations: *A tells B (within hearing of C), that he (A) is the owner of an article, which in fact belongs to C.C does not react or object to this statement made by A. Later after sometime, B buys the article from A. C is estopped from preventing the sale and B gets a better title than A to the article purchased.*

(1) Estopped by words: *In Henderson & Co. V Williams (1985), sugar bags belonging to one G & Co. were stored in the warehouse of Williams, the defendant. A fraudulent person induced G & Co. to sell sugar to him. G &Co. instructed the defendant to transfer the goods in his books to the order of the fraudulent person. The latter sold the goods to the plaintiffs. In response to an enquiry from the plaintiff the defendant informed them that he had the goods transferred to the order of the fraudulent person. On discovering the fraud and not having been paid by the fraudulent person, G & Co. instructed the defendant not to deliver goods to the plaintiffs. In a suit by the plaintiffs, it was held by the Court of Appeal that G & Co had held out the fraudulent person as having a right to sell and could not, therefore deny his right as against the plaintiffs who acted on the holding out. Accordingly, the plaintiffs were entitled to damages for conversion.*

(2) Estopped by conduct: *In Pickard Vs. Sears (1837), machinery belonging to the plaintiff were in possession of a person. The plaintiff allowed the machinery to be attached by the defendant in execution of a decree against the person who was in possession of the same. He did not even claim the machinery for some months. Besides, he had conversation with the defendant's solicitor about the execution of the decree without disclosing his claim. In a suit by the plaintiffs, it was held that he had sufficiently impressed upon the defendant that the person with whom the machinery was lying was himself the owner, and hence, he was stopped from denying the title of the person in possession of the machinery.*

(3) Estopped by negligence: *In Mercantitle Credit Co. Ltd. Vs. Hamblin (1965), the defendant, who wanted to borrow money on the security of her car, approached a dealer. The dealer gave some blank hire-purchase forms for her signature. She signed the forms thinking that they were necessary to complete the mortgage transaction. The dealer told her that he would find out what sum he could arrange for him to raise and also gave her a blank cheque to be filled in by her after the sum was known. The dealer made use of the hire-purchase forms for making an offer to the plaintiffs to sell the car and an offer by the defendant to buy the car from the plaintiffs on hire-purchase basis. The plaintiffs accepted both the offers. When the defendant came to know of this she repudiated the transaction. It was held by the Court of Appeal that she was not bound by the agreement since she had not authorised the dealer to make any offer to the plaintiffs and as such, was not estoopped from denying that she had authorised the dealer. She had retained the car throughout and had taken sufficient care.*

2. **Sale by a mercantile agent:** The buyer of goods from a mercantile agent, who has no authority from the principal to sell, gets a good title to the goods, provided that –
   (*a*) the person selling should be a mercantile agent
   (*b*) the agent gets the possession of goods or document of title to goods with the consent of the owner.
   (*c*) he sells them in the ordinary course of business.
   (*d*) the buyer has acted in good faith
   (*e*) the buyer has no notice of the sellers defective title when the contract of sale is made.

   Meaning of mercantile agent: A mercantile agent is a person who in the ordinary course of business, has agency, authority, either to sell or buy goods or to raise money on the security of goods [Sec 2(9)].

   Illustration: *In Lowther Vs. Harris (1926), the plaintiff was the owner of an ornamental textile used for the covering of walls, furniture and for curtains. He left the same with one Prior for the purpose of sale. Prior was* *not engaged in the agency business. He had his own shop and all his receipts and payments were in the registered name of his firm. Although he had no authority to complete the sale without the plaintiff's knowledge, he sold the goods to the defendant. In a suit by the plaintiff for damages for conversion, it was held that the plaintiff could not succeed since the defendant was a mercantile agent, although he acted for one principal namely the plaintiff and his authority was limited.*

3. **Sale by a co-owner [Sec 28] :** The Act states the '*If one of the several joint owners of goods has the sole possession of them by permission of the co-owners, the property in the goods is transferred to any person who buys them of such joint owner in good faith and has not at the time of the contract of sale notice that the seller has no authority to sell.*' The buyer of goods from a co-owner gets a good title to the goods if:

    (*a*) A co-owner is in the sole possession of the goods with the consent of the other owners.

    (*b*) The buyer has acted in good faith

    A co-owner or joint owner can sell his own share even without the application of the provisions of this Section. If he does so, the buyer acquires only the title of the owner, and thus becomes a co-owner along with the other co-owners. But , when this Section is applied the buyer becomes the owner of the whole of the goods and not merely to the extent of the share of the co-owner selling the goods. It is however necessary that the co-owner should be in possession of the same with the consent of the other co-owners and the buyer should act in good faith and without notice that the seller has no authority to sell.

4. **Sale by a person in possession under a voidable contract [Sec 29] :** When the seller of goods obtained their possession under a voidable contract (but the contract has not come to an end at the time of contract of sale), the buyer gets a good title to the goods provided the buyer buys them in good faith without notice of the seller's defective title. But if the seller obtains the goods under a void contract, then the buyer of the goods will not get a better title even if he buys in good faith.

5. **Sale by seller in possession of goods after sale [Sec 30(1)]:** When a seller after having sold the goods previously, re-sells them to another buyer than the second buyer gets a good title, provided;

    (*i*) The seller is in possession of goods or has document of title to goods as a seller

    (*ii*) The buyer has acted in good faith

    (*iii*) The buyer has no notice of the previous sale, and

    (*iv*) The second buyer has actually received the possession of the goods.

    Illustration: *In City Fur Manufacturing Co. Ltd. Vs. Fureencond (Brokers) London Ltd. (1937), one Herman purchased seven parcels of fur from Lampson and Co, a firm of brokers. The goods remained in the brokers' warehouse since Herman had not paid the amount which the brokers advanced on his behalf to the sellers. In the meantime, Herman sold the goods to the plaintiffs and received bills of exchange in payment for the same. He promised the plaintiffs that he would pay off his debt to the brokers and see that the goods are delivered to them. Instead of paying the brokers and taking delivery of the goods, he pledged the same with the defendants for £178. This amount was utilized by him to pay off the brokers. Having been paid off, the brokers held the goods to the order of Herman and delivered the same to the defendants. The defendants held the goods as pledges against £178 advanced by them. In a suit by the plaintiffs for recovery of the goods, it was held that the defendants acquired a good title since Herman was a seller in possession of the goods. Although the goods were not in actual possession of the seller, possession by Lampson and Co. his agents was considered by the court as sufficient.*

6. **Sale by the buyer in possession of goods after sale [Sec 30(2)] :** When a buyer sells the goods, which he bought or agreed to buy, to another buyer then that second buyer gets good title to the goods, if –
   (*a*) The second buyer has acted in good faith.
   (*b*) He has no notice of lien or any other right of the owner.

   Illustration: *In Belsize Motor Supply Co. Vs. Cox (1914), the plaintiffs let out a taxi cab to Alfred Burgess Ltd, under a hire-purchase agreement. According to the agreement, the Burgess Co. has to pay 24 instalments of £15-12-2 each amounting to £374-12-0. An option to purchase the vehicle for a sum of £50 was also given to them. Before exercising the option, the hirers pledged the vehicle with the defendant. In an action by the plaintiffs to recover the vehicle, it was held that Cox could not obtain a good title to the car since there was no obligation on the part of Burgess Co. to buy it but only an option to do so.*
7. **Re-sale by un-paid seller [Sec 53 (3)]:** When an un-paid seller, by using his right of lien or stoppage of goods in transit, re-sells the goods, then the buyer gets good title to the goods.
8. **Exceptions in other acts:**
   (*a*) Sale by finder of lost goods under certain circumstances [Sec 169 of Indian Contract Act 1872]
   (*b*) Sale by a pawnee or a pledge under certain circumstances [Sec 176 of Indian Contract Act 1872]
   (*c*) Sale by an Official Receiver or Liquidator or Companies.

(Thus in the above three cases, even the seller is not the owner of the goods, if he sells them, but the buyer gets good title to the goods.)

(C) Performance of Contract of Sale

Performance of Contract of Sale means the duty of the seller to deliver the goods to the buyer and of the buyer to accept and pay for them according to the terms of the contract of sale. Delivery means voluntary transfer of possession of goods from the seller to the buyer. Section 31 of the Sale of Goods Act states that '*it is the duty of the seller to deliver the goods and of the buyer to accept and pay for them in accordance with the terms of the contract of sale.*' Therefore it is the duty of the seller to be ready and willing to give delivery of the goods to the buyer and it is equally the duty of the buyer to be ready and willing to pay the price in exchange for possession of the goods. Delivery of the goods and payment for the same are concurrent conditions. However, the parties have the option to specify terms suitable and amicable between them. It may be–

(*a*) *Actual delivery:* When the goods are handed over by the seller to the buyer, then the delivery is called actual delivery.

(*b*) *Symbolic delivery:* When the goods are bulky, actual delivery is impossible. In such case, symbolic delivery is the effective type of delivery.

Illustration: *Handing over the key of the warehouse to the buyer.*

(*c*) *Constructive delivery or delivery by attornment:* When a third party (e.g., Bailee) who is possessing the goods of the seller at the time of the sale, indicates to the buyer that he holds the goods on his behalf, then it is called constructive delivery.

Illustration: *A sells to B 10 bags of wheat lying in C's godown. A gives an order to C to transfer the goods to B. C transfers the goods in his books to B. This is constructive delivery or delivery by attornment.*

(D) Rights and Duties of the Buyer

Rights of the buyer:

1. Right to have delivery as per contract [Sec 31 and 32]
2. Right to reject the goods [Sec 37]
3. Right to repudiate [Sec 38(1)]
4. Right to Notice of insurance [Sec 39(3)]; unless and otherwise agreed, where goods are sent by the seller to the buyer by a sea route. The buyer has a right to be informed by the seller so that he may get the goods insured.
5. Right to examine the goods [Sec 41]
6. Rights against the seller for breach of contract—
   (*a*) Suit for damages [Sec 57]
   (*b*) Suit for price
   (*c*) Suit for specific performance [Sec 58]
   (*d*) Suit for breach of warranty [Sec 59]
   (*e*) Repudiation of contract before due date [Sec 60]
   (*f*) Suit for interest [Sec 61 (2)(b)]

Duties of the buyer:

1. Duty to accept the goods and pay for them in exchange for possession [Sec 31 and 32]
2. Duty to apply for delivery [Sec 35]
3. Duty to demand delivery at a reasonable hour [Sec 36(4)]
4. Duty to accept instalment delivery and pay for it
5. Duty to take risk of deterioration in the course of transit [Sec 40]
6. Duty to intimate the seller where he rejects the goods [Sec 43]
7. Duty to take delivery [Sec 44]
8. Duty to pay price [Sec 55]
9. Duty to pay damages for non-acceptance [Sec 56]

(E) Rights and Duties of an Unpaid Seller

Under Section 45 of the Sale of Goods Act defines an unpaid seller as follows; *'the seller of goods is deemed to be an unpaid seller within the meaning of this Act: (a) when the whole of the price has not been paid or tendered; (b) when a bill of exchange or other negotiable instrument has been received as conditional payment, and the condition on which it was received has not been fulfilled by reason of the dishonour of the instrument or otherwise.'*

A seller of goods is deemed to be an unpaid seller when—

1. The whole of the price has not been paid or tendered
2. A Bill of Exchange or other Negotiable Instrument was received but the same has been dishonoured [Sec.45(1)]

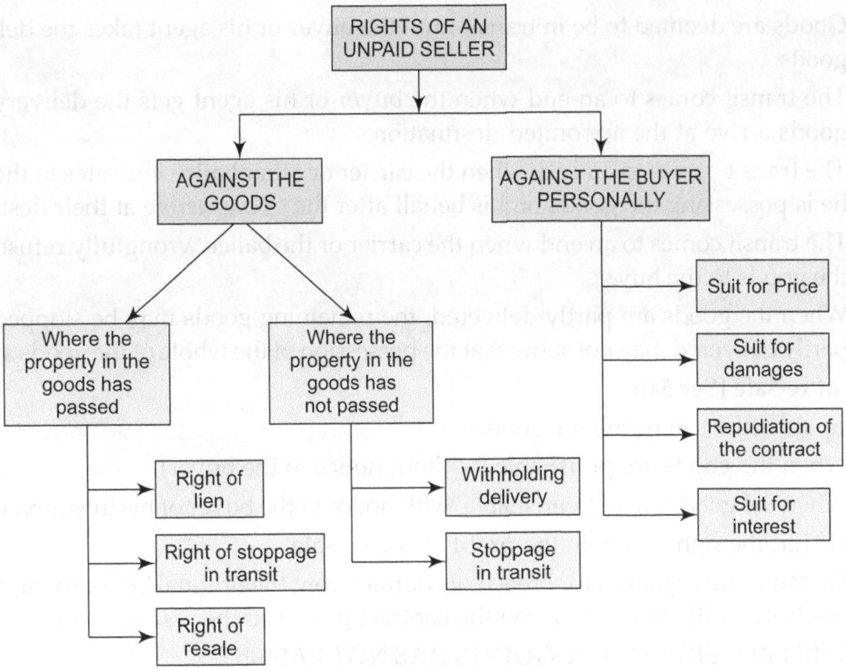

I. Right of an unpaid seller against the goods

WHERE THE PROPERTY IN THE GOODS HAS PASSED

1. **Right of lien [Sec 47 to 49]:** Lien is a right to retain the possession of goods until the payment of price or the price of the goods is paid. If the goods are partly delivered, the seller can use this right on the remaining goods , except when the part delivery made is to indicate that he has given up his right. This right can be used only:
   (*a*) When the goods have been sold on credit.
   (*b*) When the goods have been sold on credit but the credit period is over and the price is unpaid
   (*c*) When the buyer becomes insolvent

   The Seller looses his right on lien when:
   1. When the unpaid seller delivers the goods to a carrier or other bailee for the purpose of delivering the goods to the buyer.
   2. When the buyer or his agent lawfully gets the possession of the goods.
   3. When the unpaid seller has given up his right of lien
2. **Right of stoppage of goods in transit [Sec 50–52]:** This right is given to the unpaid seller to stop the goods when they are in transit. When the seller has parted with the possession of goods, he may regain or retain such possession by stopping the goods in transit before it is delivered to the buyer.[Sec 50]. This right is available:
   (*a*) When the goods are in transit and
   (*b*) When the buyer becomes an insolvent.

   Following are the rules regarding duration of transit [Sec 51]. Transit is an intermediate stage. Goods are said to be in transit from the time the goods leave the physical possession of the seller, is delivered to a carrier and until the buyer takes deliver of the goods.

1. Goods are deemed to be in transit until the buyer or his agent takes the delivery of the goods.
2. The transit comes to an end when the buyer or his agent gets the delivery before the goods arrive at the appointed destination.
3. The transit comes to an end, when the carrier or other bailee indicates to the buyer that he is possessing the goods on his behalf after the goods arrive at their destination.
4. The transit comes to an end when the carrier or the bailee wrongfully refuses to deliver the goods to the buyer.
5. When the goods are partly delivered, the remaining goods may be stopped but goods partly delivered may not show that the possession of the whole of the goods are given up.

3. **Right of re-sale [Sec 54]:**

   The unpaid seller can re-sell the goods:

   (*a*) When the goods are perishable (without notice to the buyer)

   (*b*) When the goods are not perishable, with notice to the buyer of his intention to resell and

   (*c*) He has the right to retain the profit of such resale

   (*d*) He can claim damages for breach of contract from the original buyer for any loss on the resale (the differences between the contract price and the resale price).

WHERE THE PROPERTY IN THE GOODS HAS NOT PASSED

When the property in goods has not passed: The unpaid seller can withhold the delivery of the goods when the property in goods has not passed to the buyer.

1. Withholding delivery
2. Stoppage in transit

II. Rights of an unpaid seller against the buyer personally [Sec 55,56,60 & 61]

These rights of the seller against the buyer personally are called '*right in personam*'. These rights are:

1. **Suit for prices**

   (*a*) When the property has passed to the buyer: when the goods has passed to the buyer and the buyer wrongfully neglects or refuses to pay for the goods, the seller may sue him for the price of the goods. [Sec 55(1)]

   (*b*) When the property has not passed: When the price is to be paid on a certain day as per the contract of sale. Irrespective of the delivery, if the buyer wrongfully neglects or refuses to pay such price, then the seller may sue him for the price, even though the property in goods has not passed and the goods have not been appropriated to the contract. [Sec 55(2)]

2. **Suit for damages for non-acceptance:** when the buyer wrongfully neglects or refuses to accept and pay for the goods, the seller may sue him for non-acceptance and claim damages.[Sec 56]
3. **Repudiation of the contract before the due date or anticipatory breach of contract:** When the buyer repudiates the contract before the date of delivery, the seller may either treat the contract as existing and wait till the date of delivery or treat the contract as rescinded and sue for damages for the breach of contract. [Sec 60]
4. **Suit for interest:** Where there is a specific agreement between the seller and the buyer, about the interest, on the price, the seller can recover interest on the price from the date on which

the payment of price is due. When there is no such specific agreement, the seller may charge interest on the price from the date on which he informs the buyer.

(F) Remedies to the Buyer Against the Seller

(*a*) *Damages for non-delivery:* The buyer may bring an action against the seller for non-delivery of the goods contracted for and recover damages from him. The measure of damages is the same as in the case of the action by the seller for non-acceptance by the buyer.

(*b*) *Specific performance:* Specific performance is granted to the buyer when money compensation in the form of damages would not be adequate or cannot be fairly determined. Section 58 of the Act, has accordingly, left it to the discretion of the court to order the seller to specifically perform the contract without giving him the option of retaining the goods on payment of damages. Section 58 applies only to those cases in which there is breach of contract to deliver specific or ascertained goods.

(*c*) *Remedy for breach of warranty:* Where the seller commits breach of condition, the buyer is entitled to reject the goods and treat the contract as repudiated. But, where there is a breach of warranty, the buyer cannot reject the goods . If the buyer has not paid the price, he may accept the goods and demand that the seller reduce the price to the extent of the damages caused by the breach of warranty or sue the seller for damages for breach of warranty, if he has already paid the price.

(*d*) *Repudiation of the contract:* Repudiation of the contract of sale by the seller before the date of delivery entitles the buyer to treat the contract as rescinded and sue the seller for damages for the breach.

(*e*) *Recovery of the price and interest:* Where the buyer repudiates the contract having a right to do so, he is entitled to get back the purchase money paid under the contract and in a suit by him for the refund of the price, he can also get interest.

QUESTIONS

Sections 3.1 and 3.2

1. What constitute Goods according to the Sale of Goods Act ?
2. Explain the difference between :
   (*a*) Existing goods and future goods
   (*b*) Unscertained goods and Specific goods.
3. How and on what basis is goods classified ?
4. What does Document of Title to Goods, signify ?
5. Briefly describe Actionable Claim.

Section 3.3

1. What are the essential of a contract of sale ?
2. Elucidate a Sale and an Agreement to Sell.
3. Explain Hire Purchase Agreement.
4. What are the characteristics of a contract of bailment ?

5. How would you differentiate a contract of Sale and Mortgage ?
6. Explain the effect of destruction of goods under various circumstances.

Section 3.4

1. What is the mode of determination of Price in a contract of Sale ?
2. What is the mode of payment of price ?
3. Explain Earners.
4. Explain the stipulation as to Time in a Contract of Sale.

Section 3.5

5. Define Condition.
6. Differentiate between Condition and Warranty.
3. When can a Condition be treated as a Warranty ?
4. Short Notes:
   (*a*) Implied Conditions
   (*b*) Implied Warranty
   (*c*) Caveat Emptor.
5. What are the exemptions to the rule of Caveat Emptor ?

Section 3.6

1. Write a note on the three stages laid down in the Sale of Goods Act in the performance of a Contract of Sale.
2. What is the procedure laid down in the Act when the intention of the parties with regard to transfer of property cannot be ascertained, regarding:
   (*a*) Ascertained goods
   (*b*) Unascertained goods
   (*c*) Goods sent on approval or sale or return.
3. Explain the effect of the maxim '*Nemodat quod non habet*', or sale by non-owner.
4. What are the exceptions to the maxim '*Nemodat quod non habet*' in relation to the following:
   (*a*) Estoppel
   (*b*) Sale by a mercantile agent
   (*c*) Sale by a co-owner
   (*d*) Sale by a person in possession under a voidable contract
   (*e*) Sale by a seller in possession of goods after sale
   (*f*) Sale by buyer in possession of goods after sale
   (*g*) Resale by unpaid seller.
5. Write a note on Performance of contract of sale.
6. What are the rights and duties of a buyer under the Act ?
7. Write a note on Unpaid Seller. What are his rights ?
8. What are the remedies provided by the Act against the seller ?

OBJECTIVE TYPE QUESTIONS

1. Sale of Goods Act is a _______ transaction.
   (*a*) Credit (*b*) Cash
   (*c*) Mutual (*d*) Consensual.
2. The Sale of Goods Act is applicable through out India except in the State of
   (*a*) Andaman and Nicobar islands
   (*b*) Punjab
   (*c*) Jammu and Kashmir
   (*d*) Central government ruling states.
3. Goods which are in seller's ownership and/or possession are called
   (*a*) Ascertained goods (*b*) Future goods
   (*c*) Pre-existed goods (*d*) Existing goods.
4. Specific goods are also known as:
   (*a*) Ascertained goods (*b*) Existing goods
   (*c*) Deliverable goods (*d*) Future goods.
5. Goods identified and agreed upon at the time a contract of sale is called
   (*a*) Specific goods (*b*) Unascertained goods
   (*c*) Goods on approval (*d*) Customized goods.
6. The contract of sale may take in the form of:
   (*a*) Cash (*b*) Credit
   (*c*) Both (A) and (B) (*d*) Loan.
7. Goods which are not identified at the time of making the contract is called
   (*a*) Unascertained goods (*b*) Future goods
   (*c*) Ascertained goods (*d*) Specific goods.
8. Goods which are yet to be manufactured by the producer but entered to the contract is called
   (*a*) Future contract (*b*) Existing contract
   (*c*) Contingent contract (*d*) Specific contract.
9. An agreement entered by the farmer to sell the potatoes next season of harvest to the potato chips company is an example for
   (*a*) Future contract (*b*) Quasi contract
   (*c*) Specific contract (*d*) Contingent contract.
10. Seller depends upon an event for the delivery of goods are called
    (*a*) Contingency goods (*b*) Specific goods
    (*c*) Future goods (*d*) Existing goods.
11. Certain amount has to be kept by the buyer with the seller for the fulfillment of the contract is called
    (*a*) Deposit (*b*) A and B are same
    (*c*) Earnest (*d*) None of the above.
12. A contract of sale may be
    (*a*) Conditional (*b*) Absolute
    (*c*) Optional (*d*) Certain conditions.

13. If the contract does not contain any conditions, then the contract is said to be:
(*a*) Conditional contract (*b*) Absolute contract
(*c*) Semi conditional contract (*d*) None of the above.

14. If the goods is transferred absolutely to the buyer without any conditions, then the contract is called
(*a*) Quasi contract (*b*) Contractual contract
(*c*) Absolute contract (*d*) None of the above.

15. If the goods is transferred with certain conditions then the contract is said to be
(*a*) Absolute contract (*b*) Expressed contract
(*c*) Conditional contract (*d*) Implied contract.

16. In the law of sales the major term is called
(*a*) Conditions only (*b*) Warranties only
(*c*) Both conditions and warranties (*d*) None of the above.

17. In the law of sales the minor term is called
(*a*) Conditions only (*b*) Either warranties or conditions
(*c*) Both conditions and warranties (*d*) Warranties only.

18. The breach which gives rise to a right to repudiate the contract is called
(*a*) Warranty (*b*) Both A and B
(*c*) Either A or B (*d*) Condition.

19. The right which gives rise only to a claim for damages is called
(*a*) Condition (*b*) Warranty and condition both
(*c*) Warranty (*d*) None of the above.

20. The breach of a condition may also be treated as a breach of
(*a*) Warranty (*b*) Condition
(*c*) Both A and B (*d*) None of the above.

21. The number of express conditions and warranties the parties can include is
(*a*) Limited
(*b*) Limited by the court
(*c*) Infinite
(*d*) As per the policies of the government.

22. The law presumes their existence in the contract automatically is stated in the ______ condition.
(*a*) Express (*b*) In advertisements
(*c*) Implied (*d*) None of the above.

23. Goods shall correspond with sample is stated in _________ condition.
(*a*) Explicit (*b*) Implied
(*c*) On the product (*d*) None of the above.

24. The description may be in terms of:
(*a*) The quality of the goods (*b*) The quantity of the goods
(*c*) Both the quality and quantity (*d*) Price paid.

25. When under a contract of sale, goods to be supplied should be in accordance to
   (*a*) Sample provided (*b*) As per the availability
   (*c*) As per description (*d*) A and C.
26. The dealer who sells the goods by description is bound to deliver the goods of:
   (*a*) Merchantable quality
   (*b*) Low quality
   (*c*) High quality
   (*d*) As per the description provided by the dealer.
27. The condition only applicable to the sale of eatables and provisions is mentioned in
   (*s*) Condition as to food
   (*b*) Condition as to wholesomeness
   (*c*) Condition as to name of the food manufacturing company
   (*d*) Condition as to method of consumption.
28. Doctrine of caveat emptor means:
   (*a*) Let the buyer beware
   (*b*) Let the seller explain
   (*c*) Consumerism
   (*d*) It is an Act under the Sale of Goods Act, 1930.
29. The appropriation must be
   (*a*) Implied (*b*) Concurrent
   (*c*) Intentional (*d*) Expressed.
30. Nemo det quod non habet means:
   (*a*) No one can give what he has not got
   (*b*) No person can give a better title to the goods than he possesses
   (*c*) Title to the goods belongs to the buyer
   (*d*) The seller has the right to resell.
31. Modes of delivery may take which of the following:
   (*a*) Actual delivery (*h*) Symbolic delivery
   (*c*) Constructive delivery (*d*) All of the above.
32. The seller holding the goods of the buyer after the selling procedure has been done is an best example for:
   (*a*) Constructive delivery (*b*) Symbolic delivery
   (*c*) Actual delivery (*d*) None of the above.
33. Delivery and payment are:
   (*a*) Rights of the seller (*b*) Rights of buyer
   (*c*) Concurrent conditions (*d*) None of the above.
34. Concurrent conditions include
   (*a*) Buyer and seller (*b*) Buyer only
   (*b*) Seller only (*d*) None of these.

35. Who should bear the incidental charges and the expenses relating to the delivery of goods?
(*a*) Buyer (*b*) Partly by seller and buyer
(*c*) Seller himself (*d*) Manufacturer.

36. To have reasonable opportunity to examine the goods is the right exercised by
(*a*) Seller
(*b*) Concerned authorities like excise department, income tax department
(*c*) Supplier
(*d*) Buyer.

37. To receive the compensation for damages for any loss occasioned by neglect to take delivery of the goods is the right exercised by
(*a*) Buyer (*b*) Third person
(*c*) Seller (*d*) Middle man.

38. Right of lien is exercised by
(*a*) Unpaid Seller
(*b*) Buyer
(*c*) Seller or buyer depending upon the conditions and warranties
(*d*) Third party to the contract.

39. The rights which the seller can enforce against the buyer personally is known as
(*a*) Cash payment (*b*) Payment by cheque
(*c*) Personal remedies (*d*) None of the above.

40. Repudiation of contract entitles the buyer to
(*a*) Sue the seller for specific performance
(*b*) Treat the contract as rescinded and sue the seller
(*c*) Opportunity to examine the goods
(*d*) Reject the goods.

41. Suit for damages for non-acceptance is the right of unpaid seller claimed against:
(*a*) Seller personally (*b*) Both seller and buyer
(*c*) Buyer personally (*d*) None of the above.

42. In case of failure to deliver the goods to the buyer, the seller has
(*a*) To refund the price paid by the buyer
(*b*) Make free delivery of goods
(*c*) Give free gifts to impress the buyer
(*d*) Give discount to the buyer.

43. The seller has to compensate for any
(*a*) Damage of the goods (*b*) Non performance of the contract
(*c*) Breach of contract (*d*) Late performance of the contract.

44. Who has the right to sue for damages on buyer repudiating the contract
(*a*) Seller himself (*b*) Buyer himself
(*c*) Both seller and buyer (*d*) None of the above.

45. The delivery of goods is based on terms of

(*a*) Seller (*b*) Buyer

(*c*) Both (a) and (b) (*d*) None of the above.

46. The seller of a car hands over the keys of the car to the buyer this mode of delivery is known as

(*a*) Actual delivery of the goods (*b*) Symbolic delivery of the goods

(*c*) Constructive delivery (*d*) None of the above.

47. Physical delivery of the goods is also known as

(*a*) Actual delivery of the goods (*b*) Symbolic delivery of the goods

(*c*) Constructive delivery of the goods (*d*) None of the above.

48. Voluntary transfer of possession from one person to another is known as

(*a*) Purchase of goods (*b*) Selling of goods

(*c*) Delivery of goods (*d*) All of the above.

49. The appropriation of goods refers to

(*a*) Quality (*b*) Quantity

(*c*) Both a and b (*d*) None of the above.

50. Transfer of property means the transfer of ownership of the goods from the

(*a*) Seller to the buyer (*b*) Buyer to the seller

(*c*) Seller only (*d*) Buyer only.

51. Doctrine of caveat emptor does not apply to:

(*a*) The seller deviates from the quality of the product

(*b*) Goods which are not meant for the specific purpose

(*c*) Misrepresentation made by the seller

(*d*) All of the above.

52. Right to sell means

(*a*) Seller is the owner of the goods and he can transfer title to the buyer

(*b*) Buyer becomes the owner of the goods as soon as the title of the goods is transferred

(*c*) Seller has no right to transfer the title of the goods

(*d*) None of the above.

53. Quiet possession comes under

(*a*) Standard conditions (*b*) Express warranties

(*c*) Implied warranties (*d*) None of the above.

54. The law presumes their existence in the contract automatically though they have not been put into it in express words is

(*a*) Explicit condition (*b*) Express condition

(*c*) Implied condition (*d*) Standard condition.

55. Goods identified and agreed upon at the time a contract of sale is made is called

(*a*) Ascertained goods (*b*) Unascertained goods

(*c*) Future goods (*d*) Existing goods.

56. Goods which are opposite to the specific goods are called

(*a*) Ascertained goods (*b*) Unascertained goods

(*c*) Contingent goods (*d*) Future goods.

57. Goods which are acquired by the seller after making the contract of sale is called

(*a*) Future goods (*b*) Existing goods

(*c*) Specific goods (*d*) Generic goods.

58. Unascertained goods are also called

(*a*) Specific goods (*b*) Generic goods

(*c*) Existing goods (*d*) Future goods.

59. Recovery of the price and interest is the right of

(*a*) Buyer (*b*) Supplier or seller

(*c*) Third party to the contract (*d*) All of the above.

60. Remedy to the buyer includes

(*a*) Damages for non-delivery (*b*) Specific performance

(*c*) Repudiation of contract (*d*) All of the above.

ANSWERS

1. (*d*)	2. (*c*)	3. (*d*)	4. (*a*)
5. (*a*)	6. (*c*)	7. (*a*)	8. (*a*)
9. (*a*)	10. (*a*)	11. (*c*)	12. (*b*)
13. (*b*)	14. (*c*)	15. (*c*)	16. (*a*)
17. (*d*)	18. (*d*)	19. (*c*)	20. (*a*)
21. (*c*)	22. (*c*)	23. (*b*)	24. (*a*)
25. (*d*)	26. (*d*)	27. (*b*)	28. (*a*)
29. (*c*)	30. (*b*)	31. (*d*)	32. (*a*)
33. (*c*)	34. (*a*)	35. (*c*)	36. (*d*)
37. (*c*)	38. (*a*)	39. (*c*)	40. (*b*)
41. (*c*)	42. (*a*)	43. (*c*)	44. (*a*)
45. (*c*)	46. (*b*)	47. (*a*)	48. (*c*)
49. (*c*)	50. (*a*)	51. (*d*)	52. (*a*)
53. (*c*)	54. (*c*)	55. (*a*)	56. (*b*)
57. (*a*)	58. (*b*)	59. (*a*)	60. (*d*)

4

THE INDIAN PARTNERSHIP ACT, 1932

4.1 INTRODUCTION TO THE INDIAN PARTNERSHIP ACT, 1932

(A) Scheme of the Act

Partnership is a form of business organization, where two or more people, having common interest, join together for jointly carrying on some business. The law relating to partnership in India is embodied in the Indian Partnership Act, 1932. Before this Act could come into force, the provisions of Sections 239 to 266 of the Indian Contract Act governed a partnership. This Act was given effect to from the 1st of October, 1932. However, Section 69, which deals with the effect of non-registration of firms, came into force from 1st October 1933. The Act extends to the whole of India except the State of Jammu & Kashmir. According to Sec 3, since partnership comes into existence only by a contract between people who later become partners of the firm, the provisions of the Indian Contract Act, continue to apply to partnership firms.

(B) Definition

Section 4 of the Indian Partnership Act defines a partnership as *'Partnership is the relation between persons who have agreed to share the profits of a business carried on by all or any of them acting for all'*. Partnership is therefore an association of two or more individuals who engage themselves in a commercial activity through joint efforts, labour, skill with the intention of dividing the profits and bearing the loss arising out of such association.

Essential elements and characteristic features of partnership are:

- There must be an agreement.
- Between two or more persons
- Who agree to carry on business
- With the object of sharing profit
- The business must be carried by all or any of them acting for all or Mutual Agency.

In the Act, unless there is anything repugnant in the subject or context;

(*a*) An "act of a firm" means any act or omission by all the partners, or by any partner or agent of the firm which gives rise to a right enforceable by or against the firm;

(*b*) "Business" includes every trade, occupation and profession;

(*c*) "Prescribed" means prescribed by rules made under this Act; (c-1)

(*d*) "Registrar" means the Registrar of Firms appointed under sub-section (1) of section 57 and includes the Deputy Registrar of Firms and Assistant Registrar of Firms appointed under sub-section (2) of that section;

(*e*) "Third party" used in relation to a firm or to a partner therein means any person who is not a partner in the firm; and

(*f*) expressions used but not defined in this Act and defined in the Indian Contract Act, 1872, shall have the meanings assigned to them in that Act.

1. **An agreement:** The relationship of partnership arises from an agreement between the persons concerned and not from status. Agreement as made between the persons must be valid and enforceable bylaw. This agreement may be oral or written or even inferred from the conduct of the parties. To avoid future complications and dispute amongst the persons constituting partnership, agreement in writing must be preferred. The agreement may be for a particular period, or an uncertain period, or for carrying on a particular venture.

   Illustration: *A & B enter into an agreement to start a business of manufacturing of mobile handsets and decide to share the profits and losses arising out of the business in the ratio of investment by the two. Here, a partnership is created between A & B.*

2. **Two or more persons:** There must be at least two persons to form a partnership. Only persons competent to contract can enter into partnerships. The minimum number of persons required to form a partnership is two (2) and the maximum number is ten (10) in the case of banking business and twenty (20) in the case of other type of business. If the number of partners in the respective business is above the prescribed limit, the partnership will be treated as illegal.

3. **Carrying on of business:** The agreement between the partners should be to carry on business. As per the Act, there can be no partnership agreement without a business. Sec 2(b) of the Act reads as under "business" includes every trade, occupation or profession. If the purpose is to carry on charitable work, it cannot be considered as partnership. Carrying on of the business means continuity of business activities; which is the main characteristic to consider an association of individuals as a partnership firm. Section 8, of the Act, however, provides that there can be a 'particular partnership' between partners whereby they engage in a particular adventure, project or undertaking, which, if successful, would result in profit. Thus there can be a partnership for production of a film, construction of a building, etc.

   Illustration: *In Govind Nair Vs. Maga (1948), two persons jointly purchased a tea shop by contributing in equal amounts and also incurred additional expenses in equipping it. The tea shop was then leased out on the understanding that the rent should be shared equally. It was held by the Madras High Court that the parties were only co-owners, and not partners, as they did not carry on any business.*

4. **Sharing of profit:** The essential element of partnership is to carry on business with the object of sharing profit amongst the partners. The motive of a partnership should be to earn profits. The partners may however agree to share profits in any ratio they like. Sec 13(b) however, provides that the partners are entitled to share equally in profits

earned and shall contribute equally to the loss sustained by the firm, unless otherwise, agreed. It means that the partners may make a contract contrary to this provision.

5. **Mutual agency:** The law relating to Principal and Agent is applicable to the law of Partnership in terms of mutual agency. This means that the *'business must be carried by all or any of them acting for all'*. It means all the partners should be able to represent each other and should be represented by each other with respect to the business of partnership. Thus the foundation of the relationship between the partners of a firm is the relationship of a principal and agent. In the case of partnership all the partners are essentially principals and agents to one another. Therefore as an agent, a partner binds the other partners for his acts done in the ordinary course of partnership business and similarly, each partner is bound by the acts of the other partners in his capacity as their principal. However, it may be noted that a partner can bind the firm (partners) by his act provided:
   - He acts within the scope of his authority
   - His acts are done in the name and on behalf of the firm
   - These acts are done for the benefit of the business of the firm

Illustration: *A, B and C enter into a partnership agreement for the manufacture of umbrellas. Z a dealer in umbrella material makes a deal with C for the supply of the material to the firm. Here, C has acted as an agent of A and B. In case of a default by the partnership firm, Z can file a suit against A, B and C.*

4.2 THE TRUE TEST OF PARTNERSHIP

Although a partnership is an association of persons, every such association need not be a partnership. Similarly, the business may be carried on for profit, but, if the agreement does not provide for sharing of profits, there cannot be a partnership. The existence of a business for profit and an agreement between the parties to share the profits need not make them partners of the business. There are four particular instances where a person though sharing profits with other partners, or seeking payment which is dependent upon the profits earned by the firm, but still cannot be termed or called as a partner of the firm. These class of individuals include:

- An agent or a servant as remuneration
- A moneylender to persons engaged or about to engage in any business
- A widow or child of a deceased partner as annuity
- The seller of goodwill, *i.e.*, by the previous owner or part owner of the business as consideration for the sale of the goodwill or share thereof

The Act specifies certain test to ascertain the existence of a partnership.

(*a*) Sharing of profits as a test,

(*b*) Principal-agency relationship as a test

(*c*) Existence of an express agreement between the persons.

All the elements mentioned must coexist in order to constitute Partnership. Sec 6 of Indian Partnership Act provides that *'in determining whether a group of persons is or is not a firm or whether a person is or is not a partner in a firm, regard shall be had to the real relation between the parties, as shown by all relevant facts taken together.'* The existence of a partnership can be determined when there is an express agreement between persons.

Illustrations:

Sharing of profits as a test: *(1) In Cox Vs. Coulson (1916), the defendant, who was the manager of a theatre, entered into an agreement with one Mr. Mill for making the theatre available for a play. According to the agreement, he was to pay for the lighting and other expenses, and receive 60% of the gross takings. Mr. Mill was to pay for the theatrical company, provide the scenery and receive 40% of the gross takings. The plaintiff was injured by a shot fired by an actor during performance. She made the defendant liable on the ground that he was a partner of Mr. Mill. The Court of Appeal held that the defendant could not be made liable as he was not a partner, for the sharing of gross returns did not by itself create a partnership.*

(2) In Badley Vs. Consolidated Bank (1888), money was lent to a person to enable him to construct a railway. The borrower assigned to the lender machinery, plant and securities, and agreed to pay 10% interest on the money advanced, plus 10% on the profits of the venture, subject to an allowance of £1,000, which the borrower might draw for his services in carrying out the construction work. It was held that the lender of money was not, in spite of his share of profits, a partner. Although it was true that the lender's money was required to be employed as capital in the venture, it was not risked in the construction work since it could have been recovered from the borrower if the venture had failed.

Principal-agency relationship as a test: *(1) In Walker Vs. Hirsch (1884), the plaintiff, Hirsch, previously a clerk in the firm of Walker agreed to advance £1,500 to the firm in return for a salary of £180 and one-eighth of profit. It was held that he remained a servant, and as such could not move for winding of the firm. The decision in this case was clearly based on the principle that unless person acts as an agent of another, they cannot be partners with each other.*

(2) In Mohammed Musa Sahib Vs. Mohamed Ghouse Sahib (1959), two persons agreed to carry on a business subject to the arrangement that each would run the business for two years without being accountable to the other. It was held that there was no partnership in the absence of principal-agent relationship.

Existence of an express agreement between the persons: *In Raghunandan Nanu Vs. Hormasjee Benzonjee (1927), the defendant was admitted to a partner by the plaintiff for one year, subject to the terms that the defendant would get ₹500 in lieu of profits but would not be responsible for the losses, no capital to be contributed by him and he would have all the rights of a partner. It was held that the defendant was a partner.*

4.3 DISTINCTION BETWEEN

(A) Partnership and Company

(*i*) *Formation:* A partnership is governed by the Partnership Act, while a Joint Stock Company is governed by the Companies Act. The formation of a partnership is relatively easy while a company has to observe a number of legal formalities connected with its formation.

(*ii*) *Registration:* A partnership may or may not be registered. However, a Joint Stock Company must be registered. The Certificate of Incorporation is a conclusive evidence of the registration of a company. An unregistered company becomes either a partnership or an illegal association, depending upon the number of members.

(*iii*) *Legal status:* A partnership is not a distinct legal entity. Persons who have entered into partnership with one another are called individually partners and collectively a firm. In the case of a company, however, the members are quite distinct from the company which is a juristic person. In other words, a company is an artificial person in the eyes of law enjoying a distinct entity apart from its members.

(*iv*) *Nature of contract:* The agreement between persons that brings a partnership into existence may or may not be in writing. If it is in writing, it becomes a private document. As such, outsiders cannot have recourse to its contents. However, the agreement that brings a company into existence, known as the Memorandum of Association, must be in writing. It is also a public document.

(*v*) *Number of members:* In the case of a partnership business engaged in banking activity, the maximum number of members is 10, while in the case of other types of business it is 20. The minimum is 2. In the case of a Private Joint Stock Company, the minimum number of members is 2, while the maximum is 50 excluding the employees. In a Public Company, the minimum is 7 and maximum is unlimited.

(*vi*) *Liability:* The liability of a partner is joint, several and unlimited, but the liability of a member of a company is limited to the face value of the shares held by him, or the amount guaranteed by him, depending on whether the liability of the members is limited by shares or by guarantee.

(*vii*) *Objects:* A partnership may engage itself in any business which the partners like whereas a company can engage itself only in the business mentioned under the object clause of the Memorandum. Thus, this clause restricts the powers of a company with regard to the nature of the business which it could undertake.

(*viii*) *Capital:* The capital contributions by the partners can be altered freely, but the capital of a company cannot be altered except by observing the legal formalities laid down in the Companies Act.

(*ix*) *Property:* The partnership property belongs to all the partners. As such, the property of the firm is the property of the partners. In the case of a company, however, the property belongs to the company and not to the members.

(*x*) *Management:* In the case of a partnership, every partner is entitled to take part in the management of partnership business. In the case of a company, the management of its affairs is entrusted to a Board of Directors duly elected by the members.

(*xi*) *Agency:* Principal-agency relationship is the essence of a partnership. Every partner is an agent of the firm to make contracts on behalf of the firm. In the case of a company, however, no member is an agent of the company or any other member. Consequently, no member can make contracts on behalf of the company. Such a power vests only with the Directors who have to act *intra vires* the Memorandum and Articles.

(*xii*) *Transfer of shares:* A partner cannot transfer his interests in the partnership without the consent of the other partners. If he does so, without the consent of the others, the partnership is deemed to have been dissolved. A shareholder, however, can effect a transfer of its shares without the consent of any other member. While the shares of a public company are freely transferable, those of a private company can, subject to restrictions imposed on the same.

(*xiii*) *Dissolution:* While a partnership is dissolved by the death or insolvency of a partner, a company is not affected by any such contingency. A company enjoys perpetual existence.

(*xiv*) *Accounts and audit:* The accounts of a partnership need not be audited and disclosed to the public. In the case of a company, its accounts should be audited by a registered and licensed auditor and placed before the members; a copy sent to the Registrar of Companies and in case of a public enterprise, the accounts should be made available to the public by publication in the newspaper.

(B) Partnership and Joint Hindu Family

Although a partnership resembles a Joint Hindu Family Business, Section 5 of the Act states that the members of a Joint Hindy Family are not partners in such business. Under the Income Tax Act, a Hindu Undivided Family is a distinct entity apart from its members. The manager of the family business can enter into a partnership agreement with a stranger. But the other members of the joint family do not automatically become partners in the business. This is so even if some members of the family enter into partnership with a stranger.

Partnership	Joint Hindu Family Business
A partnership arises on the basis of a contract.	A Joint Hindu Family firm arises on the basis of status i.e., by birth, and by operation of law.
A partnership may have female members as partners.	A Joint Hindu Family firm cannot have female co-parceners.
A new partner cannot be admitted into partnership without the consent of the other partners.	The membership of a Joint Hindu Family firm happens by birth to every male member of the family.
The death of a partner brings about the dissolution of the partnership.	The death of a co-parcener in a Joint Hindu Family firm does not dissolve the Hindu family business.
In a partnership all the members are entitled to take an active part in the management of the business.	In a Joint Hindu Family firm, only the senior male member of the family is entitled to take active part in the management of the business.
The existence of mutual agency enables a partner to bind the other partners for the acts done by him in the ordinary course of business.	A Joint Hindu Family firm does not have mutual agency, as such , it is only the manger who has a right to bind the other co-parceners for his acts.
The liability of a partner is joint and several and also unlimited in certain cases.	A co-parcener is liable only to the extent of his interest in the family property. It is only the manager who is personally liable to an unlimited extent.
Since a partnership arises on the basis of a contract, a minor cannot be a partner, although he may be admitted to the benefits of the firm.	In the case of Joint Hindu Family firm, even a minor can be a co-parcener.
Partnership business is disrupted by dissolution.	Joint Hindu Family firm is disrupted only by partition.
A partner has a right to demand his share of profits of the business.	A co-parcener has no such right. He can only demand partition and separate himself from the Joint Hindu Family firm's business.

(C) Partnership and Co-ownership

The Act states that '*the sharing of profits or of gross returns arising from property by prsons holding a joint or common interest in that property does not of itself make such persons partners.*'

Partnership	Co-ownership
Partnership arises on the basis of a contract.	Co-ownership arises out of relationship between the parties, status or a contract.
Business is necessary for the existence of a partnership.	Co-ownership can exist without any business.
Partnership involves sharing of profits and losses.	Co-ownership may not always involve sharing of profits and losses.
Partners are mutual agents.	Co-owners are not responsible for the acts of the other co-owner.
A partner cannot transfer his interests to a stranger without the consent of the other partners.	A co-owner can always transfer his share without the consent of the other co-owners.
A partner has a lien on the partnership property for expenses incurred by him.	A co-owner has no lien.
A partner is not entitled to claim a share in the partnership property in specie.	A co-owner can claim division of the joint property in specie.

(D) Partnership, Sole Trading Business and Company

Partnership is an improvement over the Sole Trading Concern, where one single individual with his own resources, skill and effort carries on his own business. He has limitation of resources , enjoys the profits and endures the losses incurred by himself.

In a partnership on the other hand, a number of persons could pool their resources and efforts and could start a much larger business, than could be afforded by a Sole Trader. The burden of loss is divided amongst the partners in the firm.

A company, as a form of business organization is an artificial person, distinct from its members and has a much longer life than that of a partnership. In case of a company the liability of a member is limited to the extent of the amount of shares purchased by him, whereas in case of partnership the liability of every partner is unlimited, and this factor is of great advantage in the case of a company, from the point of view of risk of investor in the business.

In certain respects a partnership is more suitable form of business organization than a company. For the creation of a partnership just an agreement between various persons is all what is required, whereas in case of a company there are lot of procedural formalities which have to be gone through before company is created. Even for the dissolution of a partnership, a mere agreement between the partners is enough, but it is not so in the case of a company, which can be wound up only after a set procedure is followed.

4.4 FORMATION OF A PARTNERSHIP

Meaning

Section 4 of the Act *'Persons who have entered into partnership with one another are called individually partners and collectively, a firm and the name under which their business is carried on is called the firm name.'* A partnership firm is an aggregate of the individuals who are partners in a business. It is not a distinct legal entity, but a name given to the partners collectively. But under the Income Tax Act, a firm is treated as a person, and the name of the firm is used in legal instruments and it is personified and treated as a separate entity for accounting purposes.

Section 2(a) of the Act defines an 'act of firm' as *'any act or omission by all the partners or by any partner or agent of the firm which gives rise to a right enforceable by or against the firm.'* Therefore, act of the firm is necessarily the act of the partners, although rights are enforceable by or aganist the firm. A partnership is formed by an agreement between the partners. The Act provides that persons who have entered into a partnership with one another are called individually 'partners' and collectively a firm and the name under which their business is carried is called the 'firm name'. The rights and obligations of the partners towards each other and towards the firm can be determined by an oral or written agreement. To avoid future dispute it is always advisable to have partnership agreement expressed in writing.

(A) Types of Formation of Partnership

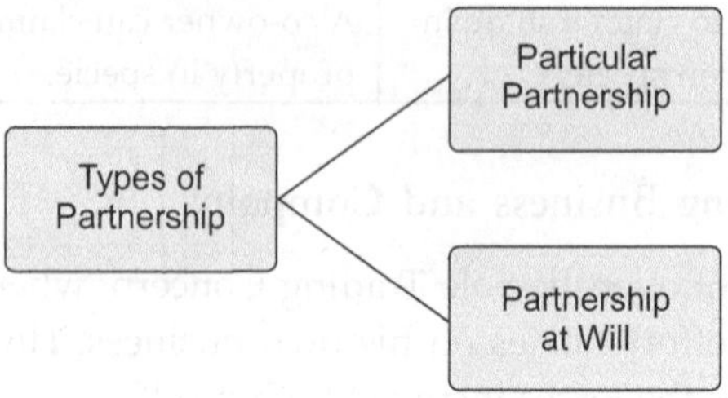

The formation of a partnership or type of partnership means, there is an agreement between parties to form the firm as per provision of the Partnership Act. A partnership may be brought into existence either for a particular period or to carry on a particular venture. When a partnership is formed for a particular purpose it is termed as 'particular partnership'. A particular partnership is automatically dissolved on completion of the venture or the transaction.

Even when a partnership is formed for a particular period or for a fixed duration, such a partnership also falls within the category of particular partnership as the relationship between the partners is automatically terminated after the expirty of the period for which it was created.

According to Section 7 of the Act, *'Where no provision is made by contract between the partners for the duration of their partnership, or for the determination of their partnership, the partnership is 'partnership at will'.* A partnership at will is one in which the contract between the partners does not provide for either duration or mode of dissolution of the partnership. In other words, a partnership at will is one for an indefinite period. As such, the partners are free to dissolve it at any time they like.

In the case of a particular partnership, just as the partners are at liberty to wind up their affairs even before the expiry of the term or the completion of the venture, they are equally at liberty to continue even after the happening of any such contingency. But, if they decide to continue their partnership, it ceases to be a particular partnership, but becomes a partnership at will.

Illustration: *In Robinson Vs. Anderson (1855), it was held that if two solicitors agree to conduct a case on behalf of a client and share the profits accruing thereform , the relationship between the solicitors would be a particular partnership.*

(B) Partnership Deed

A partnership agreement may either be express or implied. The essence of a partnership agreement lies in mutual trust and confidence. The document or the instrument containing the agreement between partners is knowns as the 'partnership deed'. A partnership agreement when put in writing is termed as partnership deed.

Before the commencement of a partnership firm, the partners usually draft the deed to ensure that the business runs smoothly and in case of dispute the terms of the partnership deed may be referred for redressal of the dispute according to the terms of the partnership deed. Just as in the case rules of contract, only legally competent persons can enter into a partnership agreement. There should be free consent between the partners to the agreement. Since the partnership is based on mutual trust and confidence, the agreement can be rescinded by a partner on the ground of fraud or misrepresentation. The object of the agreement should be lawful, legal and not opposed to public policy. What should be the exact contents in the deed depends on the particular circumstances of each case and may contain the following clauses, namely;

1. Name and address of the firm and nature of business to be carried on
2. Name and address of the partners
3. Date of commencement and duration of partnership
4. The capital and any other contribution made by partners
5. The ratio to share profit and losses amongst the partners
6. Rules as to interest on loans and capital, their salary, commission, etc.
7. Method and arrangement of keeping accounts
8. Division of task and obligation of partners
9. Rules to be followed in case of admission, expulsion/retirement or death of a partner
10. Whether a partner is allowed to carry competing business
11. The circumstances under which the partnership will stand dissolved
12. In case of dispute which course of action shall be followed *e.g.*, Court, arbitrations etc.
13. Method of valuation of goodwill in case of admission, retirement or death of a partner
14. Dissolution and distribution of assets

According to the Indian Partnership Act, 1932, a 'Partnership' is the relation between persons who have agreed to share the profit of a business carried on by all or any of them acting for all. Persons who have entered into a partnership are called by the name under which the business is carried on, which is the name of the firm. A firm is not a legal person. Partnership is, merely a relationship between persons, brought about by an agreement to share the profits of a business.

Since a partnership is the result of a contract, there must be at least two partners. The Partnership Act places no upper limit on the number of partners. However, under Section 11 of the Companies Act, 1956, it is provided that a partnership cannot have more than ten partners for carrying on the business of banking, or more than twenty partners for carrying on any other business. Thus, a partnership cannot have more than 20 partners.

A Hindu Undivided family (HUF) cannot enter into a partnership with other persons, as it is not a legal person, but the Karta of a HUF can. Two Kartas of Hindu undivided families can form a partnership, but the individual members of the two HUFs do not, automatically, become partners.

Subject to provision of this Act, mutual rights and duties maybe determined by the contract—either expressed or implied by course of dealing between the partners. Such contract can be varied by consent of all the partners and, such consent may be expressed or may be implied by the course of dealings between them, with regard to:

1. To conduct the business of the firm to the greatest common advantage.
2. To be just and faithful towards the firm and other partners.
3. To render true accounts and full information, relating to and, affecting the firm or, any partner or, his legal representative.
4. To indemnify the firm for loss, caused by his fraud, in conduct of the business of the firm.
5. To attend, diligently, to his duties in the conduct of the business.

(C) Rights of a Partner

1. To take part in the conduct of the business.
2. To express his opinion before a decision is taken. A majority may take all decision relating to ordinary matters connected with the business, but no change in nature of business may be made without the consent of all the partners.
3. To access and inspect and copy books of the firm.
4. To share the profits of the firm.
5. To be indemnified, in respect of payment made, and liabilities incurred, by him, in the ordinary and proper course of business. In case of an emergency, every partner is entitled to protect the firm from loss, as would have been done by a prudent man, in his own case.
6. To receive interest, on an amount subscribed by him, beyond the capital at the rate of 6%, per annum.

4.5 TYPES OF PARTNERS

(a) *Active Partner*: A partner who becomes a partner by an agreement and is engaged in the actual conduct of the business of the firm is called Active Partner. He works as an agent of all the partners in the firm and binds himself and all the partners to third parties for all the acts done in the name of the firm. An Active Partner is also called an Ostensible Partner. Being an Active Partner, he has authority to bind the firm and the other partners for the acts done by him in the ordinary course of business. Since he actively and publicly engages himself in the partnership business, he has to give notice of his retirement to free himself from the liability for the acts of the firm after his retirement.

(b) *Inactive or Sleeping Partner*: A Sleeping partner is also known as a Dormant partner or Secret partner. An inactive or sleeping partner is one who does not take part in the conduct of businsess of the firm, though he invests his capital in the firm and takes his share out of the profits of the firm or bears the share of its losses. His liability is also the same as that of all others or any of the active partners. Like an active partner, he invests capital and participates in the profits of the business and is also liable to an unlimited extent for the debts of the firm like an active partner. However, his liability ceases immediately on his retirement. But being in the position of an undisclosed principal, he need not give public notice of his retirement to free himself from liability for the acts of the other partners after he ceases to be a partner. If a partner is known to the public as such, but does not take an active part in the management of the business, he is called a Silent Partner.

(c) *Nominal Partner*: A nominal partner is a partner who does not have any real interest in the firm but lends his name as one of the partners in the firm. He neither invests in the firm, nor shares its profits or losses, nor takes part in the working of the firm, but he is liable to the third parties like all other active partners. A nominal partner neither contributes capital nor participates in the profits of the business. He only lends his name to the firm. Unlike a sleeping partner, he is known to the outside world and is liable for all the acts of the firm.

Illustration: *A is a renowned businessman. His son B starts the business in which A has given consent to become partner of the firm. A with the sole intention to assist his son invests in the business as a partner, (which is to be run by his son) Here, A is a nominal partner.*

(d) *Sub-Partner*: When a partner agrees to share his profits in a firm with a third person, that third person is called a Sub-Partner. Legally, he is not a partner and cannot represent the firm. He neither has any right as a partner in the firm nor is he so liable. Since there is no privity of contract between the other partners and the third party, he is a stranger to the firm. His contractual relationship is only with one of the partners of the firm.

(e) *Partner by Estoppel or Holding Out*: Sometimes, a person who is not a partner in the firm, may under certain circumstances, be liable for its debts as if he were a partner. Such a person is called a 'Partner by Estoppel or Holding out'.

According to Section 28 of the Act,'*Anyone who, by words spoken or written or by conduct represents himself, or knowingly permits himself to be represented, to be a partner in a firm, is liable as a partner in that firm, to any one who has on the faith of any such representation given credit to the firm whether the person representing himself or represented to be a partner does or does not know that the representation has reached the person so giving credit.*' Therefore, a partnership by estoppel or holdling out may arise as a result of surrounding circumstances or the conduct of the parties. A person who represents himself to be a partner in a firm, or permits himself to be so represented, becomes automatically liable as a partner in that firm to anyone who gives credit to the firm on the faith of such representation. Such a representation may be made orally or inwriting or by the conduct of the person making the representation. It is not necessary that the person making the representation should know that his representation has reached the party giving credit to the firm.

Liability by reason of holding out arises in the case of a partner who retires, but fails to give public notice of his retirement. His failure to do so makes him liable by estoppel for the debts of the firm contracted suabsequent to his retirement, to persons still knowing and believing him to be a partner. It may also arise in the case of a minor who has attained the age of majority, but has not given public notice of his willingness or otherwise to continue as a partner.

Condition for liability on the ground of Holding out: In order to render a person liable as a partner on the ground of holding out, he must have:

(i) by words spoken or written or by conduct represented himself to be a partner, or

(ii) knowingly permitted to be represented as a partner to the other person, and

(iii) Under Sec 28(1), '*the other person must have acted on the faith of such representation, and given credit to the firm. It does not matter whether the person representing himself or being represented to be a partner does or does not know that the representation has reached the other person so giving credit.*'

Illustration: *In Scarf Vs. Jardine (1882), a firm known as Rogers and Co. had two partners, Scarf and Rogers. When Scarf retired, another partner by name Beach joined in his place and the firm continued its business under the old name. No public notice of retirement was given by Scarf. Jardine, who had trading* *relationship with the old firm, sold some goods to the firm. When the firm failed to pay, Jardine sued the firm consisting of Rogers and Beach, choosing to do so. When the firm went bankrupt, Jardine sued Scarf to make him liable as an ex-partner. It was held that the ex-partner, not being a joint debtor with the partners of the new firm, the creditor might sue at his option, either the partners of the old firm or the partners of the new firm, but not all.*

(*f*) *Partners in profit only*: A partner who participates in the profits of the partnership business, without being responsible for the losses, is known as a partner in profits only. He contributes capital but does not take part in the management of the business. Like any other type of partner, his liability for the acts of the firm is unlimited. Usually such a partner is taken into the firm for some particular purpose like, huge capital investment or his vast business contacts, etc. However, such a partner is severally and jointly liable for the liabilities of the firm.

4.6 MINOR AS A PARTNER

The Contract Act does not consider a Minor as being capable of entering into a contract. Since a partnership arises on the basis of a contract, a minor cannot become a partner and be a signatory to the partnership agreement. A Minor cannot become a partner. A minor is incompetent to contract, his agreement is void and, therefore he is incapable of becoming a partner in any partnership firm. If while creating partnership, a minor is made a full-fledged partner in a partnership firm, the deed would be invalid and the document cannot be enforced even between other partners. It was held by the Supreme Court in *Commissioner of Income Tax Vs. Dwarakadas Khetan & Co. (1961)*, an agreement which makes a minor a full partner in a partnership, cannot be regarded as valid for the purpose of registration under the Income Tax Act. In another case *Commissioner of Income Tax Vs. Shah Mohandas (1966)*, the same Court held the view that a guardian of a minor cannot enter into a partnership agreement on behalf of the minor so as to enable the minor to enjoy all the rights and be subject to all the obligations of a full-fledged partner.

Position of a Minor Admitted to the Benefits of Partnership [Section 30]: Section 30(1) of the Act also lays down in this context that '*A person who is a minor according to the law to which he is subject may not be a partner in a firm, but with the consent of all the partners for the time being, he may be admitted to the benefits of partnership.*' Therefore, although a minor cannot be a partner in a firm, he may be admitted, with the consent of the other partners, to the benefits of partnership. Minor's Admission to the Benefits of Partnership.

The agreement by a minor is void but he is capable of accepting benefits. In consonance with this position of law, Section 30(1) provides that a minor may not be a partner in a firm, but with the consent of all the partners for the time being, he may be admitted to the benefits of partnership. The introduction of a minor to the benefits of partnership presupposes existence of a valid partnership between persons competent to contract. There can be no partnership of all minors, but a partnership between persons competent to contract may exist before a minor can be admitted to its benefits.

Section 30 contains the following provision regarding the position of a minor admitted to the benefits of partnership.

1. A person who is a minor according to the law to which he is subject may not be a partner in a firm but, with the consent of all the partners for the time being he may be admitted to the benefits of partnership.

2. Such minor has a right to such share of the property and of the profits of the firm as may be agreed upon, and he may have access to and inspect and copy any of the accounts of the firm.
3. Such minor's share is liable for the acts of the firm, but the minor is not personally liable for any such act.
4. Such minor may not sue the partners for an account or payment of his share of the property or profits of the firm, save when severing his connection with the firm, and in such case the amount of his share shall he determined by a valuation made as far as possible in accordance with the rules contained in Section 48 of the Act which states that ; 'Provided that all the partners acting together or any partner entitled to dissolve the firm upon notice to other partners may elect in such suit to dissolve the firm, and thereupon the Court shall proceed with the suit as one for dissolution and for settling accounts between the partners, and the amount of the share of the minor shall be determined along with the shares of the partners'.
5. At any time within six months of his attaining majority, or of his obtaining knowledge that he had been admitted to the benefits of partnership (whichever date is earlier), such person may give public notice that he has elected to become or that he has elected not to become a partner in the firm and such notice shall determine his position as regards the firm: Provided that, if he fails to give such notice, be shall become a partner in the firm on the expiry of the said six months.
6. Where any person has been admitted as a minor to the benefits of partnership in a firm, the burden of proving the fact that such person had no knowledge of such admission until a particular date after the expiry of six months of his attaining majority shall lie on the persons asserting that fact.
7. Where such person becomes a partner.
   (*a*) his rights and liabilities as a minor continue up to the date on which he becomes a partner, but he also becomes personally liable to third parties for all acts of the firm done since he was admitted to the benefits of partnership, and
   (*b*) his share in the property and profits of the firm shall be the share to which he was entitled to as a minor.
8. Where such person elects not to become a partner.
   (*a*) his rights and liabilities shall continue to be those of a minor (under this section) up to the date on which he gives public notice,
   (*b*) his share shall not be liable for any acts of the firm done after the date of the notice, and
   (*c*) he shall be entitled to sue the partners for his share of the property and profits in accordance with subsection(4) of the Act.

Illustration: *In Lachmi Narain v. Beni Ram, two persons entered into partnership under the name Beni Ram Hoti Lal in 1900. Motilal died in1920 and thereafter Beni Ram continued the business under the old name and style with the partnership funds. Lachmi Narain's minor son (the plaintiff) alleged that after his father's death he was admitted to the benefits of partnership. Held, the plaintiff (minor) could not be admitted to the benefits of partnership, as no partnership existed after the death of Hotilal. Moreover the plaintiff being a minor could not enter into a contract with Beni Ram to form partnership.*

It is possible that the major members decide to constitute partnership and admit the minors to the benefit of the said partnership. A guardian is capable of accepting benefits on behalf of a minor. Admission of a minor to the benefits of partnership can be done only with the consent of all the partners.

(A) Minor's Position During Minority

The minor thus admitted has a right to such share of the property and of the profits of the firm as may be agreed upon. He however cannot go to the court of law to enforce his rights in respect of such share so long as he continues to be admitted to the benefits of partnership. This disability is removed when he is severing his connection with the firm. He can also have access to any of the accounts of the firm and can inspect and copy them. In this matter his position is different from a partner of the firm. A partner has a right to have access to and to inspect and copy any of the books of the firm whereas a minor's right has been limited. Every partner is jointly and severally liable for all acts of the firm. Moreover his liability is unlimited and can extend to his personal property. A minor, on the other hand, is not personally liable for any such act. It is only his share which is liable for the acts of the firm. The rights and liabilities of a minor as laid down in the act include;

(i) Rights of a Minor

(*a*) A minor is entitled to such share of the property and of the profits of the firm, as may be agreed upon.

(*b*) A minor has a right of access to accounts of the firm. He can also inspect and copy them. However, this right is limited only to the account books of the firm. He cannot have access to any other book, if maintained by the firm, since the same may contain a secret of the firm and the minor's knowledge of the same would be detrimental to the interests of the firm.

(*c*) On severing connection with the firm, the minor becomes entitled to sue the other partners for accounts, payment of his share of profits or property.

(*d*) A minor has a right to elect either to become a partner or not, on attaining the age of majority.

(ii) Liabilities of a Minor

A minor's share in the profits and property of the firm is liable for the acts of the firm. The minor is not personally liable for any acts of the partners as the principle of unlimited liability, is not applicable to a minor.

A minor who has been admitted to the benefits of partnership has the option of expressing his willingness to continue being a partner after attaining age of majority by a public notice. Section 30(5) states; '*At anytime within six months of his attaining majority, or of his obtaining knowledge that he had been admitted to the benefits of partnership, whichever date is later, such person may give public notice that he has elected to become or that he has elected not to become a partner in the firm, and such notice shall determine his position as regards the firm; provided that, if he fails to give such notice, he shall become a partner in the firm on the expiry of the said six months.*' Therefore, the minor on attaining the age of majority has to give a public notice of his opinion. Such notice is required to be given within six months of attaining majority or of his obtaining knowledge that he had been admitted to the benefits of partnership, whichever date is later. If he fails to give such notice, he shall be deemed to have become a partner on the expiry of the said six months. After the minor has given his opinion and if he elects to become a partner, his rights and liabilities will be:

(a) Rights of a Minor after Electing to be a Partner

- His share in the property and profits of the firm shall be the same as that to which he was entitled when he was a minor;

- He becomes entitled to take part in the management of the partnership business, now that he has become a full-fledged partner; and
- As between himself and the other partners, his rights continue to be the same as they were before , till the date on which he becomes a partner.

(b) Liabilities of a Minor after Electing to be a Partner

- As between himself and the other partners, his liabilities continue to be the same as they were before, till the date on which he becomes a partner.
- With regard to third persons, however, he becomes liable for the acts of the firm from the date on which he was entitled to the benefits of partnership.

On the other hand if the minor does not continue to be a partner of the firm after attaining majority, his rights and liabilities will be as follows:

His right will be the same as they were before, till the notice is given; and he becomes entitled to sue the partners for his share of the property and profits. His liabilities as between himself and the other partners, his liability will be same as it was before, till the notice is given. His share of the profits and property will not be liable for any acts of the firm done after the date of the notice.

Illustration: *In Shivagouda v. Chandrakant, the Supreme Court, In this case in a partnership firm which consisted of A &B, Chandrakant, who was a minor, was admitted to the benefits of the Partnership. The firm had dealings with the appellants and it became indebted to them to the extend of ₹ 1,72,484. After that, i.e., on April 18, 1951 the partnership was dissolved. Subsequently Chandrakant attained majority but did not exercise an option under Section 30(5) declaring that he did not want to become a partner. The appellants having failed to recover the dues from A and B as they had become insolvent, brought an action against Chandrakant contending that since Chandrakant had failed to exercise an option within the period of 6 months of his attaining the majority as stipulated in Section 30(5), he had become a partner and therefore, he should also be adjudicated insolvent for the debts of the firm. It was, however, held by Supreme Court that Section 30 of the Act does not apply to Chandrakant as he had attained majority only after the firm had already been dissolved. He is not a partner of the firm, and therefore, he cannot be adjudicated insolvent for the acts of insolvency committed by the partners of the firm, i.e., A & B.*

Sometimes without the knowledge of a minor his guardian may have accepted his admission to the benefits of a partnership and the minor may have remained ignorant of his admission to the benefits of partnership even after he has attained majority. According to Section 30(6) the burden of proving the fact that such person had no knowledge of such admission until a particular date after the expiry of six months of his attaining majority shall lie upon the person asserting that fact. The Act, however, is silent as to who will have to prove that the minor obtained the knowledge of his admission after he attained majority but before the said period of six months from that date expired.

So far as his rights and liabilities in relation to partners of the firm are concerned they continue to be same up to the date on which he becomes a partner. Moreover his share in the property and profits of the firm shall be the same to which he was entitled as a minor. Towards the creditors of the firm he becomes personally liable for all the acts of the firm not from the date of his becoming a partner but retrospectively from the date of his admission to the benefits of partnership. His position under English law is different and there his liability does not extend retrospectively from the date of his admission to the benefits of partnership, but is only from the date of his attaining majority.

4.7 OBLIGATIONS OF A PARTNER

Section 9 and 10 of the Partnership Act, imposes two basic standards of conduct by the partners and to which they should adhere. These duties apply to every partnership regardless of whether the contract is in writing, and regardless of whether the contract specifies them. (1) Firstly, to act amongst themselves, in good faith. (2) And secondly, to indemnify each other for any loss.

According to Section 9 of the Act, *'Partners are bound to carry on the business of the firm to the greatest common advantage, to be just and faithful to each other, and to render true accounts and full information of all things affecting the firm to any partner or his legal representative.'* The relationship existing between partners should be one of *'Uberrimae fidei'*, which means a relationship of utmost good faith. The essence of a partnership is mutual trust and confidence. A relationship of utmost good faith can exist only when every partner is just and faithful to each other and renders true accounts and full information concerning the affairs of the firm to the other partners.

According to Section 10 of the Partnership Act, *'every partner shall indemnify the firm for any loss caused to it by his fraud in the conduct of the business of the firm.'* Section 10 focuses on encouraging honesty between the partners. This obligation is imposed upon every partner to save the other partners from loss caused to them by the fraud of a partner in conducting the business of the firm. Thereby, if the fraudulent dealings of one partner were to make the other innocent partners liable to third parties, the partner committing fraud is liable to make good the loss suffered on account of his actions .

(A) Duties of a Partners

Section 11 of the Act states that *'Subject to the provisions of this Act, the mutual rights and duties of the partners of a firm may be determined by contract between the partners, and such contract may be expressed or may be implied by a course of dealing.'* Consequently, the mutual rights and duties of partners amongst themselves are governed by their own contract, in the partnership agreement, which may either be expressed or implied. The partners are free to make their own rules for the day-to-day conduct of the business of partnership and such rules shall govern the relationship between the partners. Partners are bound to carry on the business of the firm to the greatest common advantage, to be just and faithful to each other, and to render true accounts and full information of all things affecting the firm to any partner or his legal representative. These duties are common to all partners and for all partnership firms. These duties include:

(*a*) To carry on business to the greatest common advantage of the firm and in promoting the partnership.

(*b*) To be just and faithful to the other partners and to the partnership firm as a whole.

Illustration: *In Gordon Vs Gonda (1955), upon dissolution of partnership, an active partner disposed off the partnership assets in his name and appropriated the money towards his share. The Court of Appeal held that he was accountable as a constructive trustee and hence, liable to pay interest at 5% on the share he had received.*

The principle of good faith to be observed in the mutual dealings of the partners originates from the legal maxim *'in societatis contractibus fides exuberet'*, meaning that in contractual associations, good faith must be abundantly shown.

(*c*) To render true accounts to the other partners.

(*d*) To provide full information regarding the working, and other relevant issues to the other partners.

(*e*) To indemnify for fraud committed by the partner towards the partnership firm.

(*f*) To attend diligently to his duties as a partner

(*g*) Not to claim remuneration, unless otherwise decided collectively, in the partnership agreement by all the partners.

(*h*) To share losses equally or according to the agreement decided by all the partners collectively

(*i*) Indemnity for loss due to wilful negligence by any partner, so as not to unjustly implicate the other innocent partners.

Illustration: *In Cragg Vs. Ford (1842), the partnership business carried on by the plaintiff and defendant was dissolved and the process of dissolution was left to the defendant, the managing partner. Certain bales of cotton,which were a part of partnership property, had to be sold and the plaintiff advised the defendant to dispose off the same immediately. But the defendant delayed the disposal. As a consequence, the firm sustained loss. The contention of the plaintiff that the loss should be borne by the defendant was rejected by the court on the ground that the defendant has acted in good faith and could not anticipate the sudden fall in prices.*

To hold a partner guilty of negligence, liable for the loss, it is necessary that action should be brought by the other partners in the name of the firm, and not by any partner in his individual capacity.

(*j*) To apply property only for purposes of business and not for personal gain

(*k*) To account for secret profits if any accruing to any partner. As is subject to contract between the partners, if a partner derives any profit for himself from any transaction of the firm, or from the use of the property or business connection of the firm or the firm name, he shall account for that profit and pay it to the firm. Similarly, if a partner carries on any business of the same nature as, and competing with that of the firm, he shall account for and pay to the firm all profits made by him in that business.

Illustration: *In Bentley Vs. Craven (1853), one of the partners, who was entrusted by the firm to buy sugar, sold sugar to the firm from out of his own stock, without disclosing the fact. The transaction enabled him to make substantial profit. In an action by the other partners for the recovery of the profit, it was held that the firm was entitled to it.*

(*l*) To account for the profits of a competing business by a partner, so as not to venture into a similar business that could compete with the partnership firm

(B) Determination of Rights and Duties of Partners

Subject to the provisions of this Act, the mutual rights, and duties of the partners of a firm may be determined by contract between the partners, and such contract may be expressed or may be implied by a course of dealing. Such contract may be validated by consent of all the partners, and such consent may be expressed or may be implied by a course of dealing.

Agreements in restraints of trade: Notwithstanding anything contained in Section 27 of the Indian Contract Act, 1872, such contracts may provide that a partner shall not carry on any business other than that of the firm while he is a partner.

The Conduct of the Business subject to contract between the partners,

1. Every partner has a right to take part in the conduct of the business. Section 12(a) of the Act states that, *'every partner has a right to take part in the conduct of the business.'* This right is however subject to a contract to the contrary. Which means, if the partners have by mutual agreement with other partners decided that a particular partner may abstain from exercising this right, that partner cannot take part in the conduct of the business.

2. Every partner is bound to attend diligently to his duties in the conduct of the business;
3. Any difference arising as to ordinary matters connected with the business may be decided by a majority of the partners, and every partner shall have the right to express his opinion, before the matter is decided, but no change may be made in the nature of the business without the consent of all the partners. It is natural that there may be differences in opinion between the parties on a particular issue. In such an event, Section 12(c) of the Act provides that any difference of opinion as to ordinary matters connected with the business may be settled by the will of the majority. However, even in the case of ordinary matters, the powers conferred on the majority should be exercised in good faith and for the benefit of the firm.
4. Every partner has a right to have access to and to inspect and copy any of the books of the firm. This right can be exercised either by the partner himself or by his authorised agent. The partners cannot object to inspection by the agent of a partner, unless they have reasonable ground for believing that the trade secrets might be leaked out.
5. Every partner has a right to share profits earned by the partnership firm. According to Section 13(b) of the Act, every partner is entitled to share the profits of the business in equal proportions and should contribute equally to the losses sustained by the firm. However, this provision is also subject to the contract between the parties. It is open to the parties to divide the profit, amongst themselves, according to a particular profit sharing ratio or according to a mutual agreement between the partners. The sharing of loss also follows the same principle.
6. Every partner has a right to interest on capital. Unless otherwise agreed, partners are not entitled to any interst on their capital contributions. However, Section 13(c) lays down that such interest shall be payable out of profits only.
7. Every partner has a right to interest on advances made by him to the firm. A partner need not contribute more than what he has agreed to contribute towards the capital of the partnership firm. However, if a partner has contributed more than what was necessary and if the agreement so provides, he is entitled to interest at the rate of 6% per annum on the amount so advance by him towards capital of the firm.
8. Every partner has a right to be indemnified. A partner is entitled to be indemnified for any expenditure or liability incurred by him in the ordinary course of business and secondly, where a partner does an act in an emergency to save the firm from loss. According to Section 13(e) of the Act, a partner has a right to be indemnified in respect of payment made or liabilities incurred by him either (1) in the ordinary and proper conduct of the business and (2) in doing an act in an emergency for the purpose of protecting the firm from loss. However, it is necessary that the partner should have acted in the same manner as a person of ordinary prudence would act in his own case, under similar circumstances.
9. Every partner right to partnership property. Section 14 of the Act defined partnership property as *'all property and rights and interests in property originally brought into the stock of the firm, or acquired, by purchase or otherwise, by or for the firm.'* Every partner is a joint-owner of the property of the firm. If the agreement does not specify the interest of each partner in the partnership property, the presumption is that every partner is entitled to an equal share in it. Further Section 15 of the Act states that the partnership property should be held and used by the partners only for the purposes of the business, unless and otherwise, a contract between the partners states otherwise.
10. Every partner has a right to remain in the firm. Section 33(1) of the Act protects a partner from being expelled from the partnership. The Act states that a partner cannot be expelled

from the firm by the majority partners, except in exercise of good faith of powers conferred by a contract between the partners. An expulsion can be exercised only when it can be proved that the expulsion of a particular partner is warranted for the good of the firm and in an instance where it was found that the partner has acted beyond his capacity as a partner and has either misappropriated funds, been associated with fraud towards the partnership firm or some other illegal activities against the firm.

(C) Mutual Rights and Liabilities

I. Subject to contract between the partners, a partner is not entitled to receive remuneration for taking part in the conduct of the business;

II. The partners are entitled to share equally in the profits earned, and shall contribute equally to the losses sustained by the firm;

III. Where a partner is entitled to interest on the capital subscribed by him such interest shall be payable only out of profits;

IV. Partner making, for the purposes of the business, any payment or advance beyond the amount of capital he has agreed to subscribe, is entitled to interest thereon at the rate of six per cent per annum;

V. The firm shall indemnify a partner in respect of payments made and liabilities incurred by him.

- in the ordinary and proper conduct of the business, and
- in doing such act, in an emergency, for the purpose of protecting the firm from loss, as would be done by a person of ordinary prudence, in his own case, under similar circumstances; and

VI. A partner shall indemnify the firm for any loss caused to it by his willful neglect in the conduct of the business of the firm.

4.8 THE PROPERTY OF THE FIRM

The property of the firm includes all property and rights and interests in property originally brought into the stock of the firm, or acquired, by purchase or otherwise, by or for the firm, or for the purposes and in the course of business of the firm, and includes also the goodwill of the business subject to contract between the partners. Unless the contrary intention appears, property and rights and interests in property acquired with money belonging to the firm are deemed to have been acquired for the firm.

The property of a partnership firm will consist of all the assets, moveable and immoveable brought in by any or all the partners into the firm and also include the goodwill. It may be stated that relying upon the specific provision of Section 22 of the English Partnership Act 1890, the Supreme Court has held that all property of a partnership firm, whether moveable or immoveable is moveable property and therefore, on retirement of any partner or dissolution of partnership the division of even immoveable property among the partners does not amount to transfer of property and the deed of retirement or dissolution does not require registration.

The Supreme Court has not considered the law of vesting and divesting of interest in an immoveable property. A property acquired by 'A' by purchase or otherwise is vested in him and even if 'A' brings that property into partnership and it is used for the partnership business, the property is not automatically divested from 'A' and vested in 'A' and his other partners. Vesting and divesting can take effect only by act of parties or by operation of law and therefore, the property brought in by 'A' cannot become vested in the other partners unless there is a regular transfer of the property by 'A' to himself and other partners. And similarly if property vested in the partners is divided, among them, it amounts to transfer of one partner's interest to the other, and such transfer is necessary to vest and divest the title from one to the other. Even in English law, in spite of the provisions of Partnership Act above referred to, the conveyancing practice is to affect the transfer of property brought in or taken out of the partnership by a Deed of Conveyance.

4.9 RELATION OF PARTNERS TO THIRD PARTIES

(A) Implied Authority of a Partner

Under Section 18 of the Partnership Act, *'Every partner is the agent of the firm for the purposes of the business of the firm.'* The partners of a firm are therefore agents of one another and this agency relationship makes the firm liable to third parties for its acts. He can act on behalf of the firm and bind the firm provided,

(*a*) He does the act for carrying on, in the usual way, business of the kind, carried on by the firm and,

(*b*) The act is done in the name of the firm.

Section 19(1) of the Act not only defines 'implied authority' but also determines its scope. This sub-section states that *'Subject to the provisions of Section 22 of the act of a partner which is done to carry on, in the usual way, business of the kind carried on by the firm, binds the firm. The authority of a partner to bind the firm, conferred by this Section, is called his implied authority.'*

The authority of a partner to bind the firm by his acts is called 'Implied Authority'. This authority may be either 'express' or 'implied'. It is based upon the legal relations of the partners and is founded on the principles of agency. The authority of a partner may be either actual or apparent. Even in the absence of an agreement, a partner can bind the firm for his acts done in the name of the firm, in the usual course, and in the conduct of the business. Since this authority is conferred on a partners by the Statute itself, the acts of a partner falling within his implied authority, need not be ratified by the other partners, on the ground that such a partner was not invested with express authority to do these acts. It is subject to the following conditions:

(*a*) The act done by the partner must relate to the normal business of the firm.

(*b*) The act must be such as is done within the scope of the business of the firm in the ususal way. (What is the usual way of carrying on the business of the firm depends upon the nature and circumstances of each case).

(*c*) The act must be done in the name of the firm or in any other manner expressing or implying an intention to bind the firm.

(*d*) The act done must state that it has been done in the capacity of an agent of other partners.

According to Section 26 of the Act, the firm is liable for the wrongful act or omission of each partner, if the wrongful act or omission is in the ordinary course of the firm's business or with the authority of the other partners. The wrongful act may be negligence misconduct, fraud, trespass or deceit. In case of fraud, although the firm becomes liable to a third party under this Section, it is the duty of that partner who has committed fraud to indemnify the firm for any loss caused to it according to the Act. [Sec 10].

Illustrations: *(1) In Hamlyn Vs Houston & Co. (1903), the defendants were a firm of grain merchants. The firm consisted of two partners, Houston and Strong. Houston was an active partner. He bribed the clerk of the plaintiff, who was also a grain merchant, to get secret information about the business contracts of the latter. The clerk allowed him to have access to certain books containing confidential entries concerning some contracts. The bribe was paid from out of the firm's money. As a result of the disclosure of confidential information, the plaintiff lost business to the extent of £750. When the plaintiff came to know the means adopted by the defendant, he sued the latter for damages. It was held that Strong was also liable, although the illegetimate means adopted by Houston were not known to him.*

(2) In Harrauck Chand and Govind Lal (1906), the defendants were in partnership, dealing in piece goods. Of the two partners, one was an active partner. The plaintiff firm, which was engaged in a similar business, sent some goods to the railway station for delivery to its customers. The goods were stolen on their way to the station. The stolen goods were purchased by the active partner of the defendant firm, and they were later sold by him in the name of the firm. The other partner of the firm did not know anything about the transaction. In a suit by the plaintiff firm against the defendants, for conversion, it was held that both the partners were liable to the true owner.

(B) Subjects of Implied Authority

The following acts of a partner are included within the scope of the implied authority of a partner:

1. To sell goods on behalf of the firm
2. To allow credit or advances on behalf of the firm
3. To receive payments of debts due to the firm and to issue receipts for the same
4. To purchase goods on behalf of the firm, in which either the firm deals or those which are employed in the business of the firm
5. To settle accounts with persons dealing with the creditors of the firm
6. In case of emergency, to do everything possible as a person of ordinary prudence does, to save the firm from any losses.
7. To borrow money on credit on behalf of other partners, for the purpose of the firms business.
8. To pledge any goods or property of the firm for the purpose of any borrowings for the business of the firm
9. To engage employees for the business of the firm
10. To draw, accept, endorse bills of exchange or any other negotiable instrument in the name of the firm
11. To employ a solicitor to defend any action against the firm

Illustrations: *(1) In Blair Vs. Bromle (1847), a client handed over some money to one of the partners for investment in a specific security. Although the money was credited to the joint account of the firm, one partner misappropriated the money representing to have invested it. The court held the innocent partner liable for the misapplication of money by his co-partner and his representation that the money was invested, on the ground that it was within the ordinary course of business for a solicitor to receive money for investment in a specific security.*

(2) In Plumer Vs. Gregory (1874), the plaintiff paid £1,300 to a firm of solicitors for investment and received an acknowledgement, signed by both partners. The amount was intended to be invested in a specified security. Subsequently, however, the plaintiff paid £1,700 to one of the partners for investment in some other security. The fact of payment was not known to the other partner. The partner, to whom the second sum was paid, died and both the sums were misappropriated by the other partner. It was held that the estate of the deceased partner was liable for £1,300 only but not £1,700 because, the receipt of moeny for the purpose of general investment was not normally an incident of the ordinary business of the firm of solicitors.

(C) Subjects Beyond Implied Authority

The following are the subjects for which a partner does not have Implied Authority

1. To enter into partnership on behalf of the firm
2. To acquire any immovable property on behalf of the firm
3. To transfer any immovable property belonging to the firm
4. To admit any liability in a suit or proceedings against the firm
5. To withdraw a suit filed on behalf of the firm
6. To submit a dispute related to the partnership, to arbitration
7. To compromise or relinquish any claim or a portion of a claim by the firm
8. To open a bank account on behalf of the firm in his own name

The partners in a firm may, by an agreement among themselves, extend or restrict the implied authority of any partner. However, with regard to a third party, the firm shall be liable for all such acts which come within the scope of the implied authority of a partner, unless the third party knows that the partner has no implied authority or does not know or believe him to be a partner in the firm. The third party shall also not be affected by the restrictions imposed on any particular partner regarding implied authority, unless the third party has notice of it.

(D) Rights of Transfer of Partnership Interest (Sub-partner)

A sub-partnership is created when a partner transfers his interest in the firm either absolutely or by mortgage, or by the creation of a charge on such interest. However, the sub-partner does not become entitled, to interfere with the firm's business, to check book of accounts, etc. This means that such a transfer does not entitle the transferee to become a partner in the firm. This is laid down in Section 31 of the Act which states that no person can be introduced as a partner without the consent of all the existing partners. Even to transfer the interest of a partner to a third party, consent of all the partners is required.

4.10 RECONSTITUTION OF A PARTNERSHIP FIRM

There may be instances in the firm during the course of its business that a change in the constitution of the business becomes inevitable. In such instances , where there is a change in the composition of the firm brought about by the admission of a new partner, death of an existing partner, insolvency of one or more of the existing partners, retirement of one of the partners or expulsion of a partner, there is necessarily a change in the partnership relation, but the firm continues as a new firm or a reconstituted firm. A change in the constitution of the firm does not, therefore, mean dissoluon of the firm.

(A) Admission of a Partner

The consent of all partners is required to introduce a new partner into the partnership firm. The power to introduce a new partner can be exercised by anyone of the existing partners or even by a person who is not a partner at all, if the articles of partnership so provide.

Illustration: *In Byrne Vs. Reid (1902), the partnership agreement between Byrne and Reid empowered Byrne to introduce into the partnership any of his sons on their attaining majority. Accordingly, he proposed the name of one of his sons who attained the age of 21 years. But, Reid refused to consent. It was held that Reid could not prevent since the clause in the firm's articles operated as a consent.*

(B) Liability of a new Partner

Section 31 (2) states that *'A person who is introduced as a patner into a firm does not thereby become liable for any acts of the firm done before he became a partner.'* A partner, on admission, becomes liable only in respect of the liabilities incurred by the firm after his admission but not those incurred prior to his admission. However, the incoming partner may agree with the existing partners, at the time of his admission, to become liable for the debts of the firm conracted prior to his admission. But such an agreement binds only the partners. It does not give any right to the creditors to sue the incoming partner, as there is no privity of contract between them and the incoming partner.

Illustration: *In British Homes Assurance Corporation Ltd. Vs. Paterson (1902), a solicitor, who was engaged by the plaintiffs took the defendant as a partner, and notified the fact to the plaintiffs. The plaintiffs did not take any notice of the fact of admission and continued to deal with the solicitor. When the solicitor misappropriated the money paid to him by the plaintiffs, for a mortgage transaction, the plaintiffs sued the new partner. It was held that 'where 'A', knowing B and C to be partners, refuses to contract with them jointly and insists on contracting with B alone, he canot afterwards treat C as liable'. It was held in this case that a third party who had elected to continue his dealings with a solicitor, could not sue a person whom the solicitor had taken into partnership.*

(C) Right on Premium Paid by new Partner

An incoming or new partner may be required to pay a premium to seek partnership in an existing firm. This premium would be in addition to the capital investment made by the new partner. On dissolution, the new partner is entitled to demand the return of a proportion of the premium amount paid if, the partnership was for a fixed term and was dissolved before the expiry of that term. He however cannot claim the premium amount if the dissolution of the partnership was caused either by an agreement between all the partners, misconduct of the new partner or death of a partner.

(D) Outgoing Partner (Death or Retirement of a Partner)

A partner may retire from a firm in accordance with the express agreement, with the consent of all other partners or in case of partnership at will, by issuing a notice in writing to all other partners of his intention to retire. A partner may withdraw from the firm and the other partners may continue to carry on the business of the firm without the dissolution of partnership between them.

(E) Retirement

Section 32(1) of the Act mentions three modes by which a partner may seek retirement from his position as a partner of the firm, namely;

1. With the consent of all the other partners,
2. In accordance with an express agreement by the partners
3. In the case of a partnership at will, by notice in writing to all the other partners of his intention to retire.

Once the retirement of a partner is accepted by the other partners, he ceases to be a partner and the firm becomes re-constituted without dissolution. While an incoming partner is not liable to the creditors of the firm for liability incurred before his admission, the position of the retiring partner is different. He remains liable to the creditors of the firm even after his retirement for debts contracted before his retirement.

Retiring partner may be discharged from any liability to any third party for acts of the firm done before his retirement by an agreement made by him with such third party and the partners of the reconstituted firm, and such agreement may be implied by a course of dealing between such third party and the constituted firm after he had knowledge of the retirement. Under Section 32(2), the liability of the retiring partner as against third party would be discharged only if there is an agreement made by the retiring partner, with the third party, and the partners of the reconstituted firm. Of course, an agreement could be implied by the course of dealing between such third party and the reconstituted firm after retirement of a partner.

Notwithstanding the retirement of a partner from a firm, he and the partners continue to be liable as partners to third parties for any act done by any of them which would have been an act of the firm if done before the retirement, until public notice is given of the retirement. (Provided that a retired partner is not liable to any third party who deals with the firm without knowing that he was a partner).

(F) Position of a Retiring Partner

When a partner retires the relation of partnership between the retiring and the other partners come to an end. If a third party who knew of the existence of this relationship does not know that the relationship has come to an end and gives credit to the firm, he can make the retiring partner also liable. Similarly, if he gives credit to the retiring partner thinking him to be still a partner he can make the continuing partners liable. In other words from the point of view of the third parties the mutual Legacy which had earlier come into existence is still presumed to be continuing until public notice of retirement is given. Sec,32(3) provides that "Notwithstanding the retirement of a partner from a firm, he and the partners continue to be liable as partners to third parties for any act done by any of them which would have been an act of the firm if done before the retirement, until public notice is given of the retirement.'

Such public notice may be given either by the retired partner or by any partners of the reconstituted firm. The reason for liability even after the retirement is that the absence of the notice of revocation of an agents's authority makes the principal liable to those who act on the supposition that the agency still continues. No public notice is needed by the retirement of a dormant partner *i.e.*, a partner who is not known as such to third parties, because the Partnership Act further provides that a retired partner is not liable to any third party who deals with the firm without knowing that he was a partner. The object of public notice being to remove the impression from the mind of the third parties that a certain person was a partner, no public notice is needed when the third parties had no such impression.

An important point came for consideration in Scarf v. Jardine where a third party was ignorant of either the retirement of a partner or the introduction of a new partner, when both the changes had taken place simultaneously. In that case a firm consisted of two partners, A and B. A retired and C joined the partnership in his place. No notice of the change was given. A customer of the old firm, who was not aware of the above stated change, supplied goods to the reconstituted firm. To recover the price of the goods he brought an action against B and C. Having failed to recover the price from them, he brought another action against A. The question before the court was, whether the third party who had supplied goods to the firm, could successfully bring action against A, B and C.

It was held that when the customer is ignorant of the retirement of A as well as the introduction of C, he has an option to sue either A and B on the ground of estoppel or B and C on the basis of actual facts. Since A never held himself out as a partner along with B and C , the customer could not make A , B and C all of them liable. Therefore, after having elected to sue B and C he cannot bring an action against A. The position would have been different if he was aware of the introduction of C to the firm but was not aware of the retirement of A. Then he could presume that C had joined the firm which already consisted of A and B and in that situation could make all the three partners liable.

The position of an expelled partner is the same as that of a retired partner and in this case also a public notice of expulsion should be given to avoid his liability for the acts done after the date of expulsion.

(G) Death of a Partner

On the death of a partner there is automatic dissolution of a firm unless there is a contract to the contrary between the partners. When there is a contract between the partners by virtue of which the firm is not dissolved viz., the remaining partners continue the business the fact that the business of the firm is continued in the old firm name, does not of itself make the legal representatives or the estate of the deceased partner liable for an act of the firm done after his death. The position of the legal representatives of a deceased partner is different from that of a retired partner, as the former will not be liable for the acts of the firm done after the death of the partner even though no public notice of partner's death is given, whereas a retiring partner will continue to be liable for the acts of other partners until public notice of retirement is given.

No public notice is necessary in the case of death, to relieve the estate of the deceased from future liability. However, the surviving partners continue to be liable to third parties even after dissolution of the firm for any act done on behalf of the firm, until they give public notice of dissolution of the firm.

(H) Expulsion of a Partner

According to Section 33(1) of the Act, a partner may be expelled from a firm provided the power of expulsion is conferred upon the partners by a contract between them, and such pose is exercised in good faith. Accordingly, expulsion is justified only if (a) the power is conferred by contract (b) the power is exercised in good faith and (c) by the majority of partners. No partner can otherwise be expelled from a firm by any majority of partners.

Illustrations: *(1) In Blisset Vs. Daniel (1853), the articles of partnership empowered the majority of partners to buy up the share of the outgoing partner. In exercise of the power, two-thirds of the majority of partners expelled a partner. It was held that the exercise of the power merely for the purpose of buying up the share was not bona fide.*

(2) In Carmichael Vs. Evans (1904), the court upheld the expulsion of a partner who was convicted for travelling without a railway ticket, with intent to avoid payment.

(3) In Greenaway Vs. Greenaway (1940), where friction between two partners culminated in an assault by one partner upon another and the articles of partnership provided for expulsion of a partner in the event of his conduct being prejudicial to the interests of all the partners, the expulsion of the offending partner, by notice, was valid, although friction by itself was no ground for expulsion.

When a partner is expelled in accordance with the requirements laid down in this Act, he ceases to be a partner and occupies the same position as that of a retiring partner in so far as his rights and liabilities are concerned. If expulsion is done fraudulently or *mala fide*, the partner who is so expelled is entitled to be reinstated. However, he is not entitled to damages for wrongfull expulsion unless his expulsion was given malicious publicity so as to be harmful to the partner who was wrongfully expelled.

(I) Rights of an Outgoing Partner

An outgoing partner is empowered by the Act [Sec. 36(1)] to carry on any business, even if it may be similar to the partnership firm where he was a partner or it may compete with the business of the firm in which he was a partner. He may even advertise such business but, under certain conditions that he:

(*a*) May no use the name of the firm in his newly constituted business,

(*b*) May not represent himself as carrying on the business of the firm, or

(*c*) May not solicit the customers or persons who were dealing with the firm before he ceased to be a partner.

The law imposes these restrictions to prevent unfair competition between the firm's business and similar business which the outgoing partner may begin. Section 37 of the Act also confers the right on the outgoing partner to share subsequent profits. This is applicable when a partner dies or ceases to be a partner and the surviving or continuing partners continue to carry on the business without settling the accounts of the outgoing partner , either by arrangement with the executors of the deceased or the outgoing partner himself. In such situations, the deceased partners executors or the outgoing partner may be given a ratio of the profits earned by the firm or interest at the rate of 6% on the amount of his share. However, this right is subject to an agreement in the partnership deed made by the partners.

(J) Dissolution of a Partnership Firm

Dissolution of a firm signifies the end of the partnership and the business venture. Dissolution of a firm necessarily means dissolution of partnership also, but dissolution of partnership need not necessarily mean dissolution of the firm. When partners close down the business, dissolution of the partnership firm takes place. According to Sec 39 when the dissolution of partnership between all the partners of the firms occurs, this is called dissolution of the firm.

(K) Difference between Dissolution of Partnership and Dissolution of a Firm

The dissolution of partnership between all the partners of a firm is called the dissolution of the firm. [Section 39]. Partnership is the relation between persons who have agreed to share profits of business carried on by all or any of them acting for all. Thus, if there is admission or retirement or death of a partner, the relationship between the partners changes and hence the partnership comes to an end or is dissolved but the firm continues. Hence, the change is termed as 'reconstitution of firm'. However, complete breakage between relations of all partners is termed as 'dissolution of firm'. After such dissolution, the firm ceases to exist. Thus, 'Dissolution of partnership' is different from 'dissolution of firm'. 'Dissolution of partnership' is only reconstruction of firm, while 'dissolution of firm' means the firm no more exists after dissolution.

4.11 MODES OF DISSOLUTION OF A PARTNERSHIP FIRM

MODES OF DISSOLUTION OF A PARTNERSHIP FIRM

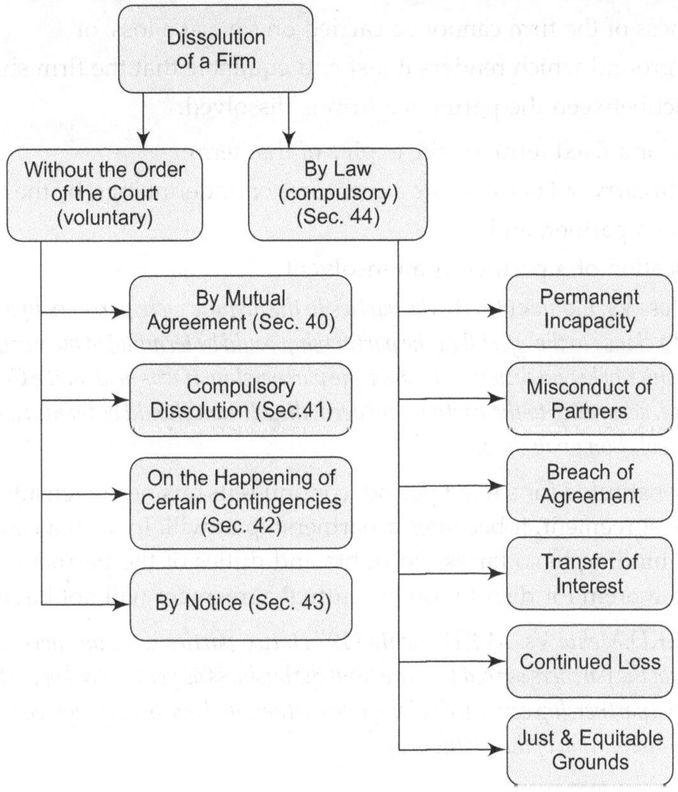

(A) Dissolution of a Firm without Intervention of the Court

(*a*) By agreement (Section 40)
(*b*) Compulsory dissolution in case of insolvency (Section 41)
(*c*) Dissolution on happening of certain contingency (Section 42)
(*d*) By notice if partnership is at will (Section 43)

(B) Dissolution of a Firm with the Intervention of the Court

At the suit of a partner, the court may dissolve a firm on any of the following grounds, namely:

(*a*) that a partner has become of unsound mind, in which case the suit may be brought as well by the next friend of the partner who has become of unsound mind as by any other partner;
(*b*) that a partner, other than the partner suing, has become in any way permanently incapable of performing his duties as partner;

(*c*) that a partner, other than the partner suing, is guilty of conduct which is likely to affect prejudicially the carrying on of the business, regard being had to the nature of the business;

(*d*) that a partner, other than the partner suing, willfully or persistently commits breach of agreements relating to the management of the affairs of the firm or the conduct of its business, or otherwise so conducts himself in matters relating to the business that it is not reasonably practicable for the other partners to carry on the business in partnership with him;

(*e*) that a partner, other than the partner suing, has in any way transferred the whole of his interest in the firm to a third party, or has allowed his share to be charged under the provisions of the Act.

(*f*) that the business of the firm cannot be carried on save at a loss; or

(*g*) on any other ground which renders it just and equitable that the firm should be dissolved.

Subject to contract between the partners a firm is dissolved.

(*a*) if constituted for a fixed term, by the expiry of that term;

(*b*) if constituted to carry out one or more adventures or undertakings, by the completion thereof;

(*c*) by the death of a partner; and

(*d*) by the adjudication of a partner as an insolvent.

Illustration: *In Moss Vs. Elphick (1910), the parties to the dispute were partners in a business. The deed of partnership, contained a clause to the effect that the partnership could be terminated by mutual arrangement only. Moss gave notice to Elphick of his intention to dissolve the partnership. It was held by the Court of Appeal that the notice was invalid since, according to the partnership deed, dissolution should be by mutual agreement, and one partner cannot force dissolution upon the other.*

Where a firm is constituted for a fixed period, continues its business even after the expiry of that term without a new agreement, it becomes a partnership at will. In such a case, even though the original articles are binding in so far as the rights and duties of the partners are concerned, any provision contained therein for dissolution by mutual agreement will not have any effect.

Illustration: *In E.F.D.Mehta Vs. M.F.D Mehta (1971), two parties were brothers, who had entered into partnership. When one of the partners agreed to retire from the business as per the deed of partnership, the Supreme Court held that 'when the partnership consisted of only two partners and one partner agreed to retire, there can be no doubt it will amount to dissolution of the partnership.'*

4.12 CONSEQUENCES OF DISSOLUTION

Since dissolution initiates the process of winding up the affairs of the firm some rights are inferred and some obligations are imposed upon the partners to do the needful in this regard. On deciding to dissolve the partnership, the partners need to make a public notification. Until such notice is given the partners continue to be liable to third parties.

After a firm is dissolved, every partner or his representative may, in the absence of a contract between the partners to the contrary, restrain any other partner or his representative from carrying on a similar business in the firm name or from using any of the property of the firm for his own benefit, until the affairs of the firm have been completely wound up: PROVIDED that where any partner or his representative has bought the goodwill of the firm, nothing in this Section shall affect his right to use the firm name. Secondly, if a new partner had been admitted into the partnership and he had paid a premium along with his investment in capital, such partner is entitled to demand return of a proportion of the premium if the partnership was for a fixed term and was dissolved before the expiry of that term. The exemption for payment of the premium amount exists only if such dissolution was caused because of the misconduct of the new partner or by mutual agreement between the partners to wind up the firm or by the death of a partner.

(A) Agreements in Restraint of Trade

Partners may, upon or in anticipation of the dissolution of the firm, make an agreement that some or all of them will not carry on a business similar to that of the firm within a specified period or within specified local limits; and notwithstanding anything contained in Section 27 of the Indian Contract Act, 1872, such agreement shall be valid if the restrictions imposed are reasonable.

(B) Sale of Goodwill after Dissolution

1. In settling the accounts of a firm after dissolution, the goodwill shall, subject to contract between the partners, be included in the assets, and it may be sold either separately or along with other property of the firm.
2. Rights of buyer and seller of goodwill. Where the goodwill of a firm is sold after dissolution, a partner may carry on a business competing with that of the buyer and he may advertise such business but subject to agreement between him and the buyer, he may not.
    (*a*) use the firm name,
    (*b*) represent himself as carrying on the business of the firm, or
    (*c*) solicit the customer or persons who were dealing with the firm before its dissolution.

The process of distribution of surplus amongst the partners after payment of liabilities of the firm is called as winding up of the firm. When the firm is dissolved, the partnership ceases and the authority of the partners to act on behalf of the firm terminates. However according to Section 47 of the Act, the authority of a partner to bind the firm and the mutual rights and obligations of the partners continue to the extent necessary to wind up the affairs of the firm. Every partner or his representative is entitled to have the firm's property applied in payment of the debts and liabilities of the firm and to have the surplus distributed amongst the partners. On the sale of the goodwill after dissolution, a partner of the dissolved firm is free to carry on a business competing with that of the buyer. He may also advertise such business, but not in the name of the firm unless there is an agreement between the buyer of goodwill and the partners of the firm. However, the partners are free to apply certain restrictions on the buyer of goodwill by an agreement entered into with him. Such agreements do not violate Section 27 of the Contract Act, provided the restraint is reasonable.

(C) Methods of Settling Accounts

The partnership deed mentions the mode of settlement of accounts after dissolution of the firm. In the absence of any agreement, the settlement of accounts has to be done according to the mode specified in Section 48 of the Act. According to this Section, *'(a) Losses, including deficiencies of capital, shall be paid first out of profits, next out of capital, and lastly, if necessary, by the partners individually in the proportion in which they were entitled to share profits.'*

Sub-section (b) of Section 48 lays down the order of the application of the assets. The order being, *'(i) in paying the debts of the firm to third parties; (ii) in paying to each partner rateably what is due to him from the firm for advances as distinguished from capital; (iii) in paying to each partner rateably what is due to him on account of capital; and (iv) the residue, if any, shall be divided among the partners in the proportions in which they were entitled to share profits.'*

Accordingly, in settling accounts between the partners after a dissolution of partnership, the following rules shall be observed (unless there is a contract to the contrary);

- Lossees, including deficiencies of capital shall be paid first out of undistributed profits, next out of capital, and lastly, if necessary, by the partners individually in the proportion in which they were entitled to share profits.
- The assets of the firm, including the sums contributed by the partners to make up losses or deficiencies of capital shall be applied in the following manner and order:
  1. In paying outside creditors
  2. In repaying advances made by partners (distinct from investment of capital)
  3. In repaying capital to partners
  4. The ultimate residue, if any, shall be divided among the partners in the ratio in which profits were divisible.

However, if the assets after realisation are not sufficient to satisfy the creditors, the partners have to bear the loss in equal shares, similarly as they would share profits. Nevertheless, under the rule in *Garner Vs.Murray,* if such deficiency is attributable to the insolvency of one of the partners, that deficiency must be borne by the other partners in the proportion of their last agreed shares in the capital, and not in the proportion in which they share profits and losses.

Illustration: *A,B and C are partners with capital investment of ₹5,000, ₹4,000 and ₹3,000 respectively. A has advanced ₹2,000. Upon dissolution of the firm the assets realise ₹10,000. Outside creditors of the firm amount to ₹5,000.After the creditors and A's advance are paid off, the amount left is ₹3,000. This being insufficient to repay the partners towards their capital, the loss on capital amounting to ₹9,000 should be borne by the partners equally, assuming that the articles of partnership do not have a provision to the contraty. Thus A is entitled to repayment of ₹2,000, B ₹1,000 and C, nil (Norwell Vs. Norwell, 1869).*

However if C's capital had been ₹2,000 only, he ought to have contributed to the firm's assets ₹1,000. Assuming that C is unable to contribute anything owing to his insolvency, the deficiency, which is a capital loss, should be borne by A and B in proportions of their last agreed capitals and not in the profit sharing proportions. This was the rule of law enunciated in Garner Vs. Murray, (1904)

(D) Restrictions on Partners

After the firm is dissolved, every partner or his representative, may restrain the other partners or representatives from carrying on similar business using the name of the firm or its property, until the affaris of the firm are completely wound up. The restriction is subject to a contract to the contraty and does not apply to a partner or his representative, who has bought the goodwill of the firm. Partners may also make an arrangement that they will not carry on a similar business within a specified period or within specified local limits. Such restrictions are perfectly valid but only for a reasonable period of time and not perpetually.

4.13 NEED FOR REGISTRATION OF FIRMS

Registration of Partnership: Registration of firm means the recording of the firm name along with the prescribed particulars, in the register of the firm, kept in the office of the Registrar of Firms. The registration provides a reliable evidence and conclusive proof of the existence of a partnership firm. The Partnership Act does not insist on registration of a firm or impose any penalty for non-registration. However, Section 69 of the Act which deals with the effects of non-registration, denies certain rights to an unregistered firm. These rights indirectly insist on the firms' registration.

(A) Mode of Registration

Application in the prescribed manner has to be filed with the Registrar of Firms coming within the jurisdiction of the establishment, along with the prescribed fee. The application should contain the following particulars:

(*a*) Name of the firm
(*b*) Place or principal place of business
(*c*) Names of any other places where the firm carries on business
(*d*) Date on which each partner joined the firm
(*e*) Names in full and permanent address of the partners
(*f*) Duration of the business (firm)

The application in the prescribed manner should be signed by every partner, or his agent specially authorised on his behalf after thorough verification about the contents. The name of the firm should not be misleading the public or opposed to public policy or a name that signifies patronage of any particular body, association , government or institution (except when such sanction is obtained from the concerned authorities to use or associate their name along with the firms name).

When the filled in application is submitted to the Registrar, he shall check the contents and satisfy himself about the entries made, as per the required stipulations, after which the Registrat issues a Certificate of Registration and also records the details in the Register of Firms. It is not mandatory that a firm should be registered at the time of its inception; it may be registered at any time during the course of its business also.

Section 69(2) discloses certain diabilities that an unregistered firm might experience. As such, an unregistered firm cannot enforce any right arising from a conract against the third party unless it is registered. An unregistered firm cannot sue anyone who breaches a contract with them.

Illustration: *In Ponnuchami Gounder Vs. Muthusami Gounder (1942), a divisional bench of the Madras High Court held that 'Section 69 of the Act is mandatory and that the registration of the firm is a condition precedent to its right to institute the suit and that if a firm was not registered at the time of the presentation of the plaint, but was registered subsequently, the only course open to the Court was to dismiss the suit.*

In the event of any change in the name of the Firm or the place of business or the change in name or address of any partner, an intimation of the alternation may be sent by any partner to the Registrar. Similarly , when a minor attains majority or when the partners decide to dissolve the partnership, a notice to the effect may be sent to the Registrar, notifying him of the same and thus recording and updating the details in the Register of Firms.

(B) Consequences of Non-Registration

(*i*) *Suit between partners and the firm:* In case of a dispute between the partners of an unregistered Firm or between a partner and the Firm, or between a partner and a person alleged to be or to have been a partner in the Firm, with regarad to any right arising from a contract, or conferred by the Act, no suit can be instituted in any court of law to enforce the right. Only a Firm that is registered can enforce its right by bringing a suit.

(ii) *Suit between the firm and third parties:* An unregistered Firm cannot enforce a contractual right by suing a third party. A suit against a third party will lie only if the Firm is registered and the persons suing are shown in the Register of Firms as partners in the Firm.

(iii) *Claim of set-off:* Neither a Firm nor a partner from an unregistered Firm can claim a set-off arising as a right from a contract against a third party. Further, an unregistered Firm cannot enforce an arbitration agreement made by it.

4.14 THE DOCTRINE OF HOLDING OUT

Every partner is liable for all acts of the Firm done while he is a partner. Therefore, generally a person who is not a partner in a Firm cannot be made liable for an act of the Firm. In certain cases, however, a person who is not a partner in the Firm may be deemed to be a partner or held out to be a partner for the purpose of his liability towards a third party. The basis of liability of such a person is not that he was himself a partner or was sharing the profits or was taking part in the management of the business, but the basis is the application of the law of estoppel because of which he is held out to be a partner or is deemed to be Partner by Holding Out. The Doctrine of Holding Out is a branch of the Law of Estoppel. According to the Law of Estoppel, if a person by his representation induces another to do some act, which he would not have done otherwise, then the person making the representation, is not allowed to deny what he asserted earlier.

Therefore, if a person who is not a partner, by his representation, creates an impression in the mind of the third party that he is a partner, on the basis of which the third party gives credit to the firm, the person making such a representation will be held out to be a partner.

Illustration: *A partnership firm consists of A,B & C. D, who is not a partner, makes a representation to X that he is also a partner and on the faith of this representation X gives credit tothe firm. In this case X can make D liable on the basis of the Doctrine of Holding Out and D is estopped from denying that he is partner in the firm.*

As stated in Section 28(1) for the application of the Doctrine of Holding Out, the presence of the following essentials is required:

1. The person sought to be made liable under the Doctrine of Holding Out, either has himself represented, or knowingly permitted somebody else to represent, that he is a partner in the Firm.
2. The third party who wants to bring an action must have acted on the faith of the representation and given credit to the Firm.

(A) Representation

In order to make a person liable under the Doctrine of Holding Out , it has to be proved that either he himself made a representation or knowingly permitted such a representation to be made by someone else. In other words there has to be a representation by a person by words spoken or written or by his conduct that he is a partner in the firm. Representation in any form indicating that a person is a partner in the firm will create the liability. Fraudulent intention to mislead another person is not required. Whether the liability for holding out exists or not depends not on the motive of the person making the representation but on the fact that a third party has given credit on the faith of that representation. When the third party has acted on the representation the

Section creates the liability whether the person representing himself or represented to be a partner does or does not know that the representation has reached the person so giving credit. The presence of the two essentials, i.e., the representation by one person about the fact of his being a partner and the acting by a third party on the faith of the representation are enough to create a liability under the doctrine.

Illustration: *In Snow White Food Products Pvt. Ltd v. Sohan Lal Bagla, it was held that by his verbal negotiations and subsequent correspondence, Sohan Lal represented as a partner of a firm of carriers and therefore, he was partner by Holding Out.*

Knowingly permitting the representation to be made: The liability under the Doctrine of Holding Out arises then a person has either made a representation that he is a partner or has knowingly permitted such a representation to be made by someone else.

Illustrations: *(1) In case it is being represented that a person A is a partner in a Firm but A is not aware of such a representation, the question of A's liability under the Doctrine of Holding Out does not arise.*

(2) In Munton v. Rutherford, one Beckwith published a statement in a newspaper that he and Mrs. Rutherford had formed a partnership.The statement was false and Mrs. Rutherford did not know about the same. It was held that Mrs.Rutherford was not liable as a partner by estoppel or holding out. Mere carelessness in allowing oneself to be represented may not necessarily mean that he has knowingly permitted himself to be represented as a partner.

(3) In Tower Cabinet Co v. Ingram a partnership consisted of Christmas and Ingram. The partnership was dissolved and thereafter the business was carried on by Christmas alone. Christmas used an old note paper of the Firm bearing the names of both Christmas and Ingram and placed an order for the purchase of some furniture from Tower Cabinet Co. Tower Cabinet Co. sued Ingram to make him liable on the basis of the Doctrine of Holding Out. It was held that merely because Ingram was negligent in not getting the old note papers destroyed when he left the firm, it cannot be inferred that he permitted himself to be represented as a partner and therefore he was not liable.

(4) In Oriental Bank of Commerce v. M/s S.R. Kishore & Co. a person not only represented himself to be a partner, but he signed the partnership deed, actively participated in various transactions ofthe firm, and signed various partnership documents from time to time. It was held that he was liable for the acts of the Firm on the basis of the principle of 'Holding Out'.

(B) Acting on the Faith of Representation

In order to entitle a person to bring an action under the Doctrine of Holding Out, it has to be shown that the third party acted on the faith of the representation and gave credit to the Firm. But if a person while giving credit to the Firm did not know about the representation he cannot take advantage of this doctrine and make such a person liable as a partner. The estoppel can be relied upon only by the person to whom the representation has been made, and who has acted upon the faith of it. For example, D who is not actually a partner in the Firm consisting of A, B & C , represents to X that he is also a partner in that firm. On the faith of that representation X gives credit to the firm. X can make D liable under the Doctrine of Holding Out. But if Y, who does not know of the representation, gives credit to the firm of A, B & C, he cannot make D liable.

QUESTIONS

Section 4.1

1. Define Partnership under the Indian Partnership Act 1932.
2. What are the essential elements and characteristics of partnership as per the Act ?

Section 4.2

1. What is the true test of partnership ?

Section 4.3

1. Distinguish between:
   (*a*) Partnership and Company
   (*b*) Partnership and Joint Hindu Family Business
   (*c*) Partnership and co-ownership
   (*d*) Partnership and Sole trading concern.

Section 4.4

1. Write a note on the methods of formation of partnership.
2. What is the importance of a partnership deed ?
3. What are the rights of a partner stipulated under the Act ?

Section 4.5

1. Write a note on the different types of partners.

Section 4.6

1. Write a note on the position of a minor admitted to the benefits of partnership, as a partner.
2. Explain the position of a Minor during his minority.
3. Write a note on the Rights and Liabilities of a minor.
4. What are the rights and liabilities of a minor after attaining majority and electing to be a partner ?

Section 4.7

1. Write a note on the duties of partners as stated in the Act.
2. What are the mutual rights and liabilities ?

Section 4.8

1. Write a note on Property of the Firm.

Section 4.9

1. Write a note on the implied authority of a partner.
2. Mention the acts which is included within the scope of implied authority of a partner ?

3. Mention the acts which are beyond the scope of implied authority for a partner ?
4. Who is a Sub-partner, what are his rights, liabilities and obligations ?

Section 4.10

1. Write a note on admission of a partner.
2. What is the position of a partner who wishes to retire from the partnerships ? His rights and liabilities.
3. What is the effect of death of a partner on the partnership firm ?
4. Can a partner be expelled ? What are the effects of expulsion on the partners in the firm ?
5. What are the rights of an outgoing partner ?

Section 4.11

1. Elucidiate the modes of dissolution of a partnership firm.
2. What are the implications when the partnership is dissolved under order of the Courts ?

Section 4.12

1. What are the consequences of dissolution of a partnership firm ?
2. Write a note on :
   (*a*) Agreement in restraint of trade
   (*b*) Sale of goodwill after dissolution
   (*c*) Methods of settling accounts.

Section 4.13

1. Explain the mode of Registration of a partnership firm.
2. What is the consequence of non-registration of a partnership firm ?

Section 4.14

1. What is meant by Doctrine of Holding out ?
2. What is Representation, according to the Act ?

OBJECTIVE TYPE QUESTIONS

1. Partnership Contract is a ________ subject.
   (*a*) Concurrent (*b*) Wonderful
   (*c*) Contractual (*d*) Wilful.
2. The Partnership Act is not applicable to the following States in India.
   (*a*) Jammu and Kashmir (*b*) Andaman and Nicobar islands
   (*c*) Goa (*d*) Karnataka.
3. Partnership firm is a ______ entity.
   (*a*) Legal (*b*) Illegal
   (*c*) Unauthorized (*d*) Statutory.

4. The authority of a partner to bind the firm conferred by the Partnership Act is called as:
   (*a*) Implied authority (*b*) Express authority
   (*c*) Legal authority (*d*) Illegal authority.
5. The rights and liabilities of each partner are determined afresh after the partnership is changed due to the death or retirement or admission of new member or any other method. This is termed as:
   (*a*) Reconstitution of a firm (*b*) Restructuring of the firm
   (*c*) Dissolution of the firm (*d*) None of the above.
6. Obtaining legal identity to the company is known as
   (*a*) Registration (*b*) Advertisement
   (*c*) Promotion (*d*) None of the above.
7. Sleeping partner in partnership firm means
   (*a*) The partner who sleeps in the office of the partnership firm
   (*b*) The partner who is active in the day to day running of the business
   (*c*) The partner who is inactive in the partnership firm
   (*d*) The partner who does the job of marketing.
8. The relation between persons who have agreed to share the profit of a business carried on by all or any of them acting for all is known as
   (*a*) Partnership (*b*) Joint Stock Company
   (*c*) Sole Trading Concern (*d*) Multi National Company.
9. The partner who is authorized to carry out the day to day activity of the concern is known as
   (*a*) Active partner (*b*) Sleeping partner
   (*c*) Partner for benefit only (*d*) Minor partner.
10. Active partner means
    (*a*) One who is very active in his life
    (*b*) One who is eager to run the business
    (*c*) One who looks after the concern on the day to day basis
    (*d*) None of the above.
11. Active partner is also called as
    (*a*) Ostensible partner (*b*) Dormant partner
    (*c*) Sleeping partner (*d*) Friendly partner.
12. Sleeping partner is also known as
    (*a*) Dormant partner (*b*) Active partner
    (*b*) Ostensible partner (*d*) None of the above.
13. Partners who make investments but do not enter into the business are known as
    (*a*) Partners in profit only (*b*) Active partners
    (*c*) Minor partner (*d*) None of the above.
14. Nominal partner means
    (*a*) One who lends his name for the growth of the firm
    (*b*) One who is nominated by the partners of the firm
    (*c*) One who is interested in the firm
    (*d*) One of the representative of the partners of the firm.

15. Minor's liability to the firm is limited to

(*a*) He is liable to profits as well as losses

(*b*) Minor cannot be admitted to the firm

(*c*) Minor's admission to the firm is invalid

(*d*) Profits only.

16. Partner by estoppel means

(*a*) Active partner (*b*) Dormant partner

(*c*) Partner by holding out (*d*) None of the above.

17. Actual partner are also called as

(*a*) Sleeping partner (*b*) Partner for profit only

(*c*) Active partner (*d*) Nominal partner.

18. Silent partners are

(*a*) Remain silent in the business

(*b*) Inactive partners

(*c*) Sleeping partners

(*d*) Have no power in the management decision making.

19. The person who represents the firm for the credit to the firm is known as

(*a*) Person by estoppel (*b*) Creditor

(*c*) Financier (*d*) Financing person to the firm.

20. Which of the following is the fundamental right of the partner

(*a*) Right to express his opinion

(*b*) Right to access the books of the partnership firm

(*c*) Right to share profits of the business proportionately

(*d*) All of the above.

21. Partnership deed is also known as

(*a*) Articles of association (*b*) Memorandum of association

(*c*) Draft agreement (*d*) Articles of partnership.

22. If there are only two as partners, then the partnership is known as

(*a*) Company (*b*) Association of members

(*c*) Duality of partnership (*d*) Association of persons.

23. Which of the following is the essentials of partnership

(*a*) Plurality of partners (*b*) Mutual agreement

(*c*) Common objective (*d*) All of the above.

24. Obtaining the legal identity to the business is known as

(*a*) Registration (*b*) Dissolution

(*c*) Legalization (*d*) Licensing.

25. Which of the following methods may take place in the dissolution of firm by court order

(*a*) Insanity (*b*) Misconduct

(*c*) Breach of agreement (*d*) All of the above.

26. The partner who transfers part of his share in the business is known as

(*a*) Sub partner (*b*) Nominal partner

(*c*) Partner by estoppel (*d*) Partner in profit only.

27. The dissolution of partnership takes place without intervention of the court when

(*a*) the expiry of the fixed term for partnership

(*b*) By dispute

(*c*) Both (a) and (b)

(*d*) Only (a).

28. Who is an incoming partner

(*a*) Ajay is the incoming partner who joined the firm since its inception

(*b*) Ajay is the incoming partner, as he is added as a partner by his father without the consent of the partners of the firm

(*c*) Ajay is the incoming partner, as he comes to the firm everyday without fail

(*d*) Ajay joined the firm after several years of establishment of the firm.

29. The power to introduce the new partner can be exercised by

(*a*) No partner has the right

(*b*) The partner in undue influence of the stakeholder can introduce the new partner

(*c*) Any of the existing partner

(*d*) The stakeholders can introduce a new partner.

30. The liability of the incoming partner starts

(*a*) When the incoming partner is admitted to firm

(*b*) The incoming partner is held liable for the entire debts of the firm

(*c*) When the incoming partners name is proposed by one/ other partners

(*d*) When the incoming partner decides to become a partner.

31. Implied authority is also known as

(*a*) Expressed authority (*b*) Apparent authority

(*c*) No authority (*d*) Some authority.

32. The acts which are incidental to the normal course of business come under the purview of

(*a*) Day to day course of business (*b*) Usual activity

(*c*) Implied authority (*d*) None of the above.

33. The implied authority of a partner does not extend to his acts beyond

(*a*) Special transactions (*b*) Specific business transactions

(*c*) The day to day activity of business (*d*) Scope of the business.

34. Suing on behalf of the firm and defending suits in the name of the firm is an example of which kind of authority

(*a*) Specific business transactions (*b*) Explicit authority

(*c*) Implied authority (*d*) Assumed authority.

35. Extension authority means

(*a*) Specific business transactions

(*b*) Assumed authority

(*c*) Eligibility of making the decision beyond the day to day routine of the business

(*d*) Limited decision making authority.

36. Which of the following benefits will a registered firm enjoy
- (*a*) Can sue the third party to establish its claims
- (*b*) Goodwill is gained soon
- (*c*) Impeachment of any condition mentioned in the partnership firm
- (*d*) All of the above.

37. What happens to the partnership firm, if the firm has employed a partner who becomes insane
- (*a*) No change takes place as the firm is providing a source of sustenance for him
- (*b*) The firm has to get permission from the Registrar of Firms
- (*c*) The firm ceases its existence
- (*d*) The firm has to keep aside certain money for his survival.

38. The partnership deed should be stamped in accordance with
- (*a*) The Partnership Act
- (*b*) The Companies Act
- (*c*) The Negotiable Instruments Act
- (*d*) The Stamps Act.

39. A minor is entitled to
- (*a*) Take active part in the business
- (*b*) Share in the profits earned by the firm
- (*c*) Share in the losses incurred by the firm
- (*d*) All of the above.

40. Empowering a partner to sign a cheque of more value than that normally allowed is known as
- (*a*) Implicit authority
- (*b*) Both a and b
- (*c*) Explicit authority
- (*d*) None of the above.

41. A person who joins the firm with the consent of all the partners of the firm is known as
- (*a*) Employee of the firm
- (*b*) Incoming partner
- (*c*) Sleeping partner
- (*d*) Silent partner.

42. An outgoing partner in a partnership firm means
- (*a*) A person who comes to the office and goes out of the office after the business hours
- (*b*) A person who is declared an insolvent
- (*c*) A person who comes in the category of partners of the firm
- (*d*) None of the above.

43. Agreement in restraint of trade means
- (*a*) An agreement agreed upon by the retiring partner not to start similar business within a specified period or area
- (*b*) An agreement agreed upon by the outgoing partner not to start similar business within a specified period or area
- (*c*) Stopping other competitors from doing similar business
- (*d*) A and B.

44. Dissolution of the firm can take place by court if the firm due to
- (*a*) Insane partners
- (*b*) Incapacity of partner
- (*c*) Misconduct of partners
- (*d*) All of the above.

45. Mutual rights and duties of partners after change in the reconstituted firm

(*a*) Remain the Same

(*b*) Some rights and duties might change as per the partners of the firm

(*c*) Change as per the new partnership deed

(*d*) No changes in the rights, only the duties of the partner will change.

46. The mutual rights and duties of the partners in respect of the other adventures or undertakings will remain the same

(*a*) As those in respect of the new undertaking

(*b*) As those in respect of the original adventures or undertakings

(*c*) Either A or B

(*d*) None of the above.

ANSWERS

1. (*a*)	**2.** (*a*)	**3.** (*a*)	**4.** (*a*)
5. (*a*)	**6.** (*a*)	**7.** (*c*)	**8.** (*a*)
9. (*a*)	**10.** (*c*)	**11.** (*a*)	**12.** (*a*)
13. (*a*)	**14.** (*a*)	**15.** (*d*)	**16.** (*c*)
17. (*c*)	**18.** (*d*)	**19.** (*a*)	**20.** (*d*)
21. (*d*)	**22.** (*c*)	**23.** (*d*)	**24.** (*a*)
25. (*d*)	**26.** (*a*)	**27.** (*d*)	**28.** (*d*)
29. (*c*)	**30.** (*a*)	**31.** (*b*)	**32.** (*c*)
33. (*d*)	**34.** (*c*)	**35.** (*c*)	**36.** (*d*)
37. (*c*)	**38.** (*d*)	**39.** (*b*)	**40.** (*c*)
41. (*b*)	**42.** (*b*)	**43.** (*d*)	**44.** (*d*)
45. (*c*)	**46.** (*b*)		

GLOSSARY

1. READING AND IDENTIFYING CASE NAMES

There are two parties to a suit (case), namely the Plaintiff and the Defendant. The first name in the case identifies the person or party who has filed a suit or who requests for court action and the second name is the person or party against whom action is sought.

Illustration: *Durga Prasad Vs. Baldeo (1880). Here Durga Prasad is the plaintiff who has filed a suit or a complaint in a court of law, against Baldeo, the defendant. 1880 is the year in which the judgement was delivered or the decision was delivered by the concerned Court.*

In a criminal case the action against the accused is always brought about by the State (people/ society) against the accused.

Illustration: *Union of India Vs. Union Carbide, (the infamous Bhopal Gas Tragedy). Here the Plaintiff is the Government, on behalf of the victims against the company-Union Carbide, the negligence of whom led to the death of several people living near the vicinity.*

2. LAW REPORTERS

The case also consists of the name of the reporter followed by the year when the decision was delivered. A reporter is a multi-volume publication were the decisions of the court is found. The reporter acts as a reference for future decision making and also as a source for formulating and amending Acts. The different reporters and their abbreviations are as follows:

Abbreviation	Meaning of the Abbreviation	Source
SCC	Supreme Court Cases	The Supreme Court of India
AIR	All India Reporter	Decisions from the Supreme Court of India and High Courts of States in India.
CLJ	Company Law Journal	Decisions relating to matters concerning Company Law in India.
ITR	Income Tax Report	Decision relating to matters concerning Income Tax in India.
LR	Labour Reports	Decision relating to Labour Law in India.

3. THE INDIAN JUDICIARY

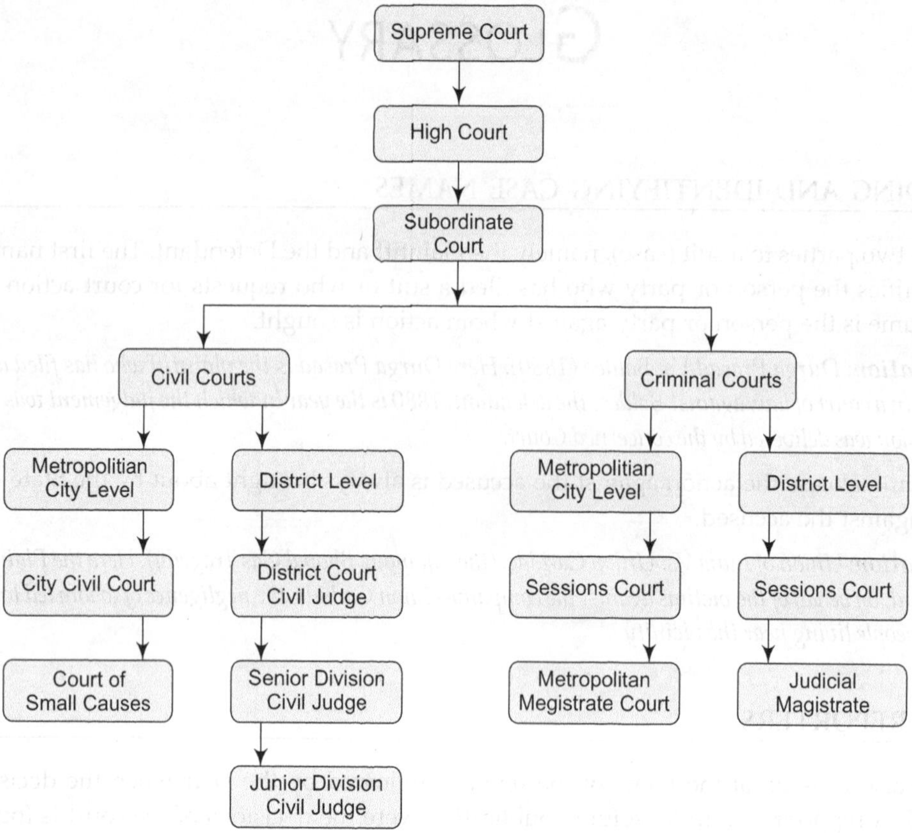

4. COMMON LEGAL TERMS AND MEANINGS

LEGAL TERMS	MEANINGS
A	
a fortiori	With stronger reason.
ab initio	From the beginning.
Abetment	a diminishment, a reduction.
Abrogate	to cancel, destroy, revoke or void.
Abscond	to vanish, to travel covertly out of the court's jurisdiction.
Abstention	a legal policy whereby one court declines to exercise. its jurisdiction and defer to a different court.
Acquittal	A final judgment by a judge or a jury that the prosecution has not proven a criminal defendant's guilt beyond a reasonable doubt. This is not a guilty verdict.

Action personalis moritur cum persona	Personal right of action dies with the person concerned.
Actionable tort	The failure to perform a legal duty created by statute or common law owed by one party to another which such failure results in injury.
Ad Damnum (latin)	The amount of damages demanded normally in the context of a lawsuit.
Ad idem	Identity of minds.
Ad litem (latin)	for the lawsuit.
Additur	An increase by the court in the amount of damages awarded by the jury.
Adjudication	A determination of the controversy and pronouncement of a judgment based on evidence presented. The decision (decree or judgment) by the court concerning the defendant(s) involved in the case.
Affidavit	A written statement made under oath.
Alinude	From another source.
Aliter	Otherwise or in other words.
Alter ego (latin)	The other self. Under this legal doctrine, the law will disregard the personal liability an individual has as a result of the existence of a corporate entity and will regard an act as the act of the individual rather than solely the act of the corporation.
Annotation	Citing a particular case of statute.
Annul	To make void, to do away with.
Annulment	A legal decree that states that a marriage was never valid. Has the legal effect of wiping out a marriage as though it never existed.
Appeal	A request to a supervisory court, usually composed of a panel of judges, to overturn the legal ruling of a lower court.
Arbitration	A method of alternative dispute resolution in which the disputing parties agree to abide by the decision of an arbitrator.
Assignment	The transfer of legal rights, such as the time left on a lease, from one person to another.
Asylum seeker	A foreigner, or any person at the border of a country, who seeks refuge, claiming an inability or unwillingness to return to the home country because of a well-founded fear of persecution.

B	
Bad-faith	Dishonesty or fraud in a transaction, such as entering into an agreement with no intention of ever living up to its terms or knowingly misrepresenting the quality of something that is being bought or sold.
Bail	The deposit-money, property, or bond that is put up by or on behalf of an arrested person to secure his or her release from jail before or after court proceedings begin.
Bailiff	A court attendant.
Bailment	A legal relationship created when a person gives property to someone else for safekeeping. To create a bailment the other party must knowingly have exclusive control over the property. The receiver must use reasonable care to protect the property.
Bankruptcy	Insolvency; a process governed by federal law to help when people cannot or will not pay their debts.
Barrister	In England, one of the two classes of legal practitioners, the other is called Trial Lawyer.
Battery	An intentional or unlawful application of force to the person of another; an unlawful touching.
Bench trial	Also called court trial. A trial held before a judge and without a jury.
Beneficiary	A person named in a will or insurance policy to receive money or property; person who receives benefit from a trust.
Bifurcation	Splitting a trial into two parts; a liability phase and a penalty phase. In some cases, a new jury may be empanelled to deliberate for the penalty phase.
Bona vacantia	Ownerless property.
Bona fide	In good faith.
Bond	A document with which one party promises to pay another within a specified amount of time. Bonds are used for many things, including borrowing money or guaranteeing payment of money.
Booking	Part of the process of being arrested in which the details of who a person is and why he or she was arrested are recorded into the police records.

C	
Capital gain	The profit made from the sale of a capital asset, such as real estate, a house, jewellery or stocks and bonds.
Case law	Also known as common law. The law created by judges when deciding individual disputes or cases.

Case of first impression	A novel legal question that comes before a court.
Cause of action	The existence of particular facts and law that create a right sufficient to merit judicial action.
Cautionary instruction	Judge's charge to a jury telling them not to allow any outside matter to influence their verdict.
Caveat (latin)	Warning or caution.
Caveat emptor	Let the buyer beware.
Cease and desist order	A court order prohibiting the person or entity to which it is directed from undertaking or continuing a particular activity or course of conduct.
Certiorari (latin)	Meaning, to be informed of. It refers to the order a court issues so that it can review the decision and proceedings in a lower court and determine whether there were any irregularities. When such an order is made, it is said that the court has granted certiorari.
Circuit court	One of several courts in a given jurisdiction; a part of a system of courts.
Circumstantial evidence	Indirect evidence that implies something occurred but doesn't directly prove it. If a man accused of embezzling money from his company had made several big-ticket purchases in cash around the time of the alleged embezzlement that would be circumstantial evidence that he had stolen the money.
Citation	A reference to a book or other source of legal authority.
Clayton Act	Prohibits price fixing and other types of discrimination.
Clean hands	The doctrine that requires that a person who seeks equitable relief must not himself have committed any impropriety with respect to the transaction.
Codicil	A supplement to a will.
Cohabitation agreement	Also called a living-together contract. A document that spells out the terms of a relationship and often addresses financial issues and how property will be divided if the relationship ends.
Collateral	An asset that a borrower agrees to give up if he or she fails to repay a loan.
Comity	A code of etiquette that governs the interactions of courts in different states, localities and foreign countries. Courts generally agree to defer scheduling a trial if the same issues are being tried in a court in another jurisdiction. In addition, courts in this country agree to recognize and enforce the valid legal contracts and court orders of other countries.
Comparative negligence	Also called comparative fault. A system that allows party to recover some portion of the damages caused by another party's

	negligence even if the original person was also partially negligent and responsible for causing the injury; the comparing of responsibility between the plaintiff and the defendant or defendants.
Compensatory damages	Money awarded to reimburse actual costs, such as medical bills and lost wages. Also awarded for things that are harder to measure, such as pain and suffering.
Complaint	A written accusation filed by a prosecutor in a justice or municipal court that accuses one or more persons of committing one or more crimes. In a civil action, the document that initiates a lawsuit. The complaint outlines the alleged facts of the case and the basis for which a legal remedy is sought. In a criminal action, a complaint is the preliminary charge filed by the complaining party, usually with the police or a court.
Compos mentis (latin)	Mentally competent
Conclusion of fact	The conclusion reached through use of facts and reasoning, without resort to rules of law.
Conclusion of law	Conclusion reached through application of rules of law.
Conclusive evidence	Evidence which is irrefutable.
Conflict of interest	A situation where the tending of one duty leads to disregard of another; refers to a situation when someone, such as a lawyer or public official, has competing professional or personal obligations or personal or financial interests that would make it difficult to fulfil his duties fairly.
Conflict of laws	Applicable law of one State Court which differs with the application law of another state jurisdiction which also has an interest in the outcome.
Consanguinity	The familial relationship of persons united by one or more common ancestors.
Consent judgement	An agreement of the parties which is placed on record with the court having jurisdiction.

D

Damages	Money compensation awarded to a person who has been injured by another;
Damnum absque injuria (latin)	Harm without injury.
De jure (latin)	By right; lawful.
Decree	A decision or order of a court, usually in equity; a final decree disposes of all matters before the court; an interlocutory decree disposes of only part of the lawsuit and often may not be appealed until the conclusion of the entire case.

Defamation	The publication of a statement that injures a person's reputation. Libel and slander are defamation.
Default	The failure to fulfil a legal obligation, such as neglecting to pay back a loan on schedule.
Deliberation	The jurors process of pondering and weighing of facts, applying the law, and coming to a verdict.
Disapproved	If the court cannot overrule an earlier case and considers the earlier case no longer to be good law.
Disposition	A final disposition is a legal action which takes place following an adult or juvenile felony arrest. Examples are dismissal, acquittal or conviction. Examples of intermediate dispositions are suspended proceedings or the placement of a defendant in one or more programs.
Distinguished	When a court finds some material difference between the facts of the two cases.
Double jeopardy	Being tried twice for the same offence.

E

Easement	Gives one party the right to go onto another party's property. Utilities often get easements that allow them to run pipes or phone lines beneath private property.
Emancipation	When a minor has achieved independence from his or her parents, often by getting married before reaching age 18 or by becoming fully self-supporting.
En banc (French)	By the full court, when all the members of an Appellate Court hear an argument, they are sitting en banc.
En banc (latin)	By the full Court.
En ventre sa mere (latin/French)	In gestation; in the womb of ones mother.
Encumbrance	Any claim or restriction on a property's title.
Erroneous	Pertaining to a mistake.
Escrow account	A special account in which a lawyer or escrow agent deposits money or documents that do not belong to him or his firm.
Estoppel	Precluding from asserting.
Ex gratia	As a matter of favour.
Ex parte	An application made by one party to the proceeding without the presence of the opposing party. Such meetings are often forbidden.
Ex post facto	Subsequently or After the event.

Executor	Person named in a will to oversee and manage an estate.
Exigent circumstances	Emergency conditions.
Express warranty	An assertion or promise concerning goods or services. Statements such as *'this washing machine will wash 5 kilos of clothes'* are express warranties.
F	
Fair use	The use of a portion of copyrighted material in a way that does not infringe the owner's rights. The use of a portion of material for educational purposes, literary criticism or news reporting is often considered a fair use.
Felony	A crime which may be punishable by imprisonment in a state prison and/or a fine or death. Probation, with or without country jail time, may also be a possible disposition.
Fiduciary duty	An obligation to act in the best interest of another party. For instance, a doctor has a fiduciary duty to his patient and an attorney has a fiduciary duty to a client.
Foreclosure	When a borrower cannot repay a loan and the lender seeks to sell the property.
Franchise	A business relationship in which the owner (the franchisor) licenses others (the franchisees) to operate outlets using business concepts, property, trade marks and trade names owned by the franchisor.
G	
Gag order	An order by the court restricting comment on, or the release of information about the proceedings.
Garnishment	A procedure to take control over a person's assets or income that have been judicially determined to be awed or to belong to another person; a Court ordered method of debt collection in which a portion of a person's salary is paid to a creditor. Often used to collect child support payments.
Good faith	A properly intentioned deed that is free from improper motive; honestly and without deception. An agreement might be declared invalid if one of the parties entered with the intention of defrauding the other.
Government immunity	A legal precept of sovereignty of the government rendering it exempt from liability for its acts or failures.
Guardian ad litem (latin)	Means, guardian at law. The person appointed by the Court to look out for the best interests of the child during the course of legal proceedings.
Guilty	The determination by a jury that the accused has committed a crime; the term is not relevant to civil law matters.

H	
Habeas corpus (latin)	Meaning, 'you have the body'. Prisoners often seek release by filing a petition for a writ of habeas corpus. A writ of habeas corpus is a judicial mandate to a prison official ordering that an inmate be brought to the court so it can be determined whether or not that person is imprisoned lawfully.
Hearsay	Second information that a witness only heard about from someone else and did not see or hear himself. Hearsay is not admitted in court because it is not trustworthy, though there are many exceptions.
Hearsay rule	A rule of evidence that requires the declarant be subject to cross examination at the hearing; many exceptions to the rule exist.
Holding order	A decision by a judge ordering one or more persons to stand trial after a preliminary hearing. A holding order is based on finding that one or more crimes have been committed and that there is sufficient cause to believe that one or more person identified at the preliminary hearing committed the crime.
Holographic will	An unwitnessed handwritten will. A few states allow such documents to be admitted to probate, but most Courts are very reluctant to accept them.
Hung jury	A jury whose members cannot agree in sufficient numbers to reach a verdict. Unanimous in criminal cases, federal civil cases and three quarters in some other States civil cases.

I	
Ibid	In the same place.
Impanel	To bring together in the courtroom, the people selected to serve as the jury.
Impleader	A rule of procedure whereby a third party is brought into an existing lawsuit.
Implied consent	A consent that is drawn from the facts of the surrounding circumstances.
In absentia (latin)	In absence.
In camera (latin)	Meaning 'in chambers'. Refers to a hearing or inspection of documents that takes place in private, often in a judge's chamber.
In forma pauperis (latin)	Meaning 'as would a pauper'. It normally refers to the right granted by the court to allow a party to proceed without the payment of costs due to financial inability.
In limine (latin)	At the beginning.
In loco parentis (latin)	In the place of the parent.
In personam (latin)	Against a person.

In presonam	Right against a particular person.
In re (latin)	In the matters of.
in rem	Right against the whole world.
In rem (latin)	An action against a thing, as opposed to an action against a person.
Indeterminate sentence	Sentences that are not fixed and may be imposed for severe felony crimes, such as murder. Examples of these sentences may be fifteen to life or twenty-five to life. Actual release dates are set by the board of prison terms after a parole hearing.
Indictment	A formal accusation of a felony, issued by a grand jury after considering evidence presented by a prosecutor; a written accusation returned by a grand jury and filed in superior court.
Injunction	An order of the Court which requires a person or entity to refrain from pursuing a particular course of conduct or activity.
Injuria absque damno (latin)	Wrong or insult without damage.
Injuria non excusat injuriam (latin)	One wrong does not justify another.
Inter alia	Among other matters.
Inter alia (latin)	Among other things.
Inter vivos (latin)	Between the living.
Interim order	A temporary order.
Interlocutory order	Temporary order issued during the course of litigation. Typically cannot be appealed because it is not final.
Interse	Between themselves.
Intestate	To die without a will.
Intra vires	Within the power.
Ipse dixit (latin)	He said it himself.
Ipso facto	On the face of itself.
Irreparable injury	A loss for which no remedy at law would be sufficient and therefore a court sitting in equity may order a special relief other than money damages.

J

Joinder	Uniting of parties to single case or litigation.
Jones act	Federal law that grants a seaman who suffers injury to his or her person during the course of employment a right to damages.

Judgment non-obstante veredicto	Also know as a judgment notwithstanding the verdict. A decision by a trial judge to rule in favourof a losing party even though the jury's verdict was in favour of the other side. Usually done when the facts or law do not support the jury's verdict.
Jurisdiction	A courts authority to rule on the questions of law at issue in a dispute, typically determined by geographic location and type of case.
Jurisprudence	The topical area of the science of law and societal order.
Jurist	A legal scholar.
Juror	An individual who has been impanelled as a member of a jury.

L

Laches	Neglecting to assert a right or claim which taken together with a lapse of time and other circumstances, causes prejudice to adverse party, thereby operating as a bar in a court of equity.
Latent defect	A defect not discoverable by the exercise of an ordinary inspection.
Lay witness	A witness that is testifying as a witness to a fact or an opinion as opposed to an opinion given by an expert about a matter beyond the expected comprehension of the jury.
Legatee	Also known as beneficiary. Person named in a will to receive property.
Lemon laws	Laws that require manufacturers to repair defective cars. If the repairs are not made within a reasonable amount of time and number of attempts, the manufacturer is required to refund the purchase price, less a reasonable amount for the use of the car.
Lex loci delicti (latin)	The place where the wrong took place.
Libel	Defamatory (false and injurious) written statements or materials, including movies or photographs.
Lien	A claim against someone's property. A lien is instituted in order to secure payment from the property owner in the event that the property is sold. A mortgage is a common lien.
Liquidated damages	A sum of money agreed upon by the parties to a contract what will be paid as damages if there is a breach of the contract.
Lis pendens (latin)	A pending suit.
Living trust	A trust created during the maker's lifetime. Some living trusts are set up so that they can be changed during the maker's lifetime. These are called 'revocable'. Others, known as 'irrevocable' are set up so that they cannot be touched.
Lord Campbell's Act	The English law that first recognized the right of the family of a decedent to bring an action for damages against the person who was responsible for the death of their family member.

M	
Malafide	In bad faith.
Malfeasance	The doing of an act in an improper, wrongful, or unlawful manner.
Malice	A spiteful state of mind.
Mens rea	A guilty mind.
Miranda warning	The statement recited to individuals taken into police custody. It warns of their right to remain silent and to have an attorney.
Misdemeanour	A crime punishable by imprisonment in the county jail for not more than one year, or by fine or both.
Misfeasance	An act of wrong doing.
Misfeasance	Improper performance of a required act.
Mistrial	An action taken by a court which terminates a trial in progress.
Mitigating circumstances	Factors that a judge may consider in reducing the penalty for committing a crime.
Mitigation of damages	A duty owned by the party who sustained injury to his person or property to minimize the loss by acting in a reasonably prudent manner.
Moot case	A case that is fictional as it is based upon a fact or right which is not recognizable or which has already been resolved.
Motion	A request asking a judge to issue a ruling or order on a legal matter.
Motion for a new trial	Request in which a losing party asserts that a trial was unfair due to legal errors that prejudiced its case.
Motion for directed verdict	A request made by the defendant in a civil case. Asserts that the plaintiff has raised no genuine issue to be tried and asks the judge to rule in favour of the defense. Typically made after the plaintiff is done presenting his or her case.
Motion in limine	A request made by a party asking the court to prohibit the discussion or other presentation of a particular matter to the jury.
Motion to suppress evidence	A request to a judge to keep out evidence at a trial or hearing often made when a party believes the evidence was unlawfully obtained.

N	
Named plaintiffs	The originators of a class action suit.
Negligence per se	An act or failure to act that is considered unreasonable conduct as a matter of law without the need to consider surrounding circumstances.
No-fault divorce	A divorce in which it does not matter who did what to whom that caused the marriage to break down; all that matters is that there is no reasonable prospect of reconciliation.

No-fault insurance	An insurance scheme wherein every person injured in an automobile accident is compensated irrespective of who was at fault.
Nominal damages	A minute (small) sum awarded, often negligible amount.
Non-feasance	The failure to perform a duty owed to another.
Non-immigrant visa	Visa granted to a foreigner who does not intend to stay in a foreign country permanently.
Nonsuit	A judgment ordered by the Court against a plaintiff who fails to proceed to trail.
Notary public	A person authorized to witness the signing of documents.
Notice of appeal	The document a person must file with the trial Court in order to pursue an appeal.
Nudum pactum	A bare promise.

O

Obiter dicta (latin)	Meaning 'sayings by the way'. They can only be of persuasive value as they do not form part of the matters at issue.
On all fours	An expression used to characterize a case where facts and law are similar to another.
Open adoption	An adoption in which the birth mother may retain some visitation privileges.
Overruled	When an appellate court decides a similar matter, in a later case, on the basis of a different legal principle, the decision in the later court is now to be followed.
Overt	Open.
Own recognizance	Sometimes called personal recognizance. A person who promises to appear in court to answer criminal charges can sometimes be released from jail without having to pay bail. This person is said to be released on his or her own recognizance. In certain cases, the judge has statutory discretion to release the defendant without posting bail. Failure by a defendant to later appear in such a case is a crime.

P

Parens patriae (latin)	Meaning 'parent of his country'. This is used when the government acts on behalf of a child or mentally ill person. It refers to the State as the guardian of minors and people who are incompetent.
Pari passu	Proportionately.
Parole	A system for the supervised release of prisoners before their terms are over.
Pecuniary damage	Financial losses incurred.

Per diem (latin)	Course of a day.
Per se	By itself.
Peremptory challenges	Limited number of challenges. Each side in a trial can use it to eliminate potential jurors without stating a reason. May not be used to keep members of a particular race or gender off the jury.
Plea bargain	A negotiated agreement between the defense and the prosecution in a criminal case. Typically the defendant agrees to plead guilty to a specified charge in exchange for an oral promise of a lower sentence.
Pre-emption	A judicial principle which states that certain federal laws apply over certain State laws.
Preponderance of the evidence	The level of proof required to prevail in most civil cases. The judge or jury must be persuaded that the facts are more probably one way (the plaintiff's way) than another (the defendant's).
Prima facie	At first sight
Prima facie (latin)	Meaning 'at first view'. It refers to the minimum amount of evidence a plaintiff must have to avoid having a case dismissed. It is said that the plaintiff must make a prima facie case.
Prima facie case	The existence of some evidence on each required point of a case.
Privity	A sufficient relationship between parties to the same rights or property.
Pro hac vice (latin)	For this one particular occasion.
pro rata	In proportion.
Pro se (latin) Pronounced pro say)	For himself; in law, it refers to a person who represents himself without a lawyer.
Probate	The legal process in which a court oversees the distribution of property left in a will.
Proffer (of evidence)	To present to the record in a trial what evidence a party has on a given point after the Court has refused its admission into evidence in order that a reviewing Court can know what was excluded at the original proceeding.
Prosecutor	The government lawyer who investigates and tries criminal cases. Typically known as a District attorney, State's attorney.
Punitive damages	An award of money to punish the wrongdoer and to stop the person or business from repeating the type of conduct that caused an injury. Also intended to deter others from similar conduct.

Q

Quantum meruit (latin)	As much as it is worth.
Quash	To annul or abandon by judicial decision; to nullify, void or declare invalid.

Quid pro quo	Something in return.
Quid pro quo (latin)	The existence of a controversy as to the actual facts of a case which must be determined by the Trier of fact-a jury in a jury trial; the judge in a bench trial.
Quitclaim deed	A deed that transfers the owner's interest to a buyer but does not guarantee that there are no other claims against the property.
R	
Ratio decidendi (latin)	Meaning 'reason for deciding'. It is capable of creating binding precedent.
Rebuttal	Evidence disproving other evidence previously given.
Reckless disregard	Behaviour or demeanour which evidences a lack of concern for consequences.
Re-cross examination	Questioning a witness about matters brought up during redirect examination.
Re-direct examination	Questioning a witness about matters brought up during cross examination.
Remittitur (latin)	To reduce, generally in law it describes a reduction to the jury's verdict made by the judge.
Replevin	Repossession. Action taken by a creditor to seize assets of a debtor.
Res ipsa loquitur (latin)	Meaning, a thing speaks for itself. In a negligence lawsuit, the plaintiff generally has the burden to prove that the defendant was negligent. The doctrine of *res ipsa loquitur* is a rule of evidence which has the effect of requiring the defendant to prove that he was not negligent in certain circumstances; refers to situations when it is assumed that a person's injury was caused by the negligent action of another party because the accident was the sort that would not occur unless someone was negligent.
Res judicata (latin)	Meaning that the thing has been decided.
Rescission	The cancellation of a contract.
Residuary estate	Also known as residue of the estate. Portion of the estate left after bequests of specific items of property are made. Often the largest portion.
Residuary legatee	The person or persons named in a will to receive any residue left in an estate after the bequests of specific items are made.
Respondeat superior (latin)	Meaning, let the superior reply. A legal principle whereby the master is responsible for the acts or omissions of his/her servant.
Restitution	Restoration.
Restitution	To make good the loss of injury or damage.
Restitution fine	A fine that a convicted perpetrator must pay to the State as part of sentencing.

Restitution order	Compensation to a crime victim by a criminal defendant for financial losses or personal injuries caused by the crime, sometimes called 'victim's restitution' or direct restitution. Every victim who suffers economic loss as a result of criminal activity is entitled to restitution upon sentencing of a defendant.
Retainer	Refers to the upfront payment a client gives a lawyer to accept a case. The client is paying to 'retain' the lawyer's services.
Reversible error	Error in a trial which is significantly sufficient to cause the entire trial to be reversed or a new trial to be granted by a reviewing appellate Court.
Routine vacatur (latin)	A procedure where a defendant settles an unfavourable determination which occurred in the trial Court while the case is on appeal and has the appellate Court vacate the determination below.

S	
Scienter(latin)	Knowledge, prior knowledge.
Scintilla	A very minute amount of evidence.
Sequester	To separate, in law, refers to the isolation of the jury from the world outside the courtroom in order that they will not be influenced from events and information not presented in the trial.
Show cause order	A command from the Court to appear before it and explain why something should not be done.
Side-bar	An area of the courtroom where the judge and attorneys can converse outside of the jury's hearing.
Slander	Defamatory (false and injurious) oral statements or gestures.
Specific performance	A remedy requiring a person who has breached a contract to perform specifically what was agreed upon and is available only when money damages would not suffice.
Spendthrift trust	A trust designed to keep money out of the hands of creditors. Often established to protect someone who is incapable of managing his or her financial affairs.
Stare decisis (latin)	To stand by what was decided; the legal principle that a lower court will follow that which has already been decided by a previous case.
Statute of limitations	The statutory law which establishes the time within which a law-suit must be brought or be forever barred.
Statutes of fraud	Laws in most States to protect against false claims for payment from contracts that were not agreed upon. The specific laws vary from State to State, but most require that certain contracts be in writing.
Statutes of limitations	Laws setting deadlines for filing lawsuits within a certain time after events occur that are the source of a claim.

Stipulation	An agreement by the attorney on both sides about some aspect of the case.
Sub judice (latin)	Before the court.
Sublet	When a party agrees to rent a space from the main tenant for a portion of the time remaining on the lease.
Summation	The closing argument in a trial.
Summons	A legal document that notifies a party that lawsuit has been initiated and states when and where the party must appear to answer the charges.

T

Testamentary trust	A trust created by the provisions in a will. Typically comes into existence after the writer of the will dies.
Testator	The person who makes a will.
Tort	A civil wrong which causes injury as a result of a breach of a legal duty owed to another.

U

Uberrimae fidei	Utmost good faith
Ubi jus ibi remedium	Where there is a right, there is a remedy.
Ultra vires	Beyond the power
Ultrahazard activity	Conduct or any activity that involves such a great potential for harm or injury that the person or entity performing such activity will be held strictly liable for the outcome.

V

Vacate	To set aside or to render void.
Verdict	The conclusion of the Court or Jury which becomes the basis for the judgment.
Vested right	An absolute right. When a retirement plan is fully vested, the employee has an absolute right to the entire amount of money in the account.
Vicarious liability	When one person is liable for the negligent actions of another person, even though the first person was not directly responsible for the injury. (a parent sometimes can be vicariously liable for the harmful acts of a child and an employer sometimes can be vicariously labile for the acts of a worker).
Vinculum juris	Legal bond
Vinculum juris	Obligation

Voir dire (French) Pronounced as 'vwa dear'	Meaning, to speak the truth; the process of interviewing prospective jurors . In law suit is that portion of the trial where the potential juror are asked questions by the attorneys or the Court to determine their qualifications and suitability to sit as juror in a particular case.
Volenti non fit injuria (latin)	A volunteer suffers no wrong; a person who consents to legal wrong has no legal right.
W	
Wanton	A heedless disregard for the outcome of one's actions.
Warrant	An official order authorising a specific act, such as an arrest or the search of someone's home.
Witness	A person who is sworn at a trial to provide evidence in a case. Also a person who comes to Court and swears under oath to give truthful evidence.
Writ	Judicial order.

INDEX

A

B

C

N

O

P

Q

R

S

T

U

V

W